BUT I JUST GREW OUT MY BANGS!

A Cancer Tale

Katya Lezin

To David,
who made my cancer journey a love story,
and to Noah, Hannah and Eliza,
the best parts of that love story.

ACKNOWLEDGEMENTS

Thank you to everyone who encouraged me to turn my Ovarian Odyssey emails into a book, and to Juli Johnsen, Nicole Lezin, David Lieberman, Carrie Nagle and Marc Lewin for reading early drafts and providing invaluable edits and insights.

Thanks to Noah, Hannah and Eliza for understanding that I had to tell my story my way, and apologies for the inevitable embarrassment that my boob photos, poop stories and family sharing entail. Just be happy you have a different last name.

CHAPTER ONE

I am a waiter's nightmare. I like extra lemon with my iced tea, I ask to taste the soup of the day before ordering it, and I want to know if the whipped cream is real or out of a can. If I see people littering or cutting in line, I feel compelled to call them on it. This inability to let idiocy get a pass includes, much to my husband's chagrin, telling the guy who just cut us off (who looks like he's got a shotgun under the seat of his beat up truck that sports not one but two bumper stickers pro- claiming his Second Amendment rights) that he needs to learn how to drive. Few thoughts remain in my head unspoken, including nice ones (*I just have to tell you how pretty you are*) but also ones that are not as well received (*I don't appreciate your attitude; it's not my fault you hate your job*). I could go on and on, but I think you get the point. I am a pain in the ass. An often loveable and charming pain in the ass, but a pain in the ass just the same.

It is ironic, then, that my cancer journey begins with just that – a pain in the ass. Ironic because I do not have anal cancer, but it is my ass that first sounds the cancer alarm. It is my ass that cries out, not once but twice, because I fail to heed the first warning, "You have ovarian cancer! Catch it now before it's too late!" Lest you worry about my mental state, I assure you I do not usually carry on conversations with my body parts, least of all my ass. But I have come to appreciate how everything in my body works in synch, and how a glitch in one part of the body can have ripple effects that appear unconnected but are, in fact, linked in an intricate and mysterious labyrinth of systems and organs and all sorts of stuff you have to go to medical school to identify that work together to keep everything running smoothly.

When you're healthy, you're blissfully ignorant of how it all works. And you don't imagine that your body parts are talking to you. But when you're ill – not cold or headache ill, but worried you might die ill - you get an immediate and often unwanted education. I am in the blissful ignorance stage when my ass sounds the alarm. I do not know that one of my ovaries has twisted and is sitting upon my rectum, nor do I know that this same twisted ovary will save my life.

All I know, and what I in fact say to my husband, which I now repeat verbatim with total certainty despite the ravaged memory that seems to be a permanent vestige of chemo brain, is "Man, my butt really hurts."

David, the hubby who no doubt says something comforting and endearing in response, like, "Uh huh," is driving our minivan up the New Jersey Turnpike. We have just celebrated a belated Chanukah with his folks in Maryland and we are headed to Westchester County, New York to visit his Uncle Carl, Aunt Beth and Grandpa Joe. It is the end of December 2010 and I am psyched I have once again convinced the non- Scrabble playing members of the family (David and Eliza, my youngest, who is 10) to spend more time in the van than out of it so that the rest of us (Noah, 16, and Hannah, 14) can indulge our Scrabble addiction and play in the Albany, NY New Year's Eve tournament. We live in Charlotte, NC, the kind of climate people from Albany seek out in the winter months; to head *from* Charlotte *to* Albany in January is either a measure of our devotion to the game of Scrabble or yet another indication (the first being my conversations with body parts) of my insanity.

To say David does not share my love of Scrabble would be putting it mildly. When I first discovered the wonderful, wacky underworld that is the competitive Scrabble circuit, thanks to a news- paper article my sister, Nicole, sent me, I took 12-year old Noah along with me to my first tournament in Atlanta so that it would be a mother- son bonding experience rather than a selfish, leave-Dad-behind-with-all- three-kids indulgence. Noah and I were both instantly hooked. We soon learned that our newfound passion did not come cheaply, especially since we do not live in a Scrabble mecca like New York or California, where local tournaments abound. In addition to the tournament fees, we also had to set aside funds for travel and lodging. Even when we win prize money, we are often still in the red. Reflecting on this one day early in our foray into competitive Scrabble, I remarked to David that a heroin addiction would actually be cheaper. David, who often put his thumb and index finger in the shape of an L on his forehead when discussing our Scrabble addiction, replied, "and less embarrassing."

Carl and Beth's house serves as a great pit stop because it is on the way, offers more comforts than any hotel ever could, and allows us to also visit with Grandpa Joe, David's then 95-year old grandfather, who lives there as well. The plan is to drive up there together and get in some good family time. David and Eliza will then take the train back to his parents' house outside of Annapolis, Maryland and cool their heels for a few days waiting for Noah and Hannah and me to finish playing -- which is why I put up with David's disdain; he does, in fact, indulge my Scrabble obsession and pretty much anything else I want to do.

The whole ride up, my butt hurts. It feels as if I am horribly constipated, but I am not. Sitting is uncomfortable, and becomes acutely so when we go out to eat with Carl and Beth that night. The discomfort is intermittent all the next day and on the third morning I finally 'fess up and ask the doctors (Carl is a retired radiologist and Beth is a retired OB/GYN) what they think could be the matter. They caution me that it could be kidney stones – which I've had twice before – that can some- times head in that direction rather than through the urethra. They have a couple other theories as well, but all end with, "You should take this seriously and check with your doctor if it continues."

I do not like doctors. I like them just fine as individual people. At the risk of sounding like a racist or bigot, who insists that some of his best friends are blacks or Jews or whomever he's claiming to like while maligning them in some other way, many of my best friends truly are doctors. But I do not like *going* to the doctor and I am notoriously bad about doing so. I do not like the inevitable waiting well past the appointment time and the malicious scales that have me weighing far more than I ever think I do. But my main objection to going to the doctor is a stubborn belief that most things work themselves out without medical intervention. I am equally bad about taking pills, icing down sore muscles, and doing anything other than just powering through whatever is bothering me. It drives everyone around me crazy, including my mom, from whom I'm convinced I inherited this attitude. She's of the belief that there's nothing a good, brisk walk won't cure, including my dad's lifelong struggle with asthma. I remember coming to her with a skinned knee when I was younger and her response was, "Why did you do that?" It obviously didn't scar me emotionally since I employ the same "joking-about-it-makes-it-go-away" approach with my own kids.

I'm not completely loony. I do believe in medicine and the irrefutable science behind it. When I have a fever, I take Tylenol. When I was pregnant, I went to every single neonatal appointment. But my pregnancies illustrate another reason I'm not good about going to the doctor. I'm pretty much the opposite of a hypochondriac. While many of my friends worried about every single aspect of their pregnancies, convinced that something was going to go wrong and that the process of bringing a baby into this world is one fraught with danger and risk aplenty, I was calm and confident. I just assumed everything would be fine. I am an optimist about most things (the sole exception being politics, where I often despair about how hatred and bigotry so often win the day) and my health is no exception. Even the fact that Hannah was born with atrial septal defect (a congenital heart defect in which the wall that separates the upper heart chambers does not close completely), a condition that cleared up on its own but rocked my confidence in my ability to sail through this world unscathed, ultimately fell in line as a confirming experience because it reinforced my belief that everything does, in fact, work out in the end.

I've had mammograms and pap smears and all the other things a woman in her 40s is supposed to do regularly, I just don't necessarily do them *regularly.* It has been two years since I've been in to see Phil Solomon, my gynecologist who also happens to be a friend. (As an aside, since I know there will be those of you scratching your heads at how I can spread my legs for someone I know socially, I will note that it's not weird at all for me. I figure the doctor's office is devoid of any- thing other than the clinical and scientific reason for my being there, and I don't feel the least bit awkward about it.) David will occasionally say, with varying levels of exasperation, "You should go get a check up," or "Aren't you due for a ...?" but for the most part I only go to the doctor when I'm in pain or quite ill.

You'd think that would translate into medical records that are sparse and reflective of how little I seek medical intervention, but the opposite is true. When I get sick, I bypass the common cold and go for the big stuff. I've been hospitalized for appendicitis, kidney stones, Toxic Shock Syndrome, bone spur surgery on my feet, three pregnancies, and a post-pregnancy unidentified virus. I've also sought medical care for a broken arm (that I managed to break again in the cast), hepatitis, a broken nose, a miscarriage and a burn to my hand from the worst Halloween night in history. The fact that two of my medical crises were in underdeveloped countries (appendectomy in Islamabad, Pakistan and Toxic Shock Syndrome in Kinshasa, Zaire) might also explain my reticence to seek medical attention.

So David and I part ways that morning with his stern admonition that I am to quit the tournament and go get medical help if the pain in my ass continues. I drive off to Albany with Noah and Hannah, while he and Eliza head to Maryland. I warn Noah and Hannah that we might have to pull out of the tournament and cut our trip short. I grimace and grit my teeth and tell them it isn't as bad as it looks. And then, after a rest stop visit on the New York Thruway, the pain is suddenly and miraculously gone. I go from agonizing discomfort one moment to absolutely no sign of anything being amiss the next. I know most people would be wondering, "What *was* that?" and would waste no time in setting up an appointment to get to the bottom of it, no pun intended. Not I. If the pain is gone, the problem is gone. I cheerily announce that I am all better and that our tournament plans are back on. We take out the Scrabble poo list (a compilation of naughty words that are acceptable in tournament Scrabble), a favorite road trip distraction en route to Scrabble tournaments, and continue on our way.

I now know that the twisted ovary has simply untwisted a bit, lifting it off my rectum and taking all the pain and pressure away. I know this because, after an almost four-month hiatus, it twists again. In April 2011, I again feel tremendous rectal pressure and pain, my ass sounding the alarm for a second time. I try to plow through for two days, thinking that whatever it is will again disappear as mysteriously as it appeared. By the third day, I am on the Internet, convinced I have either an anal fissure or anal cancer. So much for not being a hypochondriac. I lie on the couch, in agony, and decide it is time to wave the white flag.

I call Phil on the afternoon of Wednesday, April 27, 2011 (on Day Three of the second onset of Agonizing Ass Syndrome) and he tells me he will squeeze me in during his lunch hour the next day. The up-side to being notoriously bad about visiting your doctor is that he takes it seriously when you *do* call.

After describing my symptoms to him, Phil orders an ultrasound of my abdomen, something he is able to do right there in his office thanks to a new, high-tech machine and technician they have on hand. It all looks like indistinguishable white and gray blobs to me, but both Phil and the technician nod in agreement over what they are both able to instantly detect. I'm not great at reading ultrasounds, but I am quite skilled at reading people, and I watch both of their faces intently. Even though they both see something, it is clear it isn't terribly serious.

"Your ovary has torqued," Phil explains (using the fancy medical term for twisted) "and has slightly descended."

I can tell he is not worried, so neither am I. Phil explains that the ovaries are attached to the outer layer of the uterus via the ovarian ligaments, which are kind of like rubber bands that occasionally twist due to either excessive exercise or excessive sex. I joke that David will be astonished to learn we are engaging in excessive sex, so it has to be the exercise.

It is perfectly plausible that I am exercising excessively. I am a high-energy person and I do exercise a lot. It's not so much that I love to work out, but I love to eat and I am not blessed with the kind of metabolism that lets me get away with consuming calories without coming up with all sorts of ways to burn them. I walk the dogs twice each day in a mile-and-a-half loop around our neighborhood and I usually do at least an hour or two of aerobic exercise and weights on top of that. If I'm not in the gym, I'm on the tennis courts or on a walk or a run. Even though my body doesn't reflect it, in that no one would look at me and think, "Now *that's* a woman who works out a ton!" excessive exercise makes sense.

Phil recommends removing the ovary, which he can do laparoscopically in a simple outpatient surgery. As much as I want to believe I am still a young, fertile baby-making machine (even though I am 46 years old and my husband has endured not one but two vasectomies), the truth is I really have no need for the ovary. Even if Phil untwists it, the ligament attaching it to the uterus is stretched out and distorted, so there is no guarantee it won't happen again, and apparently, my rectum seems to be a good resting spot. Good for the ovary, bad for me. There are, I now know, hundreds of nerve endings in our bums that are on full pro- test when something bothers them. My nerve endings appear to be really pissed off and I do not want to anger them further.

Phil offers to squeeze me in to surgery the next day, Friday, warning me that if the ovary torques again, I will be in total agony. I call David from the parking lot and tell him I will no longer be taking the girls to Asheville, NC for a Scrabble tournament over the weekend. I actually consider delaying the surgery until Monday so that I can still go, but I conclude that a torqued ovary and the winding, mountainous roads that lead to Asheville are probably not a great combination.

It is a good call on my part. By the next morning, I am counting the minutes until my 1 pm surgery. I just cannot get comfortable. I lie on the bed with David, who has taken the day off, and I try to distract myself with one of the television shows we have recorded. David brings me the hot water bottle, I take several baths, and I try lying in a myriad of different positions, but I simply cannot get any relief. By late morning, we decide to head to the hospital in the hope that I can get checked in early and be given something for the pain.

Another good call. Within 10 minutes of arriving at Carolinas Medical Center-Pineville (after a 20-minute drive that has me cursing at David for driving too quickly, too slowly, hitting bumps – real and imagined – and basically just operating the motor vehicle I am in), I am on a morphine drip. The woman at the registration desk who is taking down our insurance information takes one look at me, my face contorted in pain, my hands gripping the back of the chair I am unable to sit in, and she asks the nurses to take me straight back while she finishes the paperwork with David. By the time David joins me in my curtained-off, pre-surgery cubicle, I am feeling infinitely better and singing the praises of narcotics.

My surgical nurse turns out to be Paula Marino, a woman I have played numerous times on the Charlotte Tennis Ladder. "I figured there could only be one Katya!" she exclaims upon seeing my name on the surgical white board for the day. Phil comes in the room and explains that I'll be getting something that will make me relaxed and loopy, prior to being knocked out entirely, and another nurse cautions that the drug works as a truth serum for some patients, who share all sorts of juicy tidbits before finally conking out.

"In that case," I tell Phil, "I should tell you, since it sounds like I'll be letting you know momentarily, that I think you're really cute."

Phil smiles, confirming that he is, in fact, very cute, and David shakes his head and announces that is his cue to leave.

I awaken in the recovery room to learn that all has gone as planned. The ovary looks perfectly fine, other than being twisted and descended, and has been removed without incident. My departure is somewhat delayed by my inability to pee (a new sensation for me since the smallness of my bladder was actually toasted at my wedding and I am the one who requires far more rest stops than the rest of the family on long car drives), but I finally manage a tiny trickle that meets the standard for release. David drives me home Friday night and I email my tennis opponent that our match is still on for Sunday morning. Easy peasy.

On Saturday, I walk the dogs with David and feel somewhat groggy and stiff, but I know I'll improve as the day progresses. I am wrong. I feel worse and worse, with my main complaint being my inability to urinate. I can feel the pressure building up in my bladder but no amount of coaxing, cajoling, water sounds and interminable toilet seat encounters produce even the slightest tinkle.

On Sunday morning, David and I return to CMC-Pineville, but this time we are instructed to go the emergency room rather than the surgical unit. Again, I am in agony. This time, however, my facial contortions and chair-gripping knuckles produce nothing more than an apology that it will be a long wait. Understatement of the year. We end up spending 10 hours there, from start to finish, and we get to experience the hospital in an entirely different, and decidedly unwelcome, way.

The emergency room doctor who finally examines me determines that I need to be catheterized. Not the most comfortable procedure, to be sure, but oh, the sweet relief as what appear to be liters and liters are drained from my bursting bladder. Unfortunately, the doc also thinks it will be a good idea to run an ultrasound, to make sure my bladder issues are nothing more than routine post-surgical complications. So no sooner have I told the nurse how much better I feel after emptying out my bladder than she apologetically hands me a 2-liter bottle of nasty contrast solution and tells me I have to drink it in preparation for the ultrasound. This is the first of many, many moments in which the only logical response, which my sister eventually has emblazoned on a t-shirt for me, is "Really?"

The ultrasound comes back clean, and I am sent home with the catheter and the understanding from the emergency room doc that Phil will remove it in his office in the morning. The night is uneventful, once I adjust to the bizarre and then somewhat liberating feeling of being able to pee without leaving (or wetting) my bed. I am not in pain or dis- comfort, but I am definitely aware of the catheter and eager to get it removed.

When I call Phil's office in the morning, he tells me there is no need for me to come in. Once I assure him that my bladder and I are back on friendly terms, he agrees that the catheter can come out but talks me through how to do that myself. He tells me he does not need to see me again and he wishes me a good trip.

I am due to fly out to Philadelphia two days later, on Wednesday, May 4th, for a conference. I am into the second year of my latest business venture, Perfect Fit College, and I have long-standing plans to attend the IECA (Independent Educational Consultant Association) annual spring conference of professional educational consultants like myself. I have been an alumni interviewer for both of my alma maters, Brown University and Georgetown University Law Center, for years and I really enjoy it. David suggested I parlay my rapport with college applicants and my desire to continue to work from home into a business that would actually bring in some revenue. I think he thought I'd be good at it, and it does seem a really good fit for me on many levels, but I think he was even more motivated by a *New York Times* article he read about what a lucrative field it has become. Nudging me into this business was his less than subtle way of letting me know that the kids are now in school for most of each day and it would be great if I spent some of that time contributing to the family income.

Don't get me wrong. David has been immensely supportive of all of my endeavors. We met at law school and he landed a job with what was then called the Bureau of Alcohol, Tobacco and Firearms after graduating in 1990, where he is still employed. I, on the other hand, clerked for a judge on the DC Superior Court, then served as a teaching fellow in the Street Law Clinic at Georgetown University Law Center before taking a position in the Career Services Office as a counselor and administrator. I planned to pursue teaching, and David was willing to follow me wherever I landed a job, even if it entailed his switching jobs and taking another bar.

We ended up in Charlotte because of his job, where he now serves as Associate Chief Counsel for ATF, but it was really my own job search that initially got the ball rolling. I was up for a position at

Emory University Law School in Atlanta, where David went to college and where my sister lived at the time. I had applied on a lark, but the further I got in the application process, the more we both got excited about the move. David was offered a lateral transfer to the ATF field office in Atlanta so we would not have to worry about his finding a new position or taking the Georgia Bar. We hadn't discussed moving as part of the master plan, but now that it was on the table, we were both excited about the prospect.

I didn't get the job. It came down to two of us and it wasn't me. We thought that was the end of it, but David's boss then asked him if he'd like to head up ATF's new legal office in Charlotte, NC. We had never been to Charlotte, save for a quick drive through on the way back from Atlanta, but we were enamored of moving at this point. With over $100,000 in student loans and two salaries that, combined, didn't even match half of what our friends were raking in at private law firms, it didn't seem possible to move without both of us having jobs. But we did the math and realized that the bulk of my salary went to daycare. If we removed that from the equation, and I was able to bring in some money from consulting and some of my part-time ventures (I had begun catering on the side and had just written a book on the death penalty, with another book in the works), then perhaps we could swing it.

I did bring in some good consulting income in our first few years in Charlotte, so much so that we were able to knock out our student loans. That took a lot of the pressure off of us financially, plus I had increasingly taken on what David likes to refer to as "full-time jobs without the hassle of paychecks or taxes," in that I volunteered up the wazoo at the kids' schools. Over the years, I earned enough from my writing (I am a freelancer for the Charlotte Observer and for some local magazines), my catering, and my occasional gigs as a consultant (primarily for a nonprofit called Street Law) to pay for our vacations and other frivolities. But it is a good thing we are not relying on my income in any way to pay the bills.

I occasionally entertained the idea of getting a more traditional job, especially after Eliza (with whom I became pregnant shortly after moving to Charlotte) started school, but it is very hard to reenter the workforce after being your own boss for so long. I remember mulling over a criminal law teaching position at a local community college but deciding that the hours were just too onerous.

"I would have to be there every Tuesday and Thursday at 9," I complained to David.

"Yes," he replied, speaking slowly and deliberately, "that's what's called a *job.*"

So he has been very supportive of my new college advising business, encouraging me to attend the conferences and workshops associated with accreditation and networking, because he wants it to succeed. He wants to see me happy and fulfilled. He also wants to see our bank account happy and fulfilled.

I leave for Philadelphia as scheduled on Wednesday. On Friday, May 6, 2011, I check my voicemail messages in between a session on *The Nuts and Bolts of Financial Aid* and *How Colleges Assess an Inter- national Baccalaureate Education.* Nestled between a call from a neighbor looking for the recipe for my pumpkin Bundt cake and a call from another neighbor asking if Hannah can babysit is a call from Phil. My heart immediately sinks.

Hey Katya. I am just calling to check on you. I know you're out of town but I just wanted to see how you're doing. I also need to chat with you about something so please call me back.

I call back, but he is with a patient. I call David. "I have cancer," I say, in tears.

"Honey, he's just calling to make sure you're not overdoing it. Like he said, he's just checking on you. You're jumping to conclusions."

"He has no need to check on me. He was done with me, remember?"

I am not to be consoled. I know David knows too.

Phil reaches me about an hour later. It is a very long hour. I can tell as soon as he says my name that it is bad. He tells me later that it is the hardest call he's ever had to make in his 20-year career.

"I don't know how to tell you this," Phil says. "But you have cancer."

I sink down to the floor, behind a ledge where the catering staff is entering one of the big ballrooms to set up for the conference luncheon.

"I want to talk to you about it but we should get David in on the call. Can you conference him in?" Phil asks.

I have no clue how to do that. Phil doesn't know how to do it. So I hang up with him and call David.

"Hi. It's me. I was right. I have cancer. You need to conference Phil in so we can discuss it."

When we are all three on the line, Phil talks us through it. The cancer was identified as serous carcinoma. I only hear little snippets, all of which sound terrifying. It is fast-moving and serious and we need to deal with it right away. I will need a hysterectomy to remove the other ovary and my uterus. Chemotherapy will begin shortly thereafter. There are two surgeons he'd recommend, both excellent. One is someone I'd really like, great guy, good doctor. The other is someone who has a reputation for not having the best bedside manner, but is top of his field and can do the hysterectomy laparoscopically.

I take notes in my datebook, notes that are surrounded by scribbles and reminders that seem ridiculously inconsequential. Hotel information for an upcoming trip, contact numbers for an interview I am lining up, a shopping list for a dinner party we've recently hosted, and then *serous carcinoma.* It is so surreal.

That call from Phil is pretty much my worst nightmare. The word cancer produces an immediate punch to the gut and conjures up a stream of images involving needles, hospitals, bandana-clad, bald and emaciated women, and death. It is something I have always feared, something I don't waste too much time worrying about or stressing over in my day-to-day life, but the fear is always there, lurking, ready to be summoned. If I hear a cancer story on the news or hear about someone who has cancer, I have a mini panic attack. In my mind, a cancer diagnosis is paramount to a death sentence – maybe not an immediate death, but a death sentence nonetheless.

No wonder that call is so hard for Phil to make. It is even harder to be on the receiving end. Phil isn't just calling to tell me I have cancer. He is calling to tell me I am dying.

CHAPTER TWO

It is a good thing I am a well-known crybaby. I cry at sappy movies, commercials, an old man eating alone in a restaurant, pretty much anything that has the potential for producing waterworks. And I can get emotionally attached in a matter of nanoseconds. I can walk by David as he's watching a track meet on TV and he will quickly fill me in on the backstory of the eight guys perched at the starting line. For one, it is his last chance to qualify before having to give up on his dream of becoming a professional runner. For another, it's his first race since a tragic accident that killed his twin sister. The guy on the end used running as his way to cope with his horrible childhood. A race I couldn't have cared less about five seconds earlier, involving eight runners whose names I don't know, is now something in which I am hugely emotionally invested. I yell at the screen and I'm devastated when the one guy I wanted to win – someone I didn't even know existed about two minutes prior to the race – doesn't place. David says I'm an advertiser's nightmare because I emote in spades what they want me to feel, but I never equate those strong emotions with a particular product. I'll be sitting on the couch, tearing up about the kid who came home from college to the little sister who waited up for him or the redhead who doesn't get asked to dance or the old couple looking lovingly at each other as they drive down a country road and David will say, "What product was that for?' and I'll say, "Umm, soap? A truck? I don't know."

So when I fly back to Charlotte on Mother's Day and tear up at the cards the girls have made for me, no suspicions are raised. The up side of being a sap is that when you are crying for other reasons – say, a recent diagnosis of cancer and the fear that this may be the last Mother's Day you'll be celebrating – it produces nothing more than rolled eyes about how pathetic you are. The fact that David and I hug for an extra long time before I get in the van doesn't alert them either. They feel that pretty much any display of affection between us is an embarrassment and avert their eyes as soon as there's any possibility of hugging or kissing, so the intimacy of our embrace – David squeezing me extra tightly, my grabbing on to him as if to make up for the fact that he wasn't there when I first got the news – is lost on Hannah and Eliza.

Noah isn't celebrating Mother's Day with us because he is in Durham, finishing up his junior year at the North Carolina School of Science and Math, a public boarding school two-and-a-half hours drive away. When he left for NCSSM, he had never been away from us for more than a night or two and I worried about how he'd transition to boarding school. During the first few weeks, as kids who couldn't hack the rigorous coursework or the homesickness dropped out, Noah stood strong. He was in his element, thrilled to be among peers who were as intellectually curious as he was, who were happy to stay up all night with him discussing super numbers and who didn't shun him because he was an eager learner. I missed him terribly, but I knew it was the right place for him.

It turns out Noah's bout with homesickness was simply delayed. By the middle of the second trimester, he was feeling run down and over- worked. He still loved the school and all of his activities there, but he'd taken on too full a load and he was overwhelmed and stressed. When I told him about my surgery – the seemingly innocuous ovary removal – he broke down.

"I don't know what I'd do if anything ever happened to you," he told me during his most recent extended weekend, hugging me as if he were still my little red-headed toddler instead of the six foot tall young man who makes me do a double take every time I catch a glimpse of him filling a doorway.

If this sounds like a mother's revisionist history of what her seventeen-year old son actually said, transforming his monosyllabic grunts into Hallmark-worthy expressions of love, know that Noah is no ordinary teenage boy. When he entered middle school and then high school, I waited for my affectionate and vulnerable sweetheart of a son to turn on me, to enter the inevitable "Mom, you are so embarrassing and I need you to stay 15 feet away from me at all times" phase, but he never did. He has never shied away from telling me how much he loves me, or how much he misses me once he started at NCSSM, so being honest about how much my surgery scared him came as no surprise. It confirmed, however, that I will not be sharing the latest development with him right away. He is about to start his final exams and I am not about to torpedo his stellar grades by distracting him with thoughts of cancer and his mom's impending surgery.

David and I agreed, in our late-night phone calls while I was lying in my hotel bed in Philadelphia and he lay on his side of the bed in Charlotte, ensconced by our dogs, Molly and Darcy, that we will delay telling the kids until the school year is over. Noah is due to come home on Saturday, June 4th and Hannah's last exam at East Mecklenburg High School, where she is finishing up her freshman year, is scheduled for Monday, June 6th. We will tell them that night. Until then, we will pretend that all is well.

The kids are not the only ones we are keeping in the dark. My parents are coming to visit (from their home in Bend, Oregon) at the end of the week and I don't want to tell them until the end of their visit. Their arrival is scheduled for Thursday, May 12th, the same day I am due to meet with my new doctor, a gynecological oncologist. (I find myself wondering if those words will ever sound right – just getting them out requires full concentration, as if I am speaking in a consonant-heavy Slavic language.) I want to see my new doc, R. Wendell Naumann, immediately, but Thursday is the earliest he can squeeze me in.

In retrospect, an appointment the week after my diagnosis seems reasonable. When you're still reeling from the news that you have cancer, though, which you picture as an insidious poison that has been festering within you, undetected, a delay of a few days seems agonizingly long. Each minute that passes provides the cancer another opportunity to latch on to you, to grow and multiply and permeate more and more of your body, and no amount of rational information about how inconsequential those minutes really are in the long run does anything to appease your fears. The only thing that gets me through the week is that it is jam-packed with activities, a hectic one even by my Queen of Multi- tasking standards, so I have plenty of distractions.

The end of the school year is always crazy. My datebook for May looks more like the military plans for the D-Day invasion, with every day crammed full of overlapping activities, carpooling logistics and no room to fit anything else in, both figuratively and literally. I can't even blame the kids because I am probably the most overextended and overscheduled person in the family. Whenever I take on something new, like telling David I've been cast in the JCC play or I'm planning to coach an Odyssey of the Mind team or start a Drama Club, his inevitable response, said with raised eyebrows and a weary shake of the head, is, "And what are you giving up?" (He also says that when I say I want another dog.) I have always enjoyed pursuing many things at once, both professionally and personally,

19

and I actually think I function best that way. David is there to warn me when I have too many balls in the air and when adding another to the mix risks having them all come crashing down, but this does not mean I always, or even frequently, heed his advice.

In the spring of 2011, I am running two clubs at Randolph Middle School. I started the Scrabble Club in 2005, when Noah was in the 6th grade, and have kept it going ever since as first Hannah and then Eliza became Randolph Raiders. (Randolph is not our home school, but we think the drive across town is worth it for its International Baccalaureate magnet program and a student body that boasts 82 nationalities.) At the end of each school year, I put together a tournament for all of the Scrabble Club participants (16 students this year) and teachers and parents are invited to participate as well. Each student pairs with a parent or teacher and gets to show off his or her mastery of good Q without U words like *mbaqanga* (a South African dance) and good vowel dumps like *ouabain* (a heart stimulant). We make a night of it, with pizza and prizes, and there is a lot to coordinate.

This year, I have also started a Drama Club, mainly to provide Eliza an outlet for all her Drama Queen ways. (I figured it'd be better for all involved if her theatrics were displayed on stage rather than at the dinner table.) I assumed I'd get a few kids like her and I'd run them through some fun improv exercises and call it a day. Jackie Menser, the RMS principal who has more foresight than I do, suggested limiting the club to 6th graders. Good call. I had 28 kids show up, and they are a wonderful mix of nationalities and socio-economic levels, far less homogenous than the group I'd envisioned. It is clear to me (although David questions my interpretation of this development) that we will have to put on a show. I come up with the theme, "Be True to Your- self," and write some skits consistent with the theme, but it is the kids who come up with most of the material for the show.

As is true of many of the Drama Club participants, Zion, an African-American boy who sports a huge Mohawk on his diminutive frame, is in Scrabble Club as well. I have become very fond of him and I convince him to perform a piece called, "Rock the Mohawk," about his difficult transition to middle school and how he'd hoped his hair would announce to would-be bullies that he should be left alone. It is clear in rehearsals that he is going to steal the show, and he does. Zion lives with his three siblings and his single mom in public housing two city bus rides away from the school. Whenever I see him walking the final stretch to Randolph, I'll pull over and give him a ride. I let him borrow one of the Scrabble Club's dictionaries over winter break and he came back proudly rattling off all the new words he'd memorized. It is kids like Zion who make volunteering at a school like Randolph so gratifying.

So the week I return from Philadelphia, consumed with the news that I have cancer, I have a lot on my plate, not just emotionally, but logistically as well. The Drama Club dress rehearsal is scheduled for Wednesday night. The Scrabble Club tournament is scheduled for Thursday night. My parents are also scheduled to arrive that night, but are getting in so late that they insist on staying at an airport hotel.

I am to pick them up on Friday morning, and they will then get to see the "Be True To Yourself" performance on Friday evening. I am also teaching a cooking class before school at Park Road Montessori, and I am scheduled to make cinnamon rolls with the 12 elementary school students in my class on Thursday morning. I am trying to enjoy the class, one of my last with a wonderful group of kids, but it is hard to shove cancer out of the way. As I roll out the dough with my class and watch their delight in painting it with butter, sprinkling it with cinnamon sugar before rolling it up and slicing it into magical little pinwheels, I have a hard time ignoring the Big C that keeps popping into my thoughts. I find myself wondering if I'll be too sick to teach in the fall and if cooking in general, not just teaching a class to would-be chefs but making meals for my family and baking for friends and teachers, will be one of the many things I'll have to give up. Despite the oohs and aahs of my young bakers as we drizzle icing over the fresh-out-of-the-oven cinnamon rolls, I am in the throes of a full-on pity party. I am trying to figure out how I will get through the first four days of my parents' visit without disclosing what is weighing so heavily on my mind, how I will handle the Drama Club performance the next night and all I still have to do for it (write and print the programs, gather the props and costumes that are still missing, and get the kids – who have been unusually unruly during their dress rehearsal – back in line) when part of me just wants to get under the covers and cry.

My thoughts are also consumed with my first appointment with Dr. Naumann that is scheduled for later in the morning. David is planning to meet me there and we are both apprehensive about what we'll find out. We have so many questions and we want answers, but we also know that this is one of those ignorance is bliss scenarios. As much as we want to know what is happening inside of me and what we can expect in the coming months, we are steeling ourselves for what we will be finding out. The general diagnosis is bad enough. The details, we fear, will be even worse.

My cell phone rings. I ignore it because I am teaching a class. A few minutes later, it rings again. The kids are happily wolfing down their still-warm, gooey cinnamon rolls, so I decide to quickly answer it.

"Ms. Katya, this is Zion's mom." I hear the distress in her voice right away. "They won't let me off work tomorrow night. I will get fired if I take any more time off." She pauses and I can tell she is fighting back tears. "I can't see the show."

We work out that I will bring Zion home with me after school, feed him dinner, and then get him back to school in time for the show. I will also drive him home afterwards, since she doesn't want him taking the buses at night by himself. And I assure her that I will have someone videotape the show so that she'll get to see her son making her proud onstage.

She thanks me, but really, I am the one who should be thanking her.

Thank you for reminding me that I could have it so much worse. I could be a single mom like you, working a job that would fire me if I took time off. *Thank you* for making me focus on all that is right in my predicament instead of all that is wrong. I am not going through this alone, but with a partner extraordinaire. Even though it has only been a few days since the Big C call, David has already shown me that this is going to strengthen our marriage, not test it. "We will get through this," he says to me that first night when we are lying in each other's arms after putting the girls to bed, and I believe him. *Thank you* for the wake up call that not everyone is blessed with good health insurance and steady employment. David's federal government job is never going to make us wildly wealthy, but it is pretty ideal in tough times. In his twenty years with ATF, he has amassed obscene amounts of sick leave and we know he can be by my side for any medical appointments, handholding, childcare, or anything else I need. All I can think, after hanging up with Zion's mom, is how much worse it would be if a single mom like her gets cancer. My pity party is officially over.

22

I tell a few close friends about my diagnosis right off the bat, while I am still in Philadelphia. My first call, after David and I hang up, is to my sister, Nicole. She is on a run when I call so I talk to Rusty, her husband, although talking is putting a generous spin on the stifled sobs and whimpers that my poor brother-in-law has to decipher to piece together that I need to talk to my sister. When Nicole gets back to the house, Rusty tells her to call me right away because someone has surely died.

Nicole is a rock. She commiserates with me but pretty instantly goes into protective older sister mode, a role she takes on with humor and compassion but also solid resolve throughout my cancer journey. As a public health consultant, she wastes no time putting her researcher skills to use and weeding through all the contacts, websites and sources at her disposal to help me figure out what lies ahead. She listens when I need her to do just that, sends funny and poignant gifts, offers up advice when it is solicited but not when it isn't, and serves as a buffer when I need her to run interference with my mom, who is sometimes convinced she knows more than my doctors. Everyone should have a Nicole in her corner when fighting ovarian cancer.

The other three people I call from Philadelphia are dear friends of mine, two in Charlotte and one in Sudbury, Massachusetts.. Nikki Levin, the one in Sudbury, is one of two life-long friends I made while a junior at Lexington High School when we lived in Massachusetts for a year while my dad took a sabbatical from the State Department to get a Master's Degree at Harvard's Kennedy School of Government. Nikki and I stayed in touch after I moved away (to spend my senior year as an exchange student in Valenciennes, France) and her family essentially adopted me when I was in college and my folks were in Africa. After graduation, Nikki and I lived together in an apartment in Cambridge (I still remember the address because it was so quaint – 16 and 1/2 Magnolia Road) while I worked at Harvard's English as a Second Language Program and Nikki got a PhD in Molecular Biology from MIT. Did I mention that Nikki is brilliant? She ended up going to medical school *after* getting her PhD and is a dermatologist in Boston.

She is one of two people (the other being my good friend Iris Cheng, also a doctor) who knew from the start that my initial ovary torqueing was not a good sign. She was concerned from the get go but she downplayed the warning flags that I did not see. When I call to tell her it is ovarian cancer, however, her worst fears are confirmed. She leaves me a voicemail that is jarring because her fear is palpable. It scares me to hear her so upset. When your dear friend, who is also a medical professional, tells you she is devastated, you know it's bad.

But Nikki quickly rebounds from her doom and gloom message, removing her distraught friend hat and replacing it with her brilliant doctor hat. By the time I return to Charlotte, she's begun rendering a service that proves invaluable throughout my diagnosis and treatment and that is to decipher the medical gobbledygook that seems to greet us at every turn and to provide clear, thoughtful and sound advice on how to proceed medically.

May 7, 2011 Hi Katya,

I'm glad we were finally able to talk today. Everything you told me about the CT scan results and the appearance of the ovary was reassuring, but the whole thing is still really upsetting. It must have been particularly awful for you to have been away from your family when you got the news. I will look forward to hearing what your gyn onc surgeon says when you meet him on Thursday. Be sure to bring a notebook for questions you might want to ask him and to take notes on what he says. You may want to ask him about whether it is possible to send your tissue for molecular studies that would predict responsiveness to chemotherapy, should it be needed.

Also, this is the web site of Dr. Berchuck at Duke, who seems to a major expert on ovarian cancer:: http://www.dukehealth.org /physicians /andrew Berchuck

You seem to be handling this news amazingly well, which does not surprise me, but know that you have license to complain, to whine,

Love, Nikki

I also call Lorrina Eastman, whose oldest son, Preston, is at Randolph with Eliza. We met when Preston and Eliza were toddlers and we have been close friends ever since, becoming intertwined in each other's lives and attached to each other's kids as good friends are prone to do. From the moment she finds out, Lorrina is a phenomenal source of support and compassion. She considers it her mission to lighten my load, and she channels all of the managerial and organizational skills that make her so successful at her full-time Bank of America job into helping me and my family.

On Mother's Day, while I am still in Philadelphia getting ready to fly home, I receive the first of many "let me help you" emails from her.

Good morning Katya,

Happy mother's day to one of the greatest moms I know!

You have been in my thoughts constantly. It hurts to think about the very difficult conversations you need to have with your kids and your parents. I wish I could fix that but know that I can't. I am here, however, in any capacity. I will clear my calendar at work whenever needed to help out. Things to consider:

How about I handle driving to randolph this week? It's one less thing for you to worry about. I can pick up noah from school whenever needed.

I can take the girls out on thursday night so you can have some privacy with your parents. Sigh ..

You will get through this. You have to. You are one of my very dearest friends and I need you!

Love, Lorrina

One thing this experience has taught me is that it is extremely helpful to have friends in the medical profession. Iris is the Chief of Residents of Internal Medicine at Carolinas Medical Center, where I'll be receiving my care. When I call her, she promises to do some digging around about my doctor and offers to come with me to my first appointment. David and I ultimately decide to go alone, but knowing Iris is at the hospital, able to pop in at a moment's notice and keep tabs on what my medical team is doing on my behalf, is a huge help.

We take Iris's advice, echoed by Nikki, and bring a notebook. David's legal training – his attention to detail and ability to distill lots of information into key facts – makes him an excellent note taker. His jottings during our first appointment and all subsequent ones prove to be immensely helpful. We are able to review them when we are away from the stress of the doctor's office and are better able to digest what we've heard. We can look up anything that is confusing or has come at us too fast to ask a question or we can refer to his notes to consult with our doctor friends and relatives. David also uses his notes to send comprehensive updates to our families, something I know they appreciate since they cannot be with us when we are getting the medical low down.

Since we are driving separately to the first appointment with Dr. Naumann, I arrive at the Blumenthal Cancer Center at Morehead Medical Plaza alone. I take the elevator up to the sixth floor and see a waiting room full of sad, sick people. There may be men among the patients waiting to be seen, but what I notice are the women. There is a woman who appears to be about my age, leaning on her walker and looking like she is about to keel over. There is another woman rocking herself in a chair against the wall, whimpering and unaware that her bandana has slid halfway off her bald head. An Indian woman is sitting next to her husband, clasping his hand tightly, her eyes large and fearful. Their four small children sit quietly in a row next to them. A TV's news feed is the only noise. It is eerily quiet and it smells like a hospital, a mixture of chemicals and disinfectant.

It feels totally surreal and my first thought is, "I don't belong here."

CHAPTER THREE

"Are you Jewish?" Dr. Naumann asks me.

The short answer is no, I'm not. I was raised a devout atheist by two parents who shunned all organized religion. My dad's parents were Russian Jewish immigrants, but he was never Bar Mitzvah'd and his Jewish identity is more cultural than religious. My mom, who grew up in a small Swiss village about an hour's train ride from Zurich, was the product of a devoutly Catholic mom and an atheist dad. Her childhood included Catholic schools and regular church attendance, but as an adult she followed in her father's footsteps.

My folks met in Zurich, where my dad was working as a diamond salesman and my mom was a stewardess for Swiss Air. My dad was smitten from the moment he met her and, after an initial rough start including my mom standing him up for their first date, they fell in love and got married in short order. When my dad brought my mom back to the States to meet his family, he took the Foreign Service exam and off they went on a life of travel and adventure. My sister was born in 1963 in Washington, DC but she was their only child born in the United States. I was born two years later in Santiago, Chile and my younger brother, Ben, was born in Bogota, Columbia in 1967.

I have lived on every continent except Antarctica and my parents always made it their mission to have us experience a country's culture, food and customs. Some families leave you scratching your head as to why they have embarked on a life in the Foreign Service because they seem to do nothing but try to recreate America when they are posted overseas. They live on American compounds, shop exclusively at the American commissary, and refuse to learn the language or interact with the locals. Not my family. My mom, a linguist extraordinaire (she had a head start with her Swiss schooling and her days as a Swiss Air stewardess) always learned how to speak the language of our host country fluently, which in turn opened us up to all sorts of opportunities and experiences. We shopped in local markets and bazaars, sampled local delicacies, and traveled off the beaten path (both my parents think of *tourist* as a swear word) as much as possible.

I have encountered plenty of people in my life – especially in the South, once we moved to the Buckle of the Bible Belt – who assume I am without morals because I am without religion. It is ironic because no one could have done a better job of teaching their kids the values that so many religions espouse than my parents. Churches, temples and mosques do not have a monopoly on values like caring for others and doing the right thing. On the contrary, I have seen many instances of supposedly devout folks who talk the talk but do not walk the walk. A former neighbor, for instance, who went to church twice each week, did not want her daughter to accompany me and my kids to deliver meals to the poor because she didn't want her going *to those parts of town.* I wanted to yell at her, "You know those people you pray for? These are they! And trust me, they'd rather have a hot meal!"

So the end result is that I do not believe in God, but I am a good person. I never envisioned marrying a man who ascribes to an organ- ized religion because that is not the way I was raised nor the way I wanted to raise my own children. By the same token, David never imagined he'd end up with someone who isn't Jewish. Unlike my dad, for whom the extent of his Jewish upbringing was knowing where to get the best bagels and whitefish, David was raised in a strong Jewish household. His dad, a doctor by trade, is the volunteer cantor for their temple in Bowie, Maryland. His mom, who was also raised Jewish, has served as the temple's president and no doubt always imagined that her kids would marry fellow Jews. David and his younger brother and sister went to religious school, were Bar and Bat Mitzvah'd, and were all involved with Jewish youth groups.

To his parents' credit, I was welcomed into the family with open arms. They chose to value their son's happiness over his beloved's lack of Judaism. We had a rabbi at our wedding (because not having one would have been much more upsetting to David and his parents than having one was to me and my parents) but there was no pressure on me to convert nor to raise our children as Jews. When we lived in Mary- land, we went to David's parents' temple for high holidays and other- wise lived our lives without our religious divide impacting us much. In fact, whenever anyone asks me about how we handle our religious differences, I tell them that our baseball divide (David roots for the New York Yankees while I am a Boston Red Sox fanatic) is a far greater marital stress.

When the kids were born, we agreed that they would be a work in progress. We'd expose them to Judaism but it would ultimately be up to them to decide whether to go with Mom's atheist ways or follow in Dad's gefilte fish ways. It was a sucker deal because we have nerds who embraced the intellectual challenge of Judaism and have continued with Hebrew school even after their Bar and Bat Mitzvahs. They are, much to my surprise and somewhat to my dismay, Super Jews. Noah won a scholarship in his confirmation class for how well he embodies the Jewish teachings of his Hebrew school and Hannah is now a Hebrew tutor, sings in the Temple's Teen Vocal Ensemble, and is often called upon to chant Torah and Haftarah at Congregational Shabbat. David takes them to temple and I drive them around in a van that proudly sports a bumper sticker that has a Darwin fish on it and reads, "We have the fossils. We win." All three kids have learned how to combine their parents' religious identities. Noah calls himself a Jagnostic and Hannah refers to herself as a Jatheist; the jury is still out on Eliza, who had her Bat Mitzvah in March 2013.

So I am married to a Jew and I'm raising three kids who pretty much self-identify as Jews. But am *I* Jewish? No.

I do not, however, go into all of that with Dr. Naumann. When he asks if I am Jewish, he really means *of Jewish descent,* and, more specifically, of Eastern European Ashkenazi Jewish lineage. I know that because Phil has already warned me that it is likely I carry the BRCA genetic mutation that is common among people who can trace their roots to Ashkenazi Jewish populations. Even though my dad was never Bar Mitzvah'd and is not a good Jew by any rabbi's standards, he is Jewish enough for medical purposes.

Dr. Naumann believes that, through my dad, I have inherited the BRCA-1 genetic mutation that greatly increases my odds of getting both breast and ovarian cancer. He tells us I'll have to get genetic testing done to confirm it but that the pathologist who studied my dissected ovary saw markings that are consistent with the BRCA-1 gene.

Dr. Naumann then washes his hands and prepares to examine me. I am sitting atop an examination table, stripped from the waist down. David is sitting in the only available chair, placed, in turns out, strategically in the corner. Before Dr. Naumann begins his pelvic exam of me, he pulls a curtain around David, shielding him from the rest of the room.

"Um, that's actually my husband over there," I remind my new doctor. "There is no need to curtain him off. We have three kids together. He has seen everything you're about to see."

Dr. Naumann looks taken aback. "This is just the way we've always done it."

"That just doesn't make sense to me," I say, wincing and forgoing any more protestations on David's behalf because a hand is now inserted where hands have no business going.

"Nobody puts Baby in the corner," I manage to get out, and the nurse laughs.

"Dirty Dancing. I love that movie," she says.

The curtain is pulled back and David smiles sheepishly from his corner perch as Dr. Naumann proceeds to fill us in on what lies ahead for us. I feel like I am being pummeled against the wall. This is partly due to Dr. Naumann's delivery, which feels like machine-gun fire. There is no gradual build up or sugarcoating of the bad news, no pause to see how we are absorbing what he is throwing at us, no softened tones or expressions of sympathy about how hard this must all be to take in.

"You will need a hysterectomy as soon as possible to remove your remaining ovary and uterus," Dr. Naumann informs us. That much we know. "Cancerous cells were found on your uterine lining, as well as in a nodule on your rectum, so it is, at a minimum, Stage II." That we don't know.

He tells us I'll be getting chemotherapy through a peritoneal port in my abdomen so that the drugs can be blasted directly to the cancerous area. The standard chemo regimen for my type of ovarian cancer involves both Taxol and Cisplatin, which is likely to make me quite ill. I am eligible for a clinical trial that would involve an even more rigorous chemo regimen and we can get back to him on whether or not we want to pursue it. He will know more about my staging when he can get in there and look around during my surgery.

After what seems like an eternity of bad news battering me against the wall, Dr. Naumann pauses, tells us the nurse will be back in with some paperwork, and that his scheduler will call us to schedule the surgery, which will likely be in June because he will be traveling quite a bit in May. He leaves the room, the door shutting with finality behind him.

I am totally demoralized, scared, and overwhelmed with every- thing we have just been told. I turn to David, convinced I'll see the same bewildered and devastated expression on his face that my own sports.

"I feel sooo much better!" David pipes up.

I look at him incredulously.

"What the hell did you find encouraging in all of that?" I ask him.

David's response illustrates our different approaches to not just this, but life in general. I am your quintessential glass is half full kind of gal. I am convinced we will make the movie, get into the school of our choice, and that everything will work out. David is not. He often assumes the worst and this is no exception. I have gone to this appointment thinking that perhaps it isn't cancer after all. Or perhaps it is, but the hysterectomy will take care of it and no chemo or follow up will be required. Even though I try to steel myself for bad news, I am hopeful that it will not be as bad as we fear. David, on the other hand, has gone straight to worst case scenarios.

"It's not Stage IV," David says, with audible relief.

We look at each other, unaccustomed to our role reversal, and burst out laughing. That is how the nurse finds us when she returns to talk me through what comes next.

"It's great that you guys have a sense of humor," she tells us. "That is so important."

CHAPTER FOUR

I don't tell my parents until the last day of their visit. This is partly due to my reluctance to share what I know will be devastating news for them. I hate the fact that I will be the source of worry and stress for them, an angst that will be compounded by their living clear across the country. I also know they'll be unable to keep their distress from the kids, from whom we are determined to keep my cancer diagnosis a secret until after they are done with exams. My mom, in particular, will think she is being discreet, but discretion is not a strong suit of hers. She'll no doubt give me knowing looks or say something cryptic that will surely raise suspicions. Best to minimize the time she overlaps with the kids with the Big C news, especially since my folks will be seeing Noah in addition to the girls.

I love when my parents visit and I wish they did so more frequently. They seem busier now, in retirement, than they ever were before, and it is difficult for them to extricate themselves from their active lives and commitments in Bend, Oregon. Even though they are older than many of my friends' parents, they are the most active and healthy (notwithstanding a few health scares every now and then) pair of senior citizens I know.

My dad is incredibly well-read and I count on him to cull the long list of things he reads on *The Huffington Post* and *The Daily Beast* and *Slate* and *The New York Times* to send me a much more manageable roster of things to read and process. At eighty-two, he hits the gym or the tennis courts every day, a feat that would be even more impressive were he not married to my mom, whose energy level is much more in keeping with someone in her thirties than someone in her mid-seventies. Whenever people marvel at my own seemingly bound- less energy, I tell them that they should see my mom in action. She can speak to pretty much any foreigner we meet in his native language (Urdu for our Pakistani taxi driver; Russian for the elderly woman we meet in a coffee shop; German for the tourists we encounter at the airport, and so on) and has many interests and talents, all of which combine to make her a truly impressive individual. My parents are interesting (their stories of our adventures overseas are always dinner party hits), liberal, funny and smart, and I genuinely enjoy their company. A visit from them is a treat, akin to a visit from good friends, albeit with a few reminders that, at forty-six, I am still their daughter.

My mom usually has something she needs to address with me each visit, some concern that needs to be vetted. My Diet Coke consumption, my neglect of our plants, the kids' TV viewing habits. This time, it is my cell phone use while driving. I point out to her that it is not illegal in North Carolina to talk on the cell phone while driving, but it is still very worrisome to her. I know she has a point and that, legal or not, it would be better not to talk while driving. But it is all I can do not to say, "Trust me, Mom, there are bigger things to stress about."

As is true of most of my parents' visits to Charlotte, this one is crammed full of activities, outings, and opportunities to see their grandchildren shine. It is also a busy weekend for me, which I hope will play in my favor. Mom and Dad will get to see me strong and active, and that will hopefully be the image they'll take back to Oregon with them. After seeing Eliza's performance in the 6th grade Review at RMS on Friday evening and seeing me direct 26 kids in the show, they get to watch me play in a tennis tournament on Saturday and cater a wedding reception for 75 people on Sunday. My dad usually comments that he's tired just watching me but I am happy to be a whirlwind of activity this time, not just because I wanted to project strength and normalcy but also because it keeps the elephant in the room at bay. On Monday, I drive my parents to Durham so that they can participate in Grandparents' Day at NCSSM and see Noah and his school.

I use the afternoon they are touring the campus with Noah to make some cancer-related calls that have built up over the last few days. I call our insurance company to get straight on what our financial obligation will be. I call a Duke University doctor Nikki recommends to see about setting up an appointment for a second opinion. (It's not like David and I are seeking a diagnosis other than cancer. We know we are in with a great doctor and medical facility, but we want some help sorting out the pros and cons of participating in the clinical study.) I call Dr. Naumann's scheduler to see if there is any way to get a date earlier than the June 8th date we've been given for surgery. I call David's Aunt Beth, who has left us several messages saying that the June 8th date is unacceptable and that she's going to arrange having my surgery in New York if we cannot get it moved up. And I place several calls to David to report back on everything and discuss any developments.

It isn't hard turning it all off when I rejoin my parents because Noah is with us. We discuss their day and the impressive research presentations they've seen, including one by a senior who is working on a cancer-related research project. We drive back to Charlotte on Tuesday morning and David meets us back at home for lunch. My parents are due to fly out the next morning and that afternoon and evening will be a flurry of picking up the girls, accompanying Eliza to dance class across town, and dinner out. This is the time we have set aside to share our news.

"David and I have something we need to tell you," I say.

Both of my parents look up.

"You're pregnant!" my mom pipes up, laughing nervously.

David and I look at each other and shake our heads.

The smiles on my parents' faces are quickly replaced with looks of concern. I try hard not to cry, because I know the way I tell them will play a big part in how they take the news. As a parent, I know that the need to protect our children is fierce, and it doesn't matter if your child is six or forty-six.

"It turns out that the ovary they removed from me was cancerous. I have ovarian cancer."

My parents take the news as well as can be expected of folks who are about to hop on a plane and head back across the country, away from their sick daughter whom they have just found out is sick. They are upset and concerned, but they also take their cues from me. The fact that I've had several days to process the news and get past the initial shock of it helps me be calm and stoic when sharing it with them. And I do not look or act sick. They'll be leaving with an image of me as they know me, crazy busy, energetic, and ready to tackle whatever challenge comes my way.

May 19, 2011
Hi Katya,
Needless to say, it is extremely hard to digest the sad news. The only consolation is that we are completely convinced that you will win the

fight 100% and be cancer free after the ugly period with chemo. I am still stunned how you were able to hide the news from us - but understand why you did itl. You are incredibly strong and it is a big help to know how appreciated and loved you are by your friends. And with good reason. You have the best support group possible. We want to help you in any way we can. I know you need to do it your way and we understand. But please - anything that comes to your mind - just let us know. David also needs to let us know how we can help him. We love you very much.
We did, as always, enjoy our time with you, David and the children. Thank you very much.
Love to all, Mom

Aside from those first terrifying moments, when my worst fears were realized and Phil called to tell me I had cancer, I pretty much go into warrior mode. I don't visualize the cancer as a foe that has to be vanquished nor do I lace up the proverbial boxing gloves, but I do feel energized and ready to battle what I perceive to be the ultimate challenge of my life. I always thought that I would rally against the injustice of getting cancer if I ever did get the big C diagnosis, but I don't. I never have a single moment of *Why me?* because, really, why *not* me? I have always lived a pretty charmed life and my happy disposition has been pretty easy to come by. It would actually be somewhat criminal of me to not be happy with everything that has fallen into place in my life. Schools, jobs, husband, kids – it's all gone really well. Sure, there were a few times along the way that I've been tested — Hannah's heart issues when she was born; discovering I was pregnant *after* David had a vasectomy following Eliza's birth and then miscarrying six weeks later; the death of our two dogs and three cats and my grandparents—but this is the first time I've faced something that is a real hardship. And it is gratifying to see that my happy disposition is not just a reflection of all that is right in my life, but that it survives something like this. Sure, it takes an initial beating, but then it bounces right back. I am ready to channel my considerable energy and positivity to fighting the cancer, and hopefully my parents hear that in my voice and see that in my demeanor.

This does not translate, however, into my mom thinking all will be well in her absence. She wants to come back for my surgery, as does Susanne, my mother-in-law. We say no to them both. It would be one thing if the kids were little and help were needed on the home front, but David is fully capable of handling things as far as the kids are concerned. The reality is that it would be *more* stressful, not *less,* having either of our mothers around for my surgery and recuperation. For one thing, I cannot turn off my hostess mode. Even if they insisted on taking care of me, I would struggle with wanting to cook for them and entertain them while they were in my house. Secondly, both moms freely give their two cents about what we should or shouldn't do, and this is not a time we want their input. David actually says as much in an email he sends out to a select number of friends and relatives after we've met with Dr. Naumann for the first time.

Obviously, chemo is going to do a number on Katya, but the doctor emphasized that it is up to her to decide how much activity she can handle. (Insert your own comment about Katya here.) Anyway, I'm sure Katya will bridle at comments about how active she is and needing to tone it down a little, so please let us take our cues from the doctor as to whether she needs to cut back on some things.

Susanne calls shortly after receiving the email. I just shake my head in frustration as she proceeds to tell me that Stuart, their former rabbi who has recently battled non-Hodgkins lymphoma, had even more energy than I do but he wound up needing to take naps every day during his treatment.

"You need to nap every day," Susanne concludes.

Really? *Really?* What part of *Don't tell Katya what to do!* did you not understand? Arghhh.

Andy Zerkle, my good friend Lisa's husband and a local OB/GYN, sends an email painting a picture of what we can expect from chemo, treading carefully on the telling Katya what to do front.

5/16

Katya, David

June 8th will be here before you know it, and I would have you use the time to plan logistics, in case you don't feel well. Possibilities include:

1) Katya muddles through and nobody else has their schedule bothered.

2) Katya can't cook because the smell of cooking food makes her feel nauseous.

3) Katya has profound fatigue and doesn't want to move from the couch

4) Katya feels really crappy, can't cook, drive, or travel, and might be in and out of the hospital with minor complications related to chemo and/or peritoneal catheter.

I don't want to sound snarky, here is a thought experiment:

Let's say Katya doesn't have cancer, but that we knew with certainty that for the next six months, every three weeks Katya was going to get laid up with the flu, and there is a 50-75% chance she couldn't cook, drive or travel, and someone might have to hang out with her for 3-7 days, every three weeks.

I think that you don't want anyone to tell you what you can and can't do. I'm not doing that. Hope for #1, plan for #4. Consider cutting all the fat from the schedule for the summer so David doesn't have to deal with a logistical nightmare. I know you met with your close friends yesterday, which is great.

Second to last thought: David, the paperwork for short term disability and FMLA can be a pain in the whatsis, can be filled out in advance, and there is a box to check where you plan on being out intermittently. Dr. Naumann has his part to fill out so you may want to drop that by, just in case.

Last thought: You can beat this, and I wouldn't say it if it wasn't true. With love, Andy

P.S. Enough with the free advice, right? Here is a good med information website www.uptodate.com/patients

------

CHAPTER FIVE

Who knew there are so many nuances to gynecological oncology? Dr. Berchuck, the head of Duke's Obstetrics and Gynecology Department, specializes in cervical cancer, gestational trophoblastic disease, gynecologic oncology, hereditary cancer risk assessment, ovarian cancer, uterine cancer, vaginal cancer and vulvar cancer. Holy moly. I am calling in the hope of making an appointment with Dr. Berchuck for a second opinion, although calling his office has the added benefit of making me feel fortunate to *just* have run-of-the-mill ovarian cancer. David and I are leaning towards not doing the clinical trial, but we feel like we need to discuss the pros and cons of participating in it with someone other than Dr. Naumann, who is involved in the trial.

As is true of so many things in life, connections help a ton. I am originally told that there is no way I can get on Dr. Berchuck's schedule prior to my surgery on June 8th, but when I now mention another doctor's name (given to me by Nikki Levin's dad, who went to medical school with him), there is suddenly a way to be squeezed in on May 19th. I know a lot of doctors, and that makes a huge difference. I have a rolodex full of folks I can call to help clarify things, to give me advice when my own doctors aren't readily available, and to open doors for me that would otherwise be shut. I know it's not fair. There are plenty of folks out there who need the help far more than I do and don't have any doctors at their disposal to walk them through the process. I keep thinking of the Indian family in the Blumenthal Cancer Center waiting room, looking like deer in the headlights as they tried to absorb what was happening to them. Did they have anyone they could call? If they needed to head to Duke, would they be able to get in? Doubtful. David's Aunt Beth wants to exert her considerable influence on my behalf and get me to see a surgeon at NYU because she thinks the June 8th surgery date that Dr. Naumann has given me is egregiously late. David and I discuss it but decide that this is already difficult enough without adding travel and out-of-state care to the mix. It's stressful to wait, though, because my emotions are clamoring for me to excise the cancer and it's extremely disconcerting to have medical voices joining the protest.

Thankfully, Andy Zerkle sends me an email that is hugely reassuring (and also endearing in the effort I know it took to write it, since Lisa reports that Andy's keyboard skills have never emerged past single digit pecking).

Ironically, you may want the surgeon with a three week waiting list, rather than a one week wait. First, understand that gyn cancer is nearly 100% of a Gyn/Onc specialist practice, and nearly all cases of gyn cancer (cervical, uterine, and ovarian cancer) require surgery initially. Every new patient Dr. Naumann sees has a new cancer diagnosis and needs surgery. If he's worth his salt, he is operating full tilt 2-3 days per week, as much as he can without burning out.

So, assuming a Gyn/Onc doc is making best use of their training and operating full tilt, then the wait time is determined by surgical volume. If Dr. Naumann had offered to operate on you in two days time it means he is only operating on maybe 2-3 patients/week. If he's got a three week waiting list his volume is higher.

With surgery, and procedures in general, you get better with practice. Hospitals with a higher cardiac cath volumes have better patient outcomes, to use a non-gyn example.

With ovarian cancer, it is important that all visible disease is removed at surgery, no matter where it is in your abdomen. "Getting it all out" is called "optimal debulking" in the med lit, and depends on the individual patient's disease, but also on the skill of the surgeon, which may depend in some part on his surgical volume. Especially with laparoscopic surgery. Gyn/Onc surgery wasn't even done laparoscopically 10 years ago, all cases were done "open" with a big abdominal incision and the surgeon getting both his hands in there and really making sure he got it all out. In general, when a procedure moves to being done laparoscopically, and nearly all gyn surgery is doing so, there is a "learning curve", meaning a surgeon has to have a certain volume to achieve equivalent outcomes laparoscopically as open. Volume matters, surgical skill matters, you want the "brilliant" surgeon with the three week waiting list. I think you want Dr. Naumann.

I call Noah and arrange to have dinner with him on the night before my Duke consultation, since his school is just down the road from Duke, close enough for him to steal their Internet access since his own is terrible at NCSSM. I lie and say that I will be heading to Durham with David for one of David's hearings. I will be happy to get through the school year and tell the kids because the lies are piling up. It feels wrong to keep them in the dark, even though I know it is the best thing for them, and the big deceit leads to a surprising number of smaller deceits. I had to lie to the girls about why I had to be dropped off at the hospital on the afternoon of my initial appointment (because they'd forgotten to take my blood that morning, even though David had specifically asked if there was anything else that needed to happen before we left) and I had to lie again about why the hospital was calling me (I said it was part of a column I was writing for the paper), since they left a message on my home machine even though I'd made a point of telling them to only call me on my cell phone.

The deceit also has its funny moments. Carrie Nagle, a neighbor down the street, calls one day to say she's "just heard" and wants to see how I am doing. I explain that I am talking in hushed tones because the girls, who are upstairs, don't know.

"Really?" Carrie says, surprised. "Because David posted it on Facebook."

"What?" I nearly go through the roof.

David is a Facebook junkie. I have never taken to it, but David and Noah are on there all the time. For David, it is a great way to stay in touch with his high school and college buddies, with whom he is still quite close. It isn't like he rediscovered them through Facebook, they have always been in touch (something I find quite impressive and endearing about him), but Facebook has made it so much easier for him. It has become a daily ritual for him to check up on folks via Facebook each day and he makes a surprising (given that he's more social on Facebook than he is in person) number of posts himself.

Every once in a while, I have to rein him in. When he posted our holiday photo, which took forever to pick because we now have five people who want a say in how we each look in it, prior to my sending it out in our holiday card, I was pissed. But *this?* This is totally unacceptable. *Noah* is on Facebook. How on earth is he planning on keeping my hysterectomy a secret if he is posting it on Facebook?

"I can't believe he posted that," I stammer. "Did he mention the cancer too, or just the hysterectomy?" I ask through clenched teeth.

Silence.

"What are you talking about?" Carrie finally asks. "Oh my God, you have *cancer?*"

It turns out David simply posted about my original surgery, the ovary removal, and Carrie is only just now following up with it.

The kids being in the dark creates other issues as well. David holds them accountable for something they don't know, and he is unusually impatient with them. Hannah, whose birthday is May 19th, keeps pestering me to plan her birthday party in late May or early June, but I keep putting her off because I don't know when my surgery is going to be. She doesn't know that, of course, so she is being a typical kid and saying that she doesn't want to invite people at the last minute and that she doesn't understand why we can't just pick a date and send out the invitations already. David explodes, calling her selfish and bratty.

That night, I remind him that Hannah does not know about the cancer. It is not fair to hold her to a higher standard when she has no idea what we are going through. Even without the cancer divide, I notice that he is being unusually short with the girls (Noah is spared David's impatience because he is not under our roof at the time). David is unbelievably sweet and supportive to me, but his frustration with our predicament is finding a different outlet, and it appears to be the girls. They both notice it, asking me repeatedly why he is being so mean. I find myself playing peacemaker, and I explain to David that it is not, ultimately, supportive of *me* to be nice to me but then act in a way that necessitates my needing to comfort and placate the girls.

Little things set *me* off too. I think I am fine, and then something will go wrong or not fall into place the way it should, and I break down. Take, for example, my call to Blue Cross and Blue Shield. After an inordinately long series of preliminary recordings, transfers, and in- putting of numbers, I finally get a live person on the line. I calmly explain that I have recently been diagnosed with ovarian cancer and I discuss the surgery and chemo that lies ahead.

The agent expresses his sympathy for my predicament and I am able to thank him and continue without a Kleenex break. I tell him that I am trying to get a handle on my coverage and what my out-of-pocket expenses are going to be. He tells me that I will be responsible for 30 % of all drugs and supplies, which includes chemo. Yikes. He also explains to me that we have a catastrophic cap of $5000, so that's the most we'll owe in a given year. Phew. He says the same cap would then apply the following year, which I hope is irrelevant information. He is in the process of getting some information for me when the line goes dead.

"Hello? Hello" I say.

No answer.

Really. *Really?*

I call the 800 number back. Same series of annoying prompts, beeps, transfers. When I finally get someone on the phone, I explain that I was already pretty far into it with another agent, but the new one says that the agent with whom I'd been speaking is now on another call and I'll have to start all over with her, the new agent. That's it. That's all it takes for my calm composure, my ability to keep the tears at bay while explaining what I'm going through, what I'll need to have happen to my body, and how much it's all going to cost me, to break down. I tell her I have cancer and I am crying (not the demure, subtle crying you often see in movies, with just a single tear slowly making its way down my cheek, but the hiccupping, voice- breaking, difficult to breathe kind of crying), which I do intermittently for the duration of the call.

I get a letter from the hospital's geneticist, confirming that my blood sample is being sent off to the lab in Utah (the fact that one lab has a monopoly on this type of genetic screening no doubt explains the astronomical cost of the screening – about $3000 - and why insurance companies are rigid about the circumstances necessitating such testing). It is the first time I see in black and white *patient has ovarian cancer.* It gives me chills to read it like that. I hide the letter in the bottom drawer of my night table.

Only two more weeks to go until the end of the school year and my surgery. As if the deception isn't hard enough, my friend Lisa Zerkle tells me she thinks it is wrong for me to keep the diagnosis from the kids. It is very unlike Lisa to give unsolicited advice and it shakes me. I tell her – and myself – that I just have to trust my gut.

At book club on Monday night, the 23rd of May, Lorrina hands out teal ovarian cancer bracelets that she has ordered from the American Cancer Society. Everyone rallies around me, assuring me they will do whatever is needed to help me out. More importantly, they will take their cues from me. Another friend emailed me about wanting to start a meal drive and she concluded her kind offer with the off-putting, "Let's see if Katya is able to accept help." That felt so unfair to me, akin to the famous cross-examination question, "When did you stop beating your wife?" I either accept the meals and what strikes me at the time as invasive and unnecessary assistance, or I am a stubborn stoic who is incapable of accepting help. My book club friends – Lorrina, Juli Johnsen (who moved to Virginia Beach at the start of the school year but has come back for this book club gathering), Jen Davis-Martin, Lisa Zerkle, Lisa Miller, and Laura Lewin – epitomize the word support. They are there for me but they also *get* me.

The next morning, Tuesday, May 24th, I am playing a Charlotte Tennis Ladder match with Jodie Coulson, a woman with whom I have had friendly, competitive matches in the past. I check my messages during the set break and I see that I have missed a call from Dr. Naumann's office. I apologize to her and say that I have to quickly return the call, and when I do, I learn that they have moved my surgery up. It is now scheduled for Friday, May 27th.

"As in *this* Friday?" I ask the scheduler, incredulous that in a matter of days I will be under the knife. Or the laser, actually.

I ask how soon the chemo will start after my surgery and I notice that Jodie is looking at me in astonishment. It is impossible not to eavesdrop when you're both getting water at the same bench during a set break. I explain to her that I was recently diagnosed with ovarian cancer and that my surgery has just been moved up.

"But what are you doing *here, on the tennis courts?"* Jodie asks incredulously.

I assure her that I am fine. It actually feels good to smack the ball around. And what else should I be doing? It's not like *pre-surgery* rest is prescribed.

We get back on the court and start the second set. I have just taken the lead and I'm serving at 3-2 when Jodie sinks to her knees on the other side of the court. I run over, thinking I must have missed the fall or injury that precipitated her collapse.

"Jodie, what's wrong?" I ask. "Are you okay?"

She looks up at me, this woman I only know through the tennis ladder, whom I have only played a handful of times. Her eyes are rimmed with tears.

"I can't do this," she says. "I'm just too upset."

I console her and convince her to keep playing. I tell her the best way to support me is to let me finish the match. When I tell my friends about it later, they are amused that I was the one comforting *her* about *my* cancer. It will not be the last time. I encounter perfect strangers in grocery stores or in line at the bank, who see my bald head and feel compelled to tell me *their* stories. Most of the time, I don't mind. But one time I truly have to resist the urge to say to the woman who is literally sobbing on my shoulder, telling me about her friend who died and how much she hates this horrible disease, that my shirt is getting wet and really, I have shopping to get done. Other times the concern is endearing and touching, like when Juli visits right before my surgery and gets teary when it is time for her to hit the road to go back to Virginia.

5/26/11

Thinking all good things for you for tomorrow! Sorry I got all emotional yesterday after breakfast. It wasn't sadness so much as worry and the frustration of not being able to do anything or even to be there if needed. I know you'll come through with flying colors tomorrow and we hope David makes it through the whole thing too! Much much love, Juli & Willy

------

David is due to leave for Washington, DC. on Wednesday and return on Friday, the day of my surgery. We agree that he will come home instead on Thursday night, since I will have to be at the hospital at 5:00 on Friday morning. David wants to cancel the trip altogether, but I insist that he go. Really, what is the point of being with me in the days prior to the surgery? Far more important to be with me in the days following it. Also, his trip is the culmination of a project he's been working on for several years on a new case management system for ATF's Office of Chief Counsel. Then Steve Rubenstein, the Chief Counsel and David's boss at the time, chimes in, telling David he will not allow him to go. David replies that I am okay with it, that I am, in fact, insisting on it. Steve responds that he will not sign David's travel voucher and that, last time he checked, it said Chief Counsel on his office door. David then informs him that he has another boss and this one is pushing him out the door. So off David goes.

My next challenge is handling the girls, since our plan of keeping my cancer under wraps never included hiding a hysterectomy from them. The one advantage to the June surgery date, which everyone seemed to agree was too far away (nothing like having your doctor friends disclose, now that the surgery is rescheduled, how worried they were about its originally scheduled date and what a relief it is that it has been moved up) was that it would follow our telling the kids about my cancer. Now that it precedes the big Cancer disclosure, I will have to keep a much bigger secret.

I decide that the way to do it is to have them both spend the night out on Friday night. By the time they come home Saturday afternoon, Ill be back from the hospital and we'll pass off my bed-ridden status as a bout of the flu. What's that? You're wondering how it is that I'd be back home on Saturday if my surgery to remove my uterus and remaining ovary, a five-hour procedure, is scheduled for Friday morning? Is this a case of Katya-the-terrible-patient demanding to go home from the hospital prematurely? Nope. The insurance company deems that a laparoscopic hysterectomy is a one-night's stay procedure. Even by my bounce right back standards, that still strikes me as ridiculously brief.

Hannah and I are supposed to head to Atlanta for a Scrabble tournament that weekend and we have both been looking forward to it as much for the Scrabble (to which she is as addicted as I am) as for the chance to get away just the two of us. I worry that she'll be upset about my having to cancel it, especially since I don't really have a good reason for doing so. (I explain that with David gone all week and our having to leave before he gets back, we'd miss seeing him until Monday night and it just seems an unnecessarily long time to be apart.) She is surprisingly cool with it, aided in large part by the fact that the sleepover I've arranged is with Ivy Zerkle, our friends Lisa and Andy's daughter, who was a good friend of Hannah's in middle school but whom she does not get to see as often as she'd like now that they are both in separate high schools. Note to self: arrange sleepover with Ivy Zerkle to offset all future cancer-related disappointments.

On Thursday, I am working out at the Jewish Community Center and I see Susan and Stephen Gundersheim. They have directed me and the girls in JCC theatrical productions and I haven't seen them in a while. I fill them in on what is going on with me.

"Wait," Stephen says, trying to process it all. "Your surgery is *tomorrow?*"

I nod.

"This sure isn't what *I'd* be doing the day before my surgery," he says.

I am getting that a lot. I honestly don't know what people expect of me. Am I supposed to hang out at home, curtains drawn, a box of Kleenex at hand, reflecting on how much my world has been rocked? Life goes on, people. Like it or not (and, for the record, I like it), life continues. For me, the best way to cope with all that is happening to me is to march on, maintaining as much normalcy in my life as possible. My biggest fear – other than dying, of course – is to become an invalid or be treated as one. To the extent it is within my power to continue living my life through all of this, to be out in the world rather than in my bed, that is the route I'll take. Sometimes consciously, most times not, often to the dismay of family and friends, I am going to face this cancer in my own way, not in the prescribed way that people think I should.

After my workout, I join some of my neighbors for lunch at Fran's Filling Station, one of my favorite Charlotte restaurants. I have become friendly with the owner, Fran Scibelli, after writing a column about her, and she has some special tables lined up in the back, adorned with fresh wildflowers and pitchers of basil strawberry lemonade for us. My friend and neighbor Amy Marx has organized the luncheon, not knowing it will double as my last meal before my surgery, and has put together a gift basket of magazines and restaurant gift cards from everyone. Amy is one of the first people I met in Charlotte; she lives around the corner and her three kids are roughly the same ages as mine. Even though she is originally from Pennsylvania, Amy epitomizes Southern charm and is just about the sweetest person on the planet. Amy orders several plates of Fran's award-winning fries, unaware that I have been told to avoid fried foods before the surgery. It is torture watching them get devoured all around me, and poor Amy feels awful. Okay, torture is maybe a little bit strong, especially in light of other hardships I am about to endure (I'm thinking French fry deprivation is easier than the slicing of one's vagina) but you get the picture.

I pick up the girls from school and decide to take them to a movie, even though it is a school night, because I need to fill the time and distract myself from what is now looming in the immediate future. I announce that we will not be buying popcorn (knowing that I can't endure another round of let's eat what Katya is not allowed to consume right in front of her) but that news is met with the kind of protestations you'd think would be reserved for an announcement that I am giving our dogs Molly and Darcy away. I relent and spend the next few hours sitting between my girls, passing a big tub of popcorn back and forth to them. The surgery will be easy compared to this, I think.

David gets home that night, after the girls have gone to bed, and we do our best to get a good night's sleep. The surgery itself isn't so worrisome – although it is a relatively major surgery and any time you are under anesthesia is risky – but our thoughts are instead consumed with what the surgery will reveal. We will find out within the next 24 hours what the staging of my cancer is, how pervasive it is, and if we've caught it in time.

Not exactly the stuff of sweet dreams.

CHAPTER SIX

I can't remember who sent the card, but it is a perfect fit for my take on what I'm going through. So many get well cards, especially the ones that are geared specifically to cancer, are schlocky and overly sentimental. But this one has a cartoonish plane that says something about how it doesn't matter how bumpy the ride, and then inside, with the plane on the ground, it concludes *as long as you have a safe landing.* I like the fact that it doesn't sugarcoat the reality that some of my journey is going to suck, but that all will be well as long as I can get through it.

My mailbox – both the metal one in front of our house and the electronic one on my computer – yields all sorts of well wishes every day. A good way for friends and family to show their support and express their concern in those first few weeks, when calls would be awkward because of the kids not knowing, is to send me emails and cards. I can only speak to what works for me, but I find *all* outreach – no matter how bumbling, the short and sweet and the long-winded and erudite, from folks I know well and folks I've only met recently or I haven't heard from in a while – to be extremely comforting. Again, I can only speak to my experience, and it may very well only be relevant to me, but I think there are some universal rights and wrongs in how to respond to someone facing a health crisis.

One of the rights, and I'm going to go out on a limb and say I think this applies to everyone, not just extroverted, open book me, is to go ahead and let the person know you're thinking about her. Don't show up on her doorstep or catch her unaware, but you can't go wrong with a call or email. I believe that the fear of inadvertently offending someone, the very person you are trying to help and comfort, makes many people reticent to reach out to folks who are sick or facing some kind of calamity. But I can't imagine anyone being offended by a well- meaning *I'm thinking about you* gesture.

The emails I receive when I am first diagnosed, as word gets out to family, friends, neighbors, and teachers, are energizing and uplifting. Any time I doubt my ability to persevere or handle all that is coming at me, someone sends me a card or email confirming that I am strong and resilient. You will need to take your cues from the person you are trying to support, but for what it's worth, the many expressions of concern and love and support and awe at my perseverance and strength that I receive in the immediate aftermath of my diagnosis are just what I need.

I also think folks worry too much about how to say something, when really, the way you express it is somewhat moot. It is the fact that you are saying something, that you are reaching out and letting me know you're thinking of me, that matters.

May 18, 2011
Katya,
Mom told me about your latest diagnosis and it has obviously been on my mind all day. She and Dad also told me that you were remarkably stoic which doesn't surprise me. I know you have what it takes to kick it.
Please let me and Celine know if we can do anything. I'll try to call you when I get a chance during the day.
Love, Ben

This is from my brother, Ben. We've been somewhat estranged in recent years so I credit cancer with bringing him back into my life. It means a lot to me that my diagnosis touches him as deeply as it does, as does his assessment of my stoicism.

May 18, 2011
Oh crap, Katya. For all my love of words, I can think of nothing to say but oh crap. I'm really sorry to hear this news, and I just want you to know that although you have 400 friends already, I hope you'll count me high on the list of those who have your back.
Ok, so here's the deal. I've only known you for nine months, but you may be the strongest, brightest, most energetic, sparkly woman I have ever met. Seriously, it's in your eyes. Something tells me that this diagnosis is going to be very sorry it crossed your particular path, because you are one formidable opponent. I'm sure you have fantastic docs which means you're going to be in great hands. Meanwhile, we'll be here to support you and your family any way we can.

I'll be around all morning tomorrow if you want to talk or even get the calendars out and plan some times we can have Eliza and/or Hannah.
Lisa

I have only met Lisa Rubenson recently, at the start of that school year, our friendship a happy outcome of Eliza's friendship with her daughter, Blaine. I love the way she calls it like it is. Cancer sucks, and just acknowledging that fact goes a long way. No need to sugarcoat it or make it into something grand or poetic. It just sucks. To me, commiserating with me about the sucky situation is preferable to trying to draw some conclusions about why it is happening to me (God only picks those who can handle is something I get a few times, problematic both because I don't believe in God and because that is a bunch of crap) or advising me how to proceed (you must read the scriptures every day is another beauty I receive – wrong on even more levels than the God picking me sentiment). And Lisa's is one of many missives I receive that has me facing off against cancer, with cancer going down, not standing a chance, losing, being vanquished, waving the white flag. I have mixed feelings about the fighting metaphor. The truth is, I do feel like I am in the fight of my life, and while I don't exactly visualize cancer as my foe, decked out in boxing gloves and facing me across the ring, I do think of my diagnosis and treatment as a battle.

I know, though, that my armor of positive thinking, unbelievable support, a good sense of humor, and a fit and strong body, are only part of the equation. When people lose their fight with cancer, it is almost always a function of things that are out of their control, and I hate the implication that they simply didn't fight hard enough. I also think it's much easier to have a positive mentality and warrior spirit when you are given a good prognosis. If I were told I was Stage IV and I had been given a slim chance of surviving, who knows if my attitude and spirit would have been the same. I kind of doubt it.

But I am tickled by Lisa's perception of the cancer as not knowing whom it is messing with and running away with its tail between its legs. I get this kind of imagery from several people and it makes me feel strong and, if not invincible, then at least able to handle whatever is going to come my way.

5/22/11

Hey Katya,

After reading your message, I was very angry and revolted against these disease and the fact that one of my best friends is one of her prey. Sorry for the delayed answer but I couldn't find the right words to express my fellow feelings.

In any case our family is here for you and ready to help. And yes you are a very strong person and keep your wonderful smile and attitude.

Grosses bises et a tres bientot Annie

My French neighbor, Annie Fromm, needn't worry about her ability to express herself in English. I laugh out loud at the concept of her revolting against mean ol' cancer and I truly appreciate her feeling pissed off on my behalf.

I receive several cards and emails telling me that folks are praying for me. I usually take these as the well-intentioned gestures they are meant to be, but there are times when the religious overtones really irritate me, especially the cards that reference God as a way of making me feel better. Anyone who knows me at all should know that isn't the least bit comforting to me, so really that kind of card or sentiment is all about *you* and what works for *you,* not *me.*

There are also times when the religious divide is downright comical. I remember walking around the neighborhood one day, shortly after my surgery, and a neighbor down the street runs out of his house to intercept me.

"Katya, I just want you to know I'm lifting you up every day," he says.

I just stare at him, completely baffled. Then it hits me. Lifting me up, as in prayer. Got it.

But that doesn't bother me because, as is true of all of the times folks tell me they are praying for me, I take it the way it is intended, as his way of expressing concern and good thoughts. I am not offended by anyone praying for me just as I hope they under - stood that if something bad were to befall them, I *wouldn't* be praying for them. I'd be doing my version of that, which is thinking good thoughts.

52

The other way the religious overtones burn my cookies (as they say here in the South) is when folks assure me I am going to be okay because God has a plan for me or He needs me on Earth. So my neighbor down the street who died of lung cancer, leaving behind three kids, or the other neighbor who had a heart attack while out biking, even though he was an exercise and health nut, are their lives somehow less valuable? Is God somehow okay with calling *them* up? Please. Sometimes, as the bumper stickers and baby bibs proclaim, shit happens. Trying to make sense of a senseless tragedy isn't helpful to me, nor is the implication that an illness or death fits in to some master plan.

A few of the cards and emails I receive go over the top with the religious platitudes, especially considering that anyone who knows me at all should know that quoting Bible verses or referring to God's love of me does not lift my spirits, just the opposite, in fact. One of David's colleagues sends me a card that says, "In your resolve against cancer, remember God is with you." My first reaction is who at Hallmark said, "Man, we should have cards just for cancer patients." It just strikes me as cheesy to have a card focused exclusively on my disease. I envision rows of cards in the store, categorized by type of cancer instead of by holiday or type of celebration. Let's see, for Sally's second bout with breast cancer, let's go to the repeat diagnosis section. For my neighbor's kidney cancer, I'll go to the non-gender-specific cancer section and for my daughter's PE teacher, who has a sense of humor about it all, let's peruse the humorous cancer card section. Give me a break. My second sentiment is even less charitable because inside the card says, "God's healing is in your treatments, His wisdom guides your caregivers, His love flows through the people who care so much about you – people like me." I don't want God giving my caregivers wisdom! And I certainly don't want Him interfering with my treatments. I'd much rather have my doctors, who have medical training I believe in, overseeing my care.

But the worst is from a woman from the tennis ladder whom I barely know. Upon hearing I have cancer, she sends me an email that makes me gasp.

We have come along way in being able to cure cancer in the uterus. The good news is that God is in control and heals. We know this through scripture and in what we've witnessed here on earth. We have to keep our faith and read his word, daily, for encouragement. Joel Osteen's bible is the best resource.

Seriously? If that works for you, go for it. But how friggin' presumptive to assume that it not only works for *me,* but to tell me – someone who doesn't read the bible at all –which bible to read! But most missives I receive are lovely and loving, striking just the right note of sympathy and encouragement.

Dear Katya,
I hope you don't mind that Lorrina just told me your devastating news. I took some time to read about so about some of things you must be going through/ and must still go through. I read some really encouraging things from survivors, and know that as you are one of the strongest women I know if they can beat it, so can you. I just want to get on a plane and see you. I wish I could be there to bring you meals (nothing like you cook), hold your hand, drive the kids around, walk your dogs. ANYTHING and EVERYTHING you need. I mostly want you to know how much I care about you. You mean a great deal to me, and have helped me many, many times. Lorrina is sending me a bracelet and I will think of you everyday. It will be so hard, and there is nothing that any- one can say to make it easier. But maybe with all the love you've given out you can feel some of the energy coming back to you.
Many of my best memories of Charlotte have you in them, and I want you to know how very sorry I am, and that I am thinking of you every minute, and love you.
Kelly

My friend Kelly Simmons, who has recently moved from Charlotte to Montana, expresses what a lot of out-of-towners feel, and that is the need to be close and to do concrete things to help out. Many of the folks who are reaching out from afar are amazingly creative in their gestures of support and love, which I will chronicle later, but just letting me know you're thinking of me goes a long way. And Kelly's hope that I can feel the good will I've put out in the world coming back at me is exactly what I am experiencing. It's certainly not a tit for tat, line up to return the favor if I've ever shown you a kindness kind of scenario, but a catastrophic illness sure does let you know how many friends you have in the world.

I have always felt that a wake, or any kind of post-death celebration of someone's life, is somewhat bittersweet because the person who is being eulogized so eloquently is not around to hear all the ways he touched people's lives. In many ways, my cancer diagnosis is a way to be around for my own wake. I don't mean this in a morbid way. I do not feel that I am dying. But facing a disease that often does result in death has almost everyone I know scrambling to tell me how much I mean to them.

And that, I am here to say, is incredibly empowering and uplifting.

My entire bout with cancer is one big manifestation of that lesson we all try to impart to our kids about treating people the way you'd like to be treated. I put a lot of kindness and compassion out in to the world, and, wow, has it come back to me! I feel so empowered by all of my friends and well-wishers, near and far, and I really do think of all of their positive energy and thoughts as my armor, my insulation against the insidious cancer, who has no friends, no one on its side.

Cancer has me feeling vulnerable and alone, but all of the emails, cards, and calls I receive in those first few weeks build me back up.

I feel loved.

CHAPTER SEVEN

I wake up from my hysterectomy glad to have it over with. I am pretty out of it, but I register that I am in a private room, for which I am grateful.

"My turn," I think to myself, as waves of pain and nausea roll over me.

The surgery is actually easy for me because I am sedated. For David, though, that day is a mighty long and hard one, especially since the surgery will yield a definitive staging of my cancer and a better sense of my prognosis.

There isn't much my friends can do for me while I am being operated on, but they can support me by supporting my family. This is the first of many, many instances when they show their love for me by caring for my kids and my husband, and I think David and the girls, in particular, become a lot closer to some of my friends as a result of this new dimension to our friendship.

If he had his druthers, David would probably have opted to spend the day alone. He's not a loner, but he doesn't draw comfort and energy from other people the way I do. But I think he is ultimately pleased that he is not alone in the Carolinas Medical Center waiting room. Marni and David Eisner bring bagels and the New York Times and sit with him for a while. Lisa Zerkle brings the Wall Street Journal, to counter- balance the Times, which is funny since Lisa is as liberal as we are. My neighbor, Lynn MacVaugh, comes by on her way to her warehouse (she started a glass lamp business) and Iris pops in during her rounds at the hospital. Lorrina is on kid duty, picking up the girls after school and chauffeuring them to their after-school activities, where David retrieves them later. "Everyone was really nice," David tells me later, "but they couldn't take away my nerves."

Once the surgery is over, and the relief of my cancer staying at Stage IIB registers, David's hard part is over and mine is just beginning. My turn. It is difficult to believe the laparoscopic hysterectomy is an improvement over the more traditional surgery of cutting me open, because I can rattle off several down sides right off the bat. Sure, my incisions are smaller, but instead of one big one, I have four small ones. One is on my right abdomen, where Dr. Naumann has inserted the plastic peritoneal port that he will use for my chemotherapy drugs. One is on my bellybutton, where Dr. Naumann inserted the telescopic rod lens that was attached to a video camera and projected everything in my gut onto a TV monitor so that he would be able to see where everything was and manipulate his instruments accordingly. Those instruments were inserted through my third incision, on my lower left abdomen, and the fourth – the bad daddy of them all – is internal, across my vagina. This is how everything exited my body since I did not have a larger incision in my abdomen.

I thought that the laparoscopic hysterectomy would be just like the laparoscopic ovary removal, albeit on a slightly larger scale. Wrong. Not even close.

My shoulders and backache from what the nurse describes to me as gas pains. It turns out that a key feature of laparoscopy – something that escaped both me and David as the surgery was described to us – is that the abdomen is essentially blown up like a balloon with carbon dioxide gas. This elevates the abdominal wall above the internal organs like a dome to provide Dr. Naumann ample room to work and view everything. It takes our bodies a while to absorb all that carbon dioxide. Until it is removed by the respiratory system, it creates painful gas pockets as it travels through the body. It is so bizarre to me that some of my most acute pain is in areas Dr. Naumann hasn't touched.

That evening, the sole overnight the insurance company covers for what now strikes me as a pretty major surgery, Lorrina comes by and brings David dinner to my hospital room. Lorrina hangs out for a while but I insist that both she and David leave for the night. I am in a lot of pain and they make sad, sympathetic puppy dog faces every time I wince. I'd rather give in to the pain without worrying about *their* worry.

The next morning, I am able to pee. I know from my last surgery that this is a major milestone (known in medical speak as the ability to void) and that my release from the hospital is contingent on my being able to do so. When I tell the nurse, she is shocked that I braved the bathroom visit on my own without calling her. I just unplugged my IV pole (sending me a steady stream of pain-relieving narcotics and fluids) and walked the five feet to my bathroom. It was not pretty and I moved very slowly, so I am not sure why this is such a big deal, but several nurses pop their heads in to marvel at my tenacity once the word gets around. This strikes me as funny since I am supposed to be sent home later in the day, so you'd think being able to get out of bed and go to the bathroom by yourself would be an expected milestone I'd have to reach.

I complain again about my back and shoulder pain, especially the shoulder pain. It truly feels as if I have a pulled muscle back there. Another nurse explains that it probably hurts so much because my arms were pinned back behind my head for the five hours I was operated on. Makes sense, and I am again taken by surprise at the things that were done to my body.

One of Dr. Naumann's partners stops by to check on me. It is the first time I have seen a doctor since my first and only appointment with Dr. Naumann (the surgery doesn't count, since I was not conscious while he was with me) and I have a ton of questions. That first appointment was such a blur, but I've had a few weeks to process all that information that came at me so fast and furious and I have so many things I want to know. It is clear, however, that Dr. Hall is doing rounds and this is not a "ask me whatever you want" kind of visit. He checks on my port and I ask the most pressing question, the one that seems so superficial and insignificant in retrospect but is gnawing at me more than any others.

"Does the fact that I'm getting my chemo in a port, rather than intravenously, mean that I'm less likely to lose my hair?"

Dr. Hall looks over my chart. If he recognizes the vulnerability in my voice, the way this one query is my way of trying to regain some semblance of control over all the traumatic things that are suddenly and inexplicably happening to my body, he doesn't show it.

"No, you are getting both infusion and port," he says, very matter of fact. No sympathetic pat of the hand or kind empathy in his gaze. "You will definitely lose your hair. Definitely."

My friends Laura Lewin and Mara Purcell show up, bringing with them some fruits and vegetables they picked up at the Farmer's Market. I appreciate the gesture, especially the way the bright red strawberries and tomatoes brighten up the clinical, white room, but I have no desire to sample any of them. I have zero appetite, no doubt because my stomach is still protesting the fact that it was stretched to pregnancy proportions and cut and prodded.

My new nurse explains to me that I won't be released until I can get some food down. She spies the bags from the farmer's market and exclaims, a look of alarm on her face, "Are those strawberries? You need to get them out of here. I'm allergic to strawberries!"

What are the odds?

I manage a few bites of mashed potato and bland chicken, enough to get the thumbs up to leave. We are eager to get out of there because I want to get home and under the covers before the girls come home.

Once home, I muster up all of my acting skills to pretend that I am sick in bed with the flu. This is no easy feat because Molly and Darcy are also clueless about my surgery and are eager to snuggle up next to me or leap over me to bark at a squirrel that is taunting them outside the window, all with total disregard for my bruised and bandaged stomach. Even on a good night, with no surgical wounds, David and I wake up with sore necks and backs because we share our bed with these two 60 and 70 pound bed hogs. It would raise the girls' suspicions for me to banish the dogs, so I wince and grimace and try to deal with the fact that every shake of the bed, including when the girls plop down on it to tell me about their sleepovers, is painful.

Prior to my surgery, Eliza seemed the most attuned to something being amiss. She asked me on several occasions if everything was okay with me. I drive her to school each day and to activities each afternoon, so we spend a lot of one on one time together. Early on, after I send her teachers an email explaining what is going on with me, I receive this one back from her science teacher, Robin Mitchell.

May 19, 2011

Dear Katya,
I am so sorry to hear about the cancer. Damn, I hate that stuff. Thank you for letting me know so that I can be more sensitive to Eliza. Her presence in class is (as you might have guessed) one of the highlights of my day. She is a very astute young lady and I would not be surprised if she guesses something is amiss. I am available any time she needs to talk and I respect your need to reveal this

diagnosis in your own time. May you have strength, courage, and
wisdom during these difficult hours.
Sincerely,
Robin Mitchell

I have arranged a ton of activities for Eliza the weekend I come home from the hospital so that she is only home for short spurts of time. She flits in to the room in between lunch with one friend, an afternoon at the pool with another, and I am able to keep up the ruse that I am bed- ridden with the flu.

It is a tougher challenge with Hannah because she does not leave the house again after we both return on Saturday. She has just turned fifteen but has not gone through any of the teen rebellion and sullen separation I have heard is a rite of passage with girls her age. Hannah still confides in me about all sorts of things and appears to enjoy spending time with me.

A good thing, ordinarily, great in fact, but lousy on this particular weekend. She is in an out of my room constantly, asking if I want to watch a movie with her (no, I just want to take these pain pills and anti- nausea drugs and drift off) and she's eager to tell me about the raspberry cake she made at the Zerkles' with raspberries they picked themselves from the Zerkles' garden (something that would ordinarily sound delicious to me but makes me incredibly nauseated, although I somehow manage to feign both interest and regret that there wasn't a piece left over for me).

On Sunday, I send David and Hannah off to Costco. It is a blow for me to be unable to go, because it means I am off track with my expected recovery. Sure, I figured I'd be moving slowly and gingerly, but I did not anticipate that I'd still be bedridden and laid low by wave after wave of nausea. The nausea is unrelenting and has me really down. I forego all pain meds because I am concerned they are contributing to the nausea, even though the nurses at the hospital assured me they wouldn't. I learn something about myself in these early days of post-surgery recovery that has held true throughout my cancer journey. I have a relatively high pain threshold, in that I can tolerate pain without my psyche getting involved. Nausea, not so much.

I have always been prone to motion sickness of any kind. When I was younger and we had a family vacation in Venice, I got sick on the gondolas. Planes, especially the little puddle jumper that we take as our final leg from Portland to my parents' home in Bend, Oregon, make me incredibly queasy. I get carsick if I sit in the back seat of a car, especially for longer rides, and buses, with their lurching stops, are even worse. One of the worst fights David and I had in our marriage was when he convinced me to ride the Space Mountain roller coaster at Disney World, assuring me it was a baby roller coaster that wouldn't upset even the weakest stomach. I was sick from the moment it ascended the first hill – which, for the record, might be significantly smaller than the inclines on more daredevil rides, but is a hill worthy of stomach-turning speed and drop all the same – and I spent the entire ride trying desperately not to throw up but also knowing that if I failed in that task, I would be sure to turn around and vomit all over David.

The worst part of this post-surgery nausea is that it is as if I am on a permanent loop of the Space Mountain ride. It shows no signs of stopping or even waning. It is constant and unrelenting and I find my spirits plummeting with each wave of queasiness.
It isn't just that I am eager to get out of the house. Being flat on my back in bed for two days is two days longer than my comfort zone, and I anticipated being on my feet by Sunday. Part of my eagerness to be up and about is due to a catering job that I am supposed to deliver on Wednesday and it would be so much easier to shop for it myself than to send David with a list. But each time I try to stand up, the room spins. Even worse, the room continues to spin when I lie back down. There is no escaping it, even closing my eyes only makes it spin in darkness, making me feel gravitationally challenged as well as nauseated.

My expectations for my recovery are unrealistic. I know most people – those who worry about me at the time and those who are reading about my struggles now – will nod their heads vigorously at this revelation of mine. I underestimate how much the surgery is going to beat me up and how difficult it will be to bounce back. The worst part of it is the nausea, which is something no one can truly anticipate and so warning me about it would have been futile, but no one really did. Had I known I'd be laid low by the cumulative effects of all that carbon dioxide collecting in painful pools in my torso and the many narcotics my bloodstream is trying to absorb and the poking, prodding and pulling that has traumatized my midsection (and especially, as they say 'round here, my "female parts"), I might have fared better emotionally. I would, as my doctors and nurses tell me in what soon becomes a familiar refrain, learn to "manage my expectations."

Yes, it would have been prudent to clear my schedule. My friends are certainly trying to get me to do just that. The catering job remains on my calendar as a big, looming obligation in the week following my surgery because I initially agreed to it when my surgery was scheduled for June 8th, well past the catering delivery date. Once my surgery date is moved up, I feel that it is too little time to reschedule and I hope – naively and erroneously, it turns out – that I will be able to pull it off anyway.

The job is for a couple of friends of ours, Alyssa Mills and Boris Krivitsky, whom we met through David's cousin, Stefanie. Alyssa and Stefanie were roommates at Yale and Stefanie hired me to make some meals for her good friend while she recovered from surgery. The irony is that my surgery is moved up so that it falls one day after Alyssa's surgery, resulting in my making meals for someone recovering from surgery on the heels of my own release from the hospital. But both Alyssa and Stefanie (neither of whom knows about my own diagnosis or surgery) have told me how excited they are that I can make the meals, and I do not want to let them down, especially with such short notice. There is no doubt they would both have insisted that I cancel if they had known and they are, in fact, mortified once it all comes out after the fact. But in my head, I have to see this catering job through.

When Hannah and David return from Costco, I give David some instructions – through gritted teeth and tearful admonitions that no, I cannot possibly eat anything – on how to begin prepping some of the food. Hannah is supposed to be helping David but she excuses herself to come see me. She knocks on the door and asks if she can talk to me. I can tell her voice is quavering and she appears to be on the verge of tears. I know she has figured it out. She may have overheard one of my conversations with Nikki or my sister or my mom. Perhaps she saw one of the many papers we've brought home from the hospital or seen one of the pamphlets we'd been given, that I have tried to stash out of sight, on ovarian cancer or chemotherapy. Or perhaps she's simply sensed, as an intuitive and sensitive 15-year old girl, that I have more going on than just the flu.

"Mommy, can I talk to you?" Hannah asks again, this time making no effort to hide how upset she is. A tear rolls down her cheek. Her lower lip trembles.

My mind is racing. Do I tell her everything? Can I count on her to keep it a secret from her siblings, especially Noah? Should I summon David to help with this conversation, since we should really be together to discuss my cancer with the kids? Should I postpone her inevitable questions until I feel better, seeing as my main focus right then, even with all of these thoughts swirling around, is to ask her to please sit still since every movement of the bed makes my stomach rise up and jump into my throat?

"Of course you can, honey. What is it?" I ask, even though I know.

Hannah just looks at me, outright crying now. She then lifts her finger to her chin, pointing at it. Full-on anguish. "Do you see it?" she asks tearfully.

I am reminded of that Gilda Radner line from Saturday Night Live, when she played Emily Litella and would get all worked up about something she'd misheard or misunderstood. (The irony of conjuring up Gilda Radner, who died of ovarian cancer, is not lost on me.) *Never Mind* is the bubble above my head. Insightful, sensitive Hannah is actually just self-absorbed, teenaged Hannah. The source of her angst is nothing more than the beginnings of a pimple, one she is convinced is a blaring, neon "I've got acne" sign on her pretty, freckled face.

Relief floods over me. My cancer secret is safe. Hannah's world will not get rocked until after her school year is safely over. The third time she comes in to complain about her nascent pimple, though, I am ready to whack her on the head with my *Chemotherapy and You* guidebook and tell her that is not a #&%@!%* problem!

Despite the unexpected moments of levity, I am in a very dark place. These first few days following my surgery are just miserable. Everyone is loving and supportive, but lives are continuing all around me while mine has just ground to an abrupt and most unwelcome halt. And the nausea has me utterly depressed because I fear that it is only going to get worse. No one warned me about the post-hysterectomy nausea, which turns out to be unbearable, but chemo-induced nausea is legendary. I truly can't imagine doing this, feeling this way, for five long months.

I send another email out to my close friends that is a testament to how low I feel, and how undeserving I am of the praise that has been heaped upon me for taking this on with such fortitude. It was easy to have a good attitude about it all when it was theoretical and on the horizon. It seems to be a reflection of my true colors that the moment it became real, the very first test of my indomitable spirit, I have collapsed into the sham that I am.

I have had a really rough day. Had to cancel the catering. No need to drive me tomorrow. David is getting new meds and hopefully they will help, Pretty miserable. I don 't think I'm a fighter after all.
Katya

I receive many encouraging emails in response, such as this one from Andy Zerkle.

Katya,
I want to encourage you. You had major abdominal surgery and most people feel mighty diminished afterward. You may feel bad physically, but there is no cause to question your character.
I tell folks to expect good days and bad days after surgery, but to expect each week to be better than the week before. Ride out the bad days, focus on the long term full recovery.
Thinking of you, David, and the kids daily,
Andy

Iris comes over to pick up Hannah (pimple and all) to take her to the pool with her girls. She quietly asks David how I'm doing and he ushers her upstairs to sit with me. I am a pitiful, tearful mess. "I can't do this," I tell Iris.

I am not usually a quitter. I have strong currents of tenacity, obstinacy and sheer pigheadedness that make me a good candidate for plowing through most things. But I am ready to throw in the towel. Prior to Iris's arrival, I have been lying in my darkened room, wondering if I have given each of my kids enough of a foundation. (My conclusion is that, while they would each miss me, I need to stick around for Eliza. She is still a work in progress and David does not have the patience to see her through her prepubescent years.) But the truth is, I want out. Or, more accurately, I want off. It feels as if I am on a whirring, dizzying and nauseating ride that won't stop or slow down, and I just want to get off of it.

Iris takes my hand and strokes it gently. "This is awful," she says, acknowledging my misery. "But it will get better."
I have encountered some people in my life who are in the wrong profession. Customer service agents who resent that helping people is part of their job titles. Lawyers who can't write or think critically. Presidents who "misunderestimate" the impact of their decisions. But every once in a while, you see someone in action who is doing exactly what she is meant to do on this earth. At this moment, holding my hand while exuding empathy and kindness, Iris is the ideal combination of a doctor and a friend.

She is able to tell me – without it coming across as a platitude that has no medical certainty – that it will get better, while simultaneously sympathizing with how badly I feel at this moment. Unlike some of the doctors I have seen so far in my cancer run, Iris is totally there for me, focused on nothing else but my symptoms and how I feel at that moment. It makes me feel so validated to have the despair that my nausea is inflicting acknowledged, but it also makes me feel hopeful to hear Iris tell me that I am not necessarily in for five more months of this hell. I will forever be grateful for the afternoon's visit, because I think it helps me come out of what is probably my darkest day.

And it helps that moments of levity keep popping up amidst all that gloom and doom, affording us some much-needed laughter. Who knew a cancer diagnosis could be so funny?

I hold my cellphone above my swollen, bruised stomach and take a picture. I send it to my sister. She writes back that she doesn't even know what she's looking at but it looks awful. I look as if I've been in a car wreck, one that involved serious trauma to my stomach. There is some satisfaction in looking as bad as I feel, because it was disconcerting to find out I have this horrible disease when I looked completely fine on the outside. Now I feel like shit *and* look like shit – hooray. There is order in the universe.

I send Boris and Alyssa an email asking if it would be okay to delay bringing them the meals I'm catering for them. They reply that they are inundated with food and that it is perfectly fine to wait until Thursday, but it feels like such a defeat. I still think I can pull off dinner Wednesday night for Eliza's teachers. This is not just because I am stubborn or an eternal optimist (both true) but because I see the dinner (something we do at the end of each school year for the kids' teachers) as a way of maintaining some normalcy in our lives. Eliza has been so excited about her turn to entertain her teachers at our house and I just don't want to deprive her of this, when there will be so many cancellations and changes in her life in the months ahead.

Iris calls and says Dr. Naumann emailed her and told her if my nausea is not better I'll have to be seen because it could be a sign of internal damage, possibly a nicked bowel or colon. I call David at work and tell him I have a 1:30 appointment and he can hear the despair and distress in my voice. He says he is on his way home. I get up in five-minute intervals to work in small stretches, doing one discrete task like chopping or dicing or giving the KitchenAid a quick whir before collapsing on the couch from dizziness and nausea.

I wait for the room to stop spinning, or at least slow down, and I get up and have another spurt of culinary activity. It is so frustrating and demoralizing to work this way because this is not me. I usually pride myself on my efficiency in the kitchen. I actually won the title of Charlotte's Best Home Chef in 2006, and a new kitchen furnished by JennAir, thanks to my ability to cook quickly and under pressure. I had to make a meal out of a bag of secret ingredients in 20 minutes, and I was able to pull it off because my ability to multi- task elsewhere in life (something most women possess, I must add) translates well to the kitchen. This efficiency serves me well in my catering jobs, especially since my profit margin is not large enough for me to be able to hire any help. Katya's Creations consists of Katya and, occasionally, David. I have delegated grilling to him on many occasions and he has also sliced meat for big parties and even peeled potatoes. But his sous chef duties end there and this is far more than I have ever asked him to do. When I tell him to dice the peppers and he asks what dicing is, I know we are in trouble.

I get up to mince jalapeno peppers for the pineapple salsa that is going to accompany the grilled mahi mahi, and the room is once again an annoying and nauseating blur. I usually take precautions when working with jalapenos, thoroughly washing my hands with soap after touching them. This time, though, I am off my game. I finish mincing them, then collapse on the couch, trying to regain enough energy to tackle the next task. I finally give up and tell David I am going upstairs to lie down until it is time to go to the hospital.

I call Nicole to fill her in because I don't want to worry my parents. Rusty answers the phone and I can hear the concern in his voice as I tearfully ask for my sister. He explains that she is on a conference call and will call me right back. I use the interval to indulge in a good cry. When Nicole calls back, I whimper about how shitty I feel, both physically and emotionally, and she says all the right things. She tells me I don't have to be a fighter all the time and that it is normal to feel despondent. Her words help and I begin to feel better. I wipe my tears away and I instantly feel a horrible burning. The burning intensifies and I realize with dismay that I have forgotten to wash the jalapenos off of my hands. I scream for David and tell Nicole I will call her back before quickly hanging up. I stumble into the bathroom and pour water over my eyes, but the damage is done. David says I look like a raccoon, my eyes bright red and swollen. The burning is horrible, a searing pain that seems to emanate from within my eye sockets. David has me lie back down and puts a wet washcloth atop my eyes. He calls Nicole back, since she doesn't know what has happened to me and I don't want to leave her hanging, imagining the worst, and all three of us have a good laugh about it.

"Where are the locusts?" Nicole asks, and that becomes our refrain. What the hell else can go wrong? It's so bad that it's funny, and David and I, alone in the house, the unfinished catering job and teacher dinner preparations strewn all over the kitchen, our entire afternoon in shambles because it now involves another trip to the hospital, just lie in bed together and laugh and laugh.

When it's time to head in to the hospital, David turns to me and says, "Come on, Raccoon Eyes, let's go."

David drops me off while he parks the car and I make my way slowly and painfully up to the sixth floor. As I enter the waiting room, I can feel it sliding slowly to one side, making me feel like I'm going to fall off of it. I grab on to the backs of chairs as I awkwardly cross the room, and I then rest my head on the receptionist's counter until they are ready for me. I know I look ridiculous but I have no choice, I am that sick. When I lift my head, I catch the pitying glances of the other people waiting to be seen. All around me, there are sympathetic smiles and even some whispers and I realize I am the person to be pitied. I am in the worst shape of anyone in an oncology waiting room, and that is mind-bogglingly pathetic. I remember striding in here for my first visit and looking around at some of the weak, incapacitated patients who were waiting to be seen and feeling so sorry for them. Oh my God, I think to myself, I am the one to be pitied now.

When we see Dr. Naumann, both he and DeLeslie, one of his two nurse practitioners, ask about my eyes. They are concerned that the redness and swelling is due to an allergic reaction I am having to one of my medications. When I explain that it is from dicing jalapenos, they just stare and me, mouths agape. I am so ill that I had to be helped up on to the examining table. What on earth was I doing chopping jalapenos? Surely that's not what I was wanting to eat in the throes of all this nausea? Oh no, I assure them, I wasn't chopping them for *me,* it was for a catering job.

"A *what??*" they both exclaim.

Dr. Naumann then lectures me about managing my expectations. "You just had major surgery," he says, in what will turn out to be a constant refrain of his. "Most people are flat on their backs for weeks."

I nod and agree and assure them I understand, thinking to myself that it's probably not a prudent time to ask about the likelihood of whether I'll be on my feet in time to host the dinner for Eliza's teachers this evening. I still haven't canceled the dinner because, as I've pointed out. I am an optimist, and I am forever hopeful that things will turn around. And my maternal instinct is on high alert, wanting to maintain normalcy for my kids as long as possible and imbuing this dinner with more significance than it warrants. Every mother wants to protect her kids from harm, from devastating news that will rock their world, and this protective mode is compounded by the fact that I will be the one dealing them this blow, I *am* the bad news I want to shield them from.

Dr. Naumann goes through all of the possible reasons for my extreme nausea, using a tree with lots of branches as his imagery. He tells me I will spend the afternoon in the infusion room, getting saline solution and anti-nausea drugs intravenously, and that will hopefully help. I ask how long that will take because, and I try to just let it slip out nonchalantly, I am still hoping to salvage our dinner plans.

Both Dr. Naumann and DeLeslie look at each other and then at me in astonishment. They remind me, yet again, that I have just had major, major surgery. They tell me, in no uncertain terms, that there will be no dinner party. David calls Jackie Menser, the principal at Randolph Middle School, and she assures him she will take care of it and let the teachers know. Everyone agrees that I am a crazy lady.

Dr. Naumann does an internal exam, which basically involves sticking his entire hand up my rectum and all the way to China. I have a whole new level of discomfort now. As I wince in pain, he explains that he thinks perhaps my colon was nicked during the surgery, and the only way to determine what is happening to me internally to account for all of this nausea is to have a CT scan. The earliest they can schedule one for me is at 5 pm that afternoon, so in the interim I will head over to the infusion room.

I am curious to see the infusion room, which is also on the sixth floor, because it will be my home away from home for the foreseeable future. I am told to go sit at a chair along the wall on the far side of the room. My slow, unsteady walk across the room gives me an opportunity to survey my fellow infusion room patients and gives me a glimpse of what is to come, the next chapter in my cancer story. It is not a pretty picture.

My first impression is that everyone is quite a bit older than I am, and then I realize with dismay that they probably don't have that many years on me, but they just look like they do thanks to cancer and chemo. I'm sure I look a hell of a lot older than my 46 years as I cling to David and shuffle across the floor.

There is an elderly woman next to us who is making me sad because she's so stoic and all alone. I tell David to look for a wedding ring, something I often do to reassure myself that the person I'm pitying and envisioning living a lonely, Campbell's Soup for One sad life is actually happily married. Her hand is under her blanket so David can't confirm it one way or the other and he tells me he will not be following her in to the bathroom to check. This is a reference to my actually requesting that he do that with an old man I was pitying in a Fuddruckers early in our marriage, and it makes me smile. We try to turn on our little TV but it is broken and we have absolutely nothing to read or do because we had not anticipated spending the afternoon there.

I ask to go to the bathroom and I am told that I will need to be unplugged and I will have to wheel my infusion pole with me into the bathroom and then get plugged back in again. The whole procedure seems like such an ordeal to me that I decide to wait instead until my meds are done, since they only have another fifteen minutes to go. DeLeslie assures me that it is no trouble but I say I'd rather just get up once because I am inherently lazy.

DeLeslie looks at me for a long moment. "I have only just met you," she says, "but I doubt that sincerely."

Susan, the infusion room nurse assigned to me, predicted I'd feel better after the fluids and she is right. I was probably dehydrated and bypassing the gag reflex, which is on high alert these days, is the right way to get me rehydrated and reenergized. I feel so much better that I insist I don't need the wheelchair to get to the wing of the hospital where my CT scan will take place, but I am overruled. I head over there in good cheer, thinking that I am finally on the other side of all the nausea.

My celebration is short-lived. When we arrive at the CT scan waiting room, we are informed that I have to drink not one but two impossibly tall glasses of contrast solution. I can pick my flavor – each option more disgusting and unappealing than the last – and I have one hour to get them both down.

I go with orange – seems to be the least offensive of the choices – and I am determined to suck it up, no pun intended, and get it over with. I take my first sip. I gag and nearly vomit on the spot. The taste is like a mixture of chalk, bitter medicine, sickly sweet syrup and, I don't know, poison, combined into a truly undrinkable potion. I look at both glasses and start to whimper. There is absolutely no way I'm going to be able to drink them both. I explain to the receptionist that I have just had surgery and that my stomach is very weak. I haven't even been able to get water down without gagging, so there is just no way I can drink this stuff. I can maybe get one of the glasses down, but I just know I can't do both. She goes to talk with the radiologist and comes back shaking her head. Sorry, you have to. No way out of it. That amount of dye is needed to provide the contrast for the CT scan to work.

I am in hell. I take little sips, big sips, I gag, I sputter, I plug my nose, I try drinking water in between, but it is just awful. And it is so discouraging how little progress I am making. I keep thinking I'll just finish it off with one, never-ending gulp, but the level just doesn't go down. David is sympathetic and tries rubbing my back or encouraging me, but he can't drink it for me, and that's really all I want him to do.

When I finally finish both glasses, I feel as if I'm going to pass out. But I am so proud of myself for finishing the vomitade and doing *my* part of the equation. Now they can get *their* part done. I expect to be called at any moment.

Fifteen minutes go by. Then twenty, then thirty.

David goes up to the desk to inquire what's taking so long and learns that there have been a lot of triage cases that trump my scheduled time. The rational part of me gets it. Of course someone who has just been shot or injured in a car accident should have access to the machine and the technician ahead of me. But the emotional part of me, that is frankly 98% of me at that moment, sitting exhausted and defeated in the waiting room, thinks, "It's *my* fucking turn."

After about an hour, I decide to go to the bathroom. I tell both David and the receptionist where I'm headed. Once there, I learn that the contrast solution is an effective remedy for constipation because my stomach and bowels are revolting against it. I am grateful no one else is in the restroom because this is definitely one of those times I would far prefer to be in the privacy of my own home.

When I come back into the waiting room, both David and the nurse are chuckling. It turns out the long-awaited technician, the one who takes me back for the procedure I have been waiting for, has come and gone.

"What are the odds," David says, sharing a laugh with his new best friend. "You just missed her."

He sees the look of incredulity on my face, and probably picks up on some of the seething rage as well. "Don't worry, though, she'll be back."

I am furious. All of the frustrations of the day are boiling up into this one moment. How could he let her *go?* Why didn't he tell her I was in the restroom and to please hold on for a minute and then run and get me? And what the hell was so goddamned funny about that?

"You're supposed to be on my team," I say, when David, genuinely perplexed as to why I'm so upset, asks me what's wrong. "You're supposed to be looking out for me, not laughing at my misfortune."

David patiently assures me that he couldn't manhandle the technician and that she really did promise she'd be right back. With each minute that passes, I glare at him in rightful indignation. When she finally comes back for me (and I'm sure David would appreciate my pointing out that the elapsed time between her first summons and her second was no more than fifteen minutes), I practically sprint to the room. I am so eager to get this over with, no matter the outcome. If it's bad, meaning it confirms that my colon was nicked, I will be admitted to the hospital for more surgery. If it's good, meaning all is well internally and it's a question of learning how to manage the nausea better, I will get to go home. Either way, there will be resolution and I can get the hell away from the waiting room that is making me gag with its sticky orange contrast drink reminders. Ugh.

We go back to the waiting room to wait for the results and I am thinking that I have never been in a room that is more aptly named because it seems as if I have spent my entire life waiting in it. When the results come, they are quite anticlimactic. No Dr. Naumann to sit with us and explain what's going on. No radiologist or doctor of any kind. Just the technician's aide to say we are free to go home.

CHAPTER EIGHT

I have a horrible night, spent mostly on the toilet. On Thursday, I get out of bed determined to finish the catering job and check it off my to do list. I am very weak, having had little more than a few bites to eat since my surgery, and I am still dizzy and nauseated, but I am glad to have a reason to get out of bed because I think I will truly go nuts lying in my bedroom for another day. David and I drop off all of the food and I feel a huge sense of accomplishment for being able to make good on my promise, albeit one Stefanie and Alyssa would not have held me to had they known my circumstances, but one that is important to me nonetheless. I also feel a swell of love and appreciation for David, because he is pretty much the only person who knew about the catering job who didn't try to get me to cancel it. In our twenty years together, he has learned what makes me tick and what I need to get through this, and that there are all sorts of things – pride, responsibility, a need to maintain a sense of normalcy and productivity –that were tied up with this one job.

I send his parents an email summing up how I feel.

Hi Norman and Susanne,

As you know, it has been an incredibly hard week for me, and the hits just seemed to escalate daily. But the one constant and bright spot has been your son. I have always known we have a strong and loving relationship, but I also knew that we'd never really been tested in any significant way.

Well, now we're being tested, and I suspect this kind of thing either strengthens your bond or dissolves it. For us, it's been a matter of falling in love all over again. David has been the perfect mate during this whole horrible ordeal and immensely loving, patient, understanding and respectful. I feel incredibly fortunate to be facing this with him at my side and he is getting lots of props from our friends for how he is handling everything. He really is a wonderful man, which is pretty lucky for me since I pretty much married the first guy who asked me out! :) Just wanted you to know that you raised a really good guy.

Love, Katya

I call the triage nurse on our way to deliver the catering job and she suggests I put something in my stomach, but to keep it plain. Alyssa's nanny gives me crackers and applesauce when we deliver the food and it seems to calm my stomach somewhat. I am still feeling somewhat weak and woozy but better (or so I keep telling myself) so our next stop is Pizza Peel, a local restaurant where my book club pals are gathered for one of our group birthday celebrations. This is yet another event I scheduled thinking my surgery was going to be in early June, and another I deemed too difficult to reschedule once the surgery date was moved up. My friends certainly tried to convince me to cancel it and find a new date, but we are celebrating two birthdays, Bridgette Trujilo's and Lisa Zerkle's, and finding another day at the end of the school year that works for everyone is an impossible task. Better to leave it as is and hope for the best.

I generally coordinate the birthday festivities and gifts for this group of friends, mainly because I have never really emerged past an eight-year old's enthusiasm for birthdays and I have enough birthday delight to fuel all the organizing and shopping and wrapping. I love celebrating my own birthday, and my family even teases me that I manage to stretch out the birthday celebrations to an annoying degree so that my actual birthday of March 7th is somewhat lost in what turns out to be my birthday month. I continue to clap my hands with delight at the prospect of my birthday even though I have hit several milestones (30, 40, 45 come to mind) when people assured me my celebratory mood would wane. The only thing that saves me from being totally obnoxious about my birthday is that I am just as excited and enthusiastic about everyone else's birthdays.

For this particular birthday celebration, Lisa Zerkle, who is a poet, has requested that we each give her a copy of our favorite poem in lieu of gifts. I tried to find a happy compromise between her request and my belief that gifts, especially when a bunch of people are able to pool their money, are an essential part of the festivities.

So we bought her some goodies for her garden and herself, but I also put together a poetry book with everyone's submissions. I could certainly hand off the gifts to someone else to give to her, but I really want to be there because I know Lisa is going to love her book of poems and I want to see her face light up with delight. I also want to be there because I have written a poem of my own for Lisa, and I want to be the one to read it to her.

David helps me carry everything in and everyone seems pleased, albeit surprised, to see me there. Seated at the table are Jen, Lisa Miller, Lisa Zerkle, Bridgette, and Lorrina. Their expressions are textbook pity. I usually move at a much faster pace, so my slow progression to the table and my weakened state overall bring home the reality of the Big C in a way no call or email could capture. I nibble on the crust of some pizza, hoping it will settle my stomach, and hand out all of the gifts. My friends offer to go out and buy me crackers, and I tell them plain bread will be just fine. When their salads are served, every one of them immediately takes the slice of bread that is adorning her salad bowl and hands it over to me. I chuckle because it will be a challenge to eat one slice, I certainly don't need five of them. But I am so touched by their little kindnesses, like Jen wiping away both a tear and the tomato sauce on her pizza crust before gently placing it on my plate.

I am close to tears already, just overcome with the emotion of being among such good friends and being out of the house for the first time in days. I then read aloud my poem, stopping several times to settle the lump in my throat and catch my breath. It serves as a good excuse for all of us to have a good cry.

Lovely Lisa

I've had a lot to ponder
As I walk my dogs each day
How will I fare, I wonder
And will I be okay
I think about what's growing
That I can't touch or see
Unfelt and unwanted
But now a part of me
These walks are when I let
My thoughts go where it's dark

And what used to be so fun
Is no longer such a lark
But when I reach the house
My steps and heart get lighter
I remind myself I'm strong
And that I am a fighter
Because there, awaiting me
In four beds, side by side
Is a garden, my garden,
A source of wonder and of pride.
The red of my tomatoes
The pea shoots, green and wild
I check their progress daily
Clap my hands like a child.
Is that pepper even bigger
That it was just days ago?
The cukes, squash and eggplants
All thrill me as they grow.
The basil peeps out timidly
From the unforgiving clay
Then seems to gain confidence
Just as I do with each day.
My family's incredulous
No one quite believes
That the arugula I've plucked
Dirt clinging to its leaves
Came from my own garden
Grew from a tiny seed
And who knew I could do this?
Who knew I had this need?
This wondrous source of sustenance
Both literal and figurative
Came from my dear friend Lisa
To whom my thanks I give.
It was Lisa who inspired me
And showed me how to plant
With her trademark patience
Each time I said, "I can't."
Lisa who got me started
And encouraged me to try

But all without judgment
No raised eyebrows. No big sigh.
Whether it's her gardening
Or a book or civic cause
She leads with quiet certitude
No need for fanfare or applause.
It's Lisa whom we turn to
For a myriad of things
And the comfort and enlightenment
That her good counsel brings.
Her solid moral compass
Her disdain for all that's fake
Are rendered more impressive
By the path she had to take
Her beauty, in and out,
Her core of who she is
Grew and flourished, like a seed
Without a gardening whiz.
For Lisa and my garden
Have both suffered from a lack
Of the nurturing and care
That keep most of us on track
Her good, her strength and fiber
Are so strong and resolute
They weathered some neglect
But nonetheless took root.
So Lisa, like my seedlings
That warm my heart and soul
In my life, you, dear friend
Play a similar role.
This life-affirming garden
Has survived my ineptitude
And both of you sustain me
With so much more than food.
I will now look to you
As I face my own tough times
Knowing I can count on...
My green-thumbed friend who rhymes!

One of the great things about poetry, something Lisa has taught me in exposing me to more and more of it, is how well it can capture a sentiment or moment. It's hard to say to someone in the midst of a significant life event, "Here, read this book, it says exactly what I want to express to you right now." A book would take too long and it's unlikely the entire book will stay on message. But a poem, both in length and the clarity of its theme, is perfect. Lisa actually sent me a poem a few days earlier, when I was in my "I can't do this" phase, that conveyed her encouragement and support better than a letter directly *to* me could have done. It is one of two poems I receive on that dark, miserable day when I pronounce that I am not, in fact, a fighter, and both lift my spirits considerably.

Lisa sends the first:

Lunch Will Be Served
by Eleanor Lerman

Just when you think that you are
on the road to success and the
medications have calmed down
your wife, plus a big sale at
the foodstore means that you
can finally buy your cat a
decent meal — that's when
you get the news that it's time
to stare calamity in the face

And what a face; it comes
At you like a speeding pie
It has three eyes. It was created
by an overdose of nuclear
radiation. Its cunning knows
no bounds. Meaning, now
you are going to pay for something
you did in a past life, or didn't
do or should have thought
about doing. If you even rated
a past life. If not, then these are
just the normal ups and downs
Which do you think is worse?

Anyway. A procession of ghosts
will carry your pencil box
down to the office from which
you will never be allowed
to retire. Lunch will be served,
but all you can expect is
a bag of blood and transfat:
In other words, to rub it in
even the cat will get a better deal

Meanwhile, the universe remains
an incomprehensible wheel of
grave attraction. Fish, swans,
and archers lie in each other's
starry embrace while dark particles
have been driving by your house
all day in their neutrino cars,
in a hurry to do a job that will
never be revealed to us. And in
some versions of this story,
the cat has magical powers
Oh my God, you say, I had no idea

Well, now you do. In fact,
in some versions of this story,
beings of faith and light
are in the kitchen, dancing
with your wife. Then your
friends arrive, still lugging
around their own dilemmas,
hoping you will feed them
from the common pot, like
in the old days. And as tired
as you are, you think you can

Reprinted with permission of Sarabande Books,
publisher of The Sensual World Re-Emerges.

Nicole sends me the second poem, Wild Geese by Mary Olliver (not reprinted here), along with her trademark encouragement.

5/31/11

Katya,
I'm so sorry you've had such a rough few days and hope you've truly turned the corner tonight. The weird thing about feeling truly awful is you can't quite imagine ever feeling better, and vice versa . . . so I hope the memory of all the nauseous misery is fading fast. I was thinking of this poem as I was listening to you, helplessly, this morning. Just because you had a bad day doesn't mean you're not strong; you don't have to be strong every minute of every day to be strong. You don't have to prove that you're strong. You don't even have to be strong. (Sometimes, it's overrated.)
So here's Mary Oliver saying all that, I think, much more elegantly. (Is tomorrow your poetry lunch? Give Lisa my birthday best. I know she will love your sweet poem and its images of a flourishing, vibrant garden, as I did.)

Love you, garden girl!
Nicole

My own poem, while very low brow in terms of veritable poetry, is a good vehicle for what I want to express and allows me to convey to Lisa how much I admire her and how I am both scared and hopeful, all things that would have been decidedly awkward in a non-poetic format. It felt cathartic to write it and even more so to read it aloud. As I laugh and cry with my dear friends, I am so glad to have made it to this birthday lunch, to have one less thing I missed, and to be back among friends and daylight.

I excuse myself to go to the bathroom. Despite the purging of the contrast solution the day before, I again feel constipated. The discomfort I feel is very similar to the rectal pain I felt when I had the descended ovary. I find out later that removing the cancerous nodule from atop my rectum involved scraping it cleanly away, which royally pissed off my nerve endings there. I can't imagine that there is much in there, since I have given my bowels very little to work with, but I feel as though I am carrying a bowling ball around.

When I try to go to the bathroom, I notice with alarm that the toilet bowl is red. I have bled a significant amount...out *of my ass.*

"This," I think to myself, "cannot be good."

I make my way back to the table, the good times at an abrupt end, and announce that I need to call David to come pick me up. Lorrina insists on driving me home instead, even though her Bank of America office is uptown, the exact opposite direction. I call Dr. Naumann's office, at her suggestion, and describe my latest development to DeLeslie. She tells me to come in, so Lorrina turns the car around and drives me all the way back to the hospital.

On the drive to the hospital, I admit to Lorrina that I have been in a very dark place. She says just the right things to prop me up. She also tells me that she has been able to see, as I have, how much David loves me.

"I know Jim loves me," Lorrina says. "But not in the way David loves you. He just loves you so much and he would do anything for you."

Lorrina goes to park (I try to convince her to leave, since David is on his way, but she insists on coming up until he gets to the hospital) so I again make my way across the waiting room alone. Even though I am again the object of pity as I stumble and weave, I spy an adorable toddler waiting with her grandmother. I give her a high five as I pass her and her whole face lights up with delight. It warms my heart because I love kids, and being able to have this moment with this child makes me feel so much more like myself.

Once I am buzzed back, I am again treated to Dr. Naumann's hand up my ass. He is apparently feeling for internal hemorrhoids, although I'm thinking that whatever is causing my bleeding cannot possibly be as bad as this invasion of both my dignity and my rectum. It is determined that my days of constipation and straining have caused some tears along the rectal wall. I have both internal and external anal fissures (lovely, just lovely) but I am not bleeding internally. I am told internal bleeding would result in a different color and quantity, information I store for future reference and then check myself because I don't want it to be relevant ever again.

I realize with dismay but also a newfound resignation that we will not be able to head to Duke that evening to see Noah and meet with Dr. Berchuck the following morning. I don't really care about the second opinion anymore but I hate that we have to cancel our dinner with Noah. I am trying to figure out how to tell him without disclosing why or the fact that I'm calling him from a hospital when I get a brilliant idea. I call Watt's Grocery, the restaurant within walking distance of his school where we are supposed to be dining that evening, and change the reservation to two instead of three. I explain to the maître d what is happening and give him my credit card number over the phone, arranging for Noah and his good friend, Morty, to dine there instead. I call DonJuan, the adult counselor who lives on Noah's hall, and get permis- sion for Noah and Morty to stay out past curfew (as soon as the sun sets on a weeknight) and it is also a good opportunity to fill DonJuan in on what is going on with me. I then call Noah and, as expected, the dis- appointment at not getting to see his parents is totally supplanted by delight at the change in plans, that he and Morty get to go have a nice dinner, in the midst of final exams, on us. I feel pretty proud of myself that I pulled off this parenting feat while wearing nothing more than a hospital gown and lying flat on my back.

While we are waiting for blood work to come back, I realize with surprise that the rumbling I'm feeling in my stomach is actually hunger. I have an appetite for the first time since my surgery, and it feels good to want food, to think about what I'd like for dinner. It feels as if a bit of me has been restored, and it is surely a good sign because I must be getting better if I want to eat. David gets me some graham crackers from the basket in the reception area (where I saw a patient's husband stuff fistfuls of crackers and Oreo packets from the basket into his pockets the last time we were in) and promises me he'll run out and get whatever takeout I want for dinner once we get home. He seems almost giddy at the thought of getting me food and I am again reminded that I have a wonderful husband. This cancer has provided us some unique opportunities for testing our relationship and demonstrating our love for each other. Not a path I would have chosen to take – I was fine thinking all was good on the marriage front without needing to prove it in such dire circumstances – but the new bond we share and the many ways David is sweet and patient and loving to me are definitely perks of the hell we are in.

Dr. Naumann appears to be in a particularly chatty mood, in that he is not staring at his watch when he plops down on the stool next to me, so I take advantage to ask him a barrage of questions. I learn that my blood work reveals a very high CA-125 level, which is good news in that it will be a strong prognosticator when I get my blood tested regularly in the five year span following my chemotherapy treatment. I'm not quite sure how I can still get ovarian cancer now that I no longer have ovaries, but apparently a microscopic ovarian cancer cell could linger and grow again. I decide not to think about that.

We discuss the clinical trial and Dr. Naumann tells me that I do qualify for it, which is not particularly good news since it doesn't accept patients in the early stages of ovarian cancer. Mine is IIB (also definitively confirmed during this visit, since my pathology is back and we are not just relying on what Dr. Naumann saw during the surgery), which I guess is far enough along to be of interest to researchers of this disease. Two key factors make me decide on the spot that I will go with the standard protocol (Cisplatin and Taxol) rather than the clinical trial. The first is that Dr. Naumann would have no flexibility with my chemo treatments if I were to do the clinical trial, which pretty much means I'd have to stay put all summer. With the standard protocol, he is in charge so he can work around my summer travel plans (taking Noah on a college visit trip up the East Coast and taking both Noah and Hannah to the National Scrabble Championship in Dallas). What really puts me over the edge, however, are the nasty side effects associated with the clinical trial, one of which is possible bowel perforation. My bowls and I have been traumatized enough – no thank you.

Dr. Naumann tells me that my Stage II diagnosis is really rare. In his extensive experience, he finds that it is either Stage I in only one ovary, discovered by removal of the ovary, or a higher stage because it has spread everywhere and the patient exhibits lots of symptoms. He reiterates how lucky I was to have had my pain manifest the way it did, although it is not completely clear that the two (my twisted and descended ovary and my ovarian cancer) are related. I ask him if it would have made a difference if I had gone to see the doctor back in January and he says no, which is immensely reassuring.

When we leave the hospital, with the agreement on everyone's part that we all like each other just fine but let's try to go a day or two without seeing each other, I am still weak and dizzy, but decidedly less so. Riding down on the elevator, I ask a woman wearing a bandana about her hair loss, because I realize I know nothing about it. Will it come out in clumps? Is it best to shave it off? She is eager to talk to us, especially since we discover we have the same cancer and the same medical team, although she is at the end of her journey and I am just beginning. As nice and forthcoming as she is, it is not a good encounter. She does not paint a pretty picture and, as we follow her into the parking lot, I see her hobble over to her car parked in the handicapped spot. "Most days," she says, " I can't even make it across the parking lot." She gives me some ginger candies to help offset the inevitable chemo nausea and her telephone number. I tell David how unbelievably discouraging it was to see her and to imagine what I will look like at the end of all this. He reminds me that she is all alone (she was diagnosed right after moving to Charlotte) and that my support system is stronger than hers and so am I. Still, it leaves an image in my mind – her frailty, her handicapped spot, her dark picture of chemo – that sours my mood.

I am still hungry and David is eager to do something to make me happy, plus we are both convinced that eating something substantive is all it will take to get me back on track. I replace the image of the sad and weak fellow patient with images of food. My comfort food tends to be ethnic. When I was pregnant with Noah, I once sent David out from our house in Silver Spring, Maryland to get me some Persian rice from an Afghani restaurant in Bethesda. So my mind does not fill with visions of mac and cheese or chocolate cake, the standard culinary comforts, but instead with colorful plates of Indian and Thai food. We decide that David will drop me off at home and then head out to pick up my dinner of choice.

Which brings us to a key piece of unsolicited cancer advice from me. I know every cancer patient has her own road to take and each cancer journey is different. What works for me may not work for you, and even two women with the same cancer could receive different treatments, have different things that push their buttons or energize them, and bring different strengths – like your health at the time of diagnosis and your support system – to the table. But at the risk of over- generalizing and extrapolating from my own experience into a truism that applies to everyone, I feel I must emphasize the one lesson I learned that night. I truly think it is a cautionary tale for everyone, not just those emerging from several days of nausea following a hysterectomy for Stage II B serous carcinoma ovarian cancer.

Do not, no matter how hungry you are and how much you think you can handle it (despite it being the first solid food you're eating in days), give in to your first cravings.

Do not send your husband out for Ped Gra Pow Duck from Thai Taste.

Bad, bad idea.

CHAPTER NINE

It is one week after my surgery and David finally braves leaving me at home alone. We are both hoping this will be a day when he is not summoned back home or to the hospital for one of my many setbacks. He leaves with the admonition that I am not allowed to walk the Grimmersborough loop (the larger of our two neighborhood walks) by my- self. I tell him that I know someone in almost every house along the way so I could stop for a rest or a glass of water or anything else I might need, but he won't budge. I decide to appease him because he has been really flexible and accommodating on everything else, especially the catering job. It seems a bizarre line for him to draw, but it clearly matters to him so I agree to be a good girl.

I decide to rest on the couch downstairs before braving the smaller neighborhood loop, the one David approved my walking. The phone rings and once I answer it, I am connected to it for the rest of the morning. I suppose I have the option of not answering it, but if I let the machine screen calls for me, the dogs go insane. There is something about voices coming out of the answering machine that riles them into a barking frenzy, one of the many things I have learned about them now that I'm home so much.

Brenda, Dr. Naumann's nurse, calls to check up on me. I complain about the nausea and how worried I am about how much worse it will be once I start chemo. She gives me the most encouraging news I've had so far. "How was your morning sickness?" she asks. It was pretty nonexistent, I reply. My labors were from hell, but my pregnancies were pretty easy. Brenda informs me that new research indicates that the same part of the brain that controls morning sickness controls chemo-induced nausea, so I should have a good run of it. I am unbelievably relieved because the anticipation of five months of this, or worse, has me really discouraged.

DeLeslie also calls to check on me and reminds me what I should look as far as troublesome signs and developments. I assure her I won't hesitate to call and she says she knows I am a good caller. I initially take this as a compliment but, after hanging up, I wonder if I'm coming across as a high-maintenance, hypochondriacal patient.

The next call is from Lisa Rubenson, who had Eliza over the weekend. She took Eliza to Blaine's art class and it turned out to be a therapy session for Eliza. I have suspected that she knows something is going on and her behavior at this art class confirms it. Lisa tells me that the teacher let Eliza go out back by herself and work with clay, but really it was more like anger therapy. Eliza beat the hell out of the clay and told the teacher she was angry at how sick I've been. Breaks my heart because she is clearly suffering. I am glad we get to tell the kids soon so that I can reassure her and put an end to all the unspoken worries.

I hang up from that call to take the next one beeping in. Lisa Miller wants to see if I have a request from Dunkin Donuts. I ask for a small cup of coffee – it's encouraging that I even want it because very few things have tempted me in the last week – and then I ask her a huge favor. I wonder if she'd be willing to pop into Harris Teeter and buy about six things I'm missing for my next culinary obligation. We are having about 20 Scrabble players over to our house on Sunday and I need to make most of the food today because I will be playing in the first day of the Scrabble tournament, which is going to be at Park Road Park, all day Saturday. Lisa assures me it is not a big favor but when she asks a follow up question about the kind of tortillas I want and I tell her it doesn't really matter since they are going to get cut into strips and fried, she lets me have it.

"Is this for another catering job?" she asks, incredulously. "You know what, don't even tell me. I don't want to know. Oh my God, you make my head hurt."

When she delivers the groceries and my coffee, which tastes great for the first few sips and then seems like a really bad idea, she alludes to emails that have been circulating about my symptoms and emotional state. It is the first I hear of emails about me flying fast and furious among my friends and it leaves me feeling irritated, even though I know they are all supportive and mean well. It makes sense that I would be left out of emails that are comparing notes and coordinating care, but I feel marginalized and somewhat paranoid.

Lisa also tells me that Cassie, her 5-year-old daughter, knows about my cancer. She had apparently been asking about cancer, no doubt having heard Lisa mentioning it, and Lisa inadvertently disclosed that I have it. I only care because I don't want it getting back to the kids before we tell them, and it's hard enough keeping the adults who know in line without having to worry about kids spilling the beans as well. I create a special handshake for Cassie that is meant to seal the secret and I make a mental note to not have Eliza accompany me on the Grimmersborough loop when we walk over the weekend so that we will not pass Lisa's house and run the risk of seeing Cassie.

Lorrina calls to say she has made us an afternoon appointment at the Ballantyne Spa for manicures and pedicures. I know I should probably decline because I have been up since 3 am and I should nap while the house is empty and quiet, but I don't. I feel so unattractive and beat up that it will be great to be pampered and have some part of me (even if it is just my toenails and fingernails) looking good. I'm also eager to get out of the house for a reason other than a trip to the hospital. I am a late convert to pedicures, having had my first one at age 45, but I am definitely a fan now. And the Ballantyne Spa is quite the treat, a far cry from the little neighborhood nail place I have frequented. We are pampered and fussed over and we then get to sit in chairs facing the golf course in our own private room while our legs are massaged and our toenails painted. I would never have woken up thinking *this is what I need to do today* but it is, in fact, exactly what I need. Lorrina insists on treating and I shudder to think how much it all costs.

Mom calls on the way home and I tell her where I've been. Mom tells me I have the best friends imaginable and I agree whole- heartedly. I then pass the phone to Lorrina so that Mom can thank her directly for taking such good care of me. I hear Lorrina say, "Katya would do the same for me." I look at Lorrina and shake my head in disagreement. "Umm, probably not the spa," I admit, and we both have a good laugh.

The next day, Saturday, David heads off to Durham to bring Noah home for the summer. I will be so glad to have all three kids under one roof. He drops off the girls and me on his way since we are all three playing in the Scrabble tournament at Park Road Park. It is a hot, muggy day and David is very concerned about my being outside for that long. I know he is being overprotective because he cares about me, and that's what I have to keep reminding myself, because it is coming across as patronizing and annoyingly restrictive. At lunch, the girls choose to stay behind and snack on the food that is up for grabs while I decide to walk to Panera Bread. It is less than a mile away but it is the most exercise I have done since the surgery.

When I return, I feel extremely out of breath. I go to the bathroom to unhook my bra, think- ing perhaps it is too tight and that is why I am struggling to breathe, and I see that two of my four incisions have opened and are oozing blood and whatever other gross bodily fluids escape from surgical wounds. Another moment of thinking, "This cannot be good."

Hannah notices the blood stain on my shirt and inquires what it is. She does so by sticking her finger directly in it. The pain is excruciating, but she has no idea what she's done so I just bite my lower lip and tell her it must be a scab that opened up. When I tell David about it when he comes to pick us up, he is furious with Hannah. He yells at her for loading the cooler back into the van incorrectly and I point out to him, when she leaves in a huff, that he is again holding her accountable for things she does not know.

David and I have both had enough of the hospital, so we decide to call on one of our many doctor friends for a weekend consult. We drop the kids at home and then head to the Lewins' house, where we pretend we are going for drinks (why the kids bought that is beyond me because it is completely out of character for us). Marc, a family doctor who insists he doesn't mind serving as the go-to neighborhood doc, examines me and says the wounds are fine. Yes, they are oozing and have come slightly open but they do not require medical attention. They are probably a result of overdoing it, Marc says, and asks if I over exerted myself.

Before I can answer, David pipes up, "Yes, she walked the dogs this morning and then, on top of that, walked 3/4 mile to Panera Bread and back. In the heat."

I say that I have got to be able to do things my way and set my own limits.

Marc plays marriage counselor.

To me, he says, "David is worried shitless about you and he loves you. That's where that's coming from."

To David, he says, "You have to let her do her thing."

He then listens to my list of ailments and explains how every- thing works in my body and what they did to me. It is extremely helpful because not one of my doctors had the time or the inclination to put it like that. When he echoes the now familiar refrain that I have to manage my expectations because I had major surgery one week ago, it makes more sense.

On the way home, I get weepy explaining to David that the reason I am pushing myself is that I have a limited window of opportunity before chemo starts. I confess that I am very fearful of chemo and he agrees that he is as well. We call a truce, each explaining where we're coming from and acknowledging the other, and all is well until we get home. David sees that the girls took a bath in our bathroom rather than the showers they'd been instructed to take in their bathroom and he goes through the roof. I direct my anger at him.

"We are about to hit them with something that is going to rock their worlds. Something no kid should have to hear and something they'll remember for the rest of their lives. I really think we can let things like the bathwater go, don't you?"

The next day is the Scrabble tournament at our house. David and I just roll our eyes at each other as some of the Scrabble players, a whiny, high-maintenance bunch for the most part, complain about not sleeping well or how hard it was to find our house. Like Hannah, they don't know what I'm going through, but I'm much less inclined to give them the benefit of the doubt. During one of the games, one player – a notorious whiner – complains bitterly about her tiles. I just look at her and say, "Well, if that's the worst problem you're going to face today, you're living a pretty charmed life."

One of my first outings after surgery to see Shrek, the Musical. Note the grown out bangs!

With Noah at a Starbucks before dropping him off at his internship at the Reelect Mayor Foxx Headquarters.

CHAPTER TEN

On Monday, June 6th, two days before my originally scheduled surgery and ten days after it actually occurs, David and I head into the Blumenthal Cancer Center to meet with the geneticist and a breast oncologist about my results. We tell the kids we are meeting with a financial advisor. The lies are really starting to pile up and I look forward to telling the kids what's really going on this evening. Hannah's last final exam is today so we have picked tonight as the first possible opportunity for the Big C talk. It won't be easy, but I'm eager to put an end to the deception and have us all on the same page.

Dr. Theresa Flippo, my breast oncologist (I've never had so many doctors overseeing my care in my life) strongly recommends a prophylactic mastectomy. My genetic mutation increases my likelyhood of getting breast cancer by a whopping 85%, so the only surefire way to prevent it is to remove the breasts. She explains that detection has come a long way and we can now stagger mammograms with breast MRIs and physical examinations by doctors, but even a microscopic amount caught early would require chemo because of my genetic mutation. That's a compelling argument but I don't even need to go that far. I haven't started chemo yet but I am highly confident it is not an experience I will want to repeat. Even more paramount, in my mind, is removing the risk so that I can live my life without worry. I already feel like I lost the cancer lottery, getting the far less statistically likely ovarian cancer, so I do not want to tempt fate by hoping for the best with my breasts.

David and I both struggle with getting our heads around this other cancer and surgery when we are still reeling from the first diag- nosis. We agree to move forward with the double mastectomy, but it will have to wait until I am done with chemo for my ovarian cancer. I tell David that my limit is one cancer at a time and he laughs, but it is a sad laugh.

We have arranged to meet with the Blumenthal Cancer Center Sociologist, Meg Turner, in the afternoon so that we can solicit her advice on how best to tell the kids. We decide to kill the time between the two appointments by walking on the Little Sugar Creek Greenway outside of the hospital. While we are walking, I have to stop multiple times because of a shooting pain in my vagina. Brenda, Dr. Naumann's nurse, tells me to take tons of ibuprofen to reduce the swelling, both there and in my anus, which is also competing for what can provide Katya with the most discomfort. I am told that I probably have a tear in my vagina and that I shouldn't walk so much. Cue the frustration about being told conflicting things. No one mentioned that I ran the risk of walking too much or that I would tear the scar tissue in my vagina if I did. In fact, I specifically asked about walking and I was told I could do as much as I wanted, as much as felt comfortable. Well, I guess I have reached my limit because stopping every few minutes convinced that needles and electric shocks are piercing my vagina is by no means comfortable.

Meg is very helpful and I can tell she thinks David and I are handling things well. What really sticks with me in what she has to say is that we should focus on looking at the softer side of each other and to be more charitable. David knows he has to really work on that one. He is a sweetheart to me, but he has continued to unload his frustration and worry on the kids. We also call Cantor Andrew Bernard at Temple Beth El because he knows the kids so well. He suggests focusing on telling them the truth and assuring them we won't lie anymore. He says kids will ask what they can handle and we should take our cues from them. David and I have a good laugh about that one and I am tempted to reply, "Have you *met* our kids?" That is exactly the advice I read in a parenting magazine before having the sex talk with Noah when he was five years old (initiated by him, not me!) and his questions never stopped! It is also a challenge when you're telling three kids together who are at very different ages and levels of maturity and comprehension. What Eliza can handle is totally different from what Noah will want to know.

After dinner, we call for a family meeting in the living room. The pretext for the gathering is to tell Hannah what we love about her. Each birthday, we take turns saying what we love about the birthday celebrant. Feel free to cue the Kumbaya music in the background, but it often transgresses into a vent session rather than a love fest. Kids who cannot remember whether or not they brushed their teeth five minutes earlier have a laser-like recall of what was said to each of their siblings at previous birthdays and will immediately call you on it if your comment about them is not equally grandiose. And each sibling's *what I love about you*

—

comment is given even more scrutiny. Did Eliza just piggyback on what Noah said? Did Noah just pick something like Hannah's freckles or her red hair, both of which are out of her control and both traits he, incidentally, possesses as well?

Since we weren't all together for Hannah's birthday, we agreed to delay the Hannah love fest. She has been bugging us ever since Noah came home, and when I finally manage to get us all together to do it, we have clearly passed the point of acceptable delay in her mind. She is so frustrated with how long it has taken that when we gather to tell her, she finds fault with everything that is said. Eliza tells her she loves hanging out with her. Hannah says that isn't really about *her*. Noah says he likes how smart she is, Hannah says he is just copying what was said about *him*. Eliza and Noah then chime in with all sorts of examples of what they *don't* love about Hannah and all three kids are ready to leave in a huff. I call them all back, got Hannah calmed down, get Noah and Eliza to give more personal accolades, and then tell them we actually have something else to discuss as well.

"You know how I've always had a phobia of sharks?" I ask. David looks at me quizzically. He is silently asking me where I am going with this, but I have a plan. My shark phobia is well known. I love swimming in the ocean but I am convinced that every brush of seaweed, every encounter with a piece of driftwood or even a particularly menacing wave is a shark, so I spend most of my time in the ocean petrified that I will not get back to the shore alive. The reason I know my fear of sharks is actually a phobia, or as close to it as a fear can get, is that I can get myself worked up about a shark in a lake or even a swimming pool, when rational thought should tell me I have nothing to fear.

"So you know how I always watch those shark programs on Animal Planet and I try to educate myself as much as possible about sharks?" I ask. Lots of nods, but I can tell the kids are also wondering where this is leading. "Well, I always figured that the more I knew about sharks, the more I learned about them, the less fearful I'd be of them."

"I'm thinking that's been a big fail," Noah says.

"Yes, it has not helped me with sharks. But another phobia I have is cancer." I take a big breath because I am determined not to cry or even let my voice quaver when getting through this next part with the kids. Just as when I told my parents, I know that they will take their cues from me. There is no way to sugarcoat the actual news, but the delivery of it can have a big impact in how it is received. "The more I've learned about cancer, though, the less scared of it I am."

I can see that Noah and Hannah are starting to see where this is going. Eliza is just looking at me quizzically, but her expression also contains excitement. I find out later that she is convinced my shark phobia intro is a segue for letting the kids know that we'll be going to Sea World for vacation.

"My view of cancer is based on an antiquated view of it, when learning you had cancer was essentially a death sentence," I say. "But I have learned a lot about it in the past month and the more I've learned, the less frightened I am of it." I pause, and David gives me an encouraging smile. "The reason I'm telling you this, the reason we called this family meeting, is that I have cancer."

All three kids instantly tear up, looking at me with total surprise and dismay. Any thoughts I'd had that they'd started guessing what was going on were instantly dismissed. They had no idea.

I tell them about my twisted ovary, which they knew, and what it ended up telling us, which they didn't. I tell them I've already had the hysterectomy, which is why I have been so weak and fragile lately.

"Wait, I don't get it," Eliza says "How did you get this cancer?"

Noah and Hannah, who have both studied cancer in school, proceed to explain cancer to her far better than any of my docs have ever explained it to me.

I tell the kids that I'll be starting chemo soon and that it will probably be a rough summer for me, but I reassure Noah that we've built the chemo schedule around his college trip, so that will not have to be cancelled, and I reassure the girls that they can still go to British Columbia with my parents this summer.

"I'm not going," Hannah pipes up, and Eliza quickly agrees. "I want to stay with you."

I tell the girls that they can't stay with me even if they want to because I'll be traveling up the East Coast at that time with Noah and David. I remind them how excited they have been about the trip and that there will be plenty of time to be with me and help me before and after the trip. My mom, in an effort to be helpful, has been asking me to send the girls out for the entire summer. Even if I wanted to do that, which I don't, I know it will be an incredibly hard sell because their natural inclination is to be near me.

After discussing it some more, including what chemo will entail and the fact that I'll be losing my hair, I ask if they have any questions. I know there is probably a limit to what they can handle that night and I assure them they can come to us with questions at any time, as they continue to process the news.

Noah, whom I'd worried would take it the worst, is surprisingly stoic. "I'm a man of science," he says. "Stage II is good. I know you are not going to die."

Hannah seems most concerned about my impending baldness. "Poor Mommy," she laments. "You *just* grew out your bangs." It is a big lament of mine too. I'd gone through months of awkward hair and had finally reached the stage where I could pin them up. Arghhhh.

Eliza's takeaway from the night has us ending the Big C Talk in laughter. "Man Mom," she says, shaking her head in disbelief, "you are *such* a good liar."

I'm of the firm belief that ice cream can solve most problems, so we all load into the van – Molly and Darcy included – and head to Brewster's, where Molly and Darcy get their own cups with a little doggy bone on top. (Interesting and completely irrelevant aside: Molly eats her ice cream first, licking under and around the bone and saving it for last. Darcy, on the other hand, scarfs the bone down first, in one swallow, *before* inhaling his ice cream.) On the way home, Hannah tells Noah that Mr. Oates, the Latin teacher at East Meck (who was his Latin teacher before he'd left for NCSSM) was asking about him.
"Well, I was going to go over there today, but noooo," Noah says, exaggerating his distress level at the fact that I couldn't take him because I had a doctor's appointment, "I couldn't because Mom had to go and get cancer."

It is just what we all need to break the tension. Humor is such an important weapon against shitty times, and this lets me know that it will not just be my own coping mechanism, but our family's as well.

That night, as I am tucking Eliza in, she needs an extra big hug but she otherwise assures me that she is okay.

"Mommy?" she asks, her blue eyes especially big, as I am

kissing her goodnight.

"What is it, honey?" I say, hoping it isn't the start of a query about what chemo will entail or whether I can guarantee her that I won't die. The night went far better than I'd anticipated but it was still emotionally draining. I am really tired.

"So are we *not* going to Sea World?" Eliza asks.

CHAPTER ELEVEN

Once the kids know, I decide it is time to let everyone else know.

I write the first missive to friends and family and put Ovarian Odyssey in the subject line. My Ovarian Odyssey emails are my way of keeping a bunch of disparate folks – some close, who would know most of what I write even if they don't receive the emails, others folks near and far whom I rarely see or call, for whom the emails not only keep them up to date on my cancer journey, but also, in a touching and completely unexpected way, bring many of them *back* into my life, sometimes in a more significant and meaningful way than before – up to date on what I am going through. They also serve as a cathartic and therapeutic outlet for me, a way for me to not only document but process what I am feeling, experiencing and thinking.

Subject: Ovarian Odyssey
Date: June 6, 2011

Hi folks.

This is my first missive to friends and family, near and far, to fill everyone in on what I'm referring to as my Ovarian Odyssey. Many of you are already aware of my recent health woes (some of you to a degree you probably wish you weren't!) but for others this will be the first you hear of my cancer, and for that, I apologize. My preference would be to tell each of you in person, but that is simply not possible. I will also use this venue for sending out periodic updates as warranted, or when I need to vent or share some of the surprisingly frequent moments of levity that crop up, often just when I've needed them most.

For those of you who find me to be a pain in the ass at times, you'll find it ironic that this all started with just that... a pain in the ass. I felt tremendous discomfort and pressure on my rectum for several days in late April and when it became unbearable, I called my

OB/GYN, Dr. Solomon. He squeezed me in to his lunch hour that day (for which I will be eternally grateful) and an ultrasound revealed that one of my ovaries was twisted and was sitting atop my rectum. He surgically removed it, laparoscopically, the next day. He said nothing else looked amiss and that I was good to go, so I left for a conference in Philadelphia.

That's where I was, alone, when I received the call that instantly created a new normal for me, and from which I am still reeling. In a conference call, David and I learned that the ovary Dr. Solomon had removed, which he'd sent off to pathology, just to be on the safe side, was cancerous. David and I met with Dr. Naumann, a renowned gynecological oncologist, at Charlotte's Blumenthal Cancer Center, in mid-May. I had a hysterectomy to remove my remaining ovary plus my uterus and fallopian tube, on Friday, May 27th.

I will pause here to say that I want to give a shout out to those "female parts" that are no longer a part of me. They served me well, giving me three of the most interesting, entertaining and loveable kids I could hope for.

We decided to keep Noah, Hannah and Eliza in the dark about my surgery and diagnosis until the end of the school year so that they could concentrate on exams and be together when we told them. It is a feat that proved quite challenging (we arranged sleepovers for the girls on the night of my surgery and when they returned I was back home, confined to bed with what we claimed was a bad case of the flu) but one I am glad we accomplished. I am back on my feet with the surgery behind me, which makes the news much more manageable from a child's perspective.

One of the standout moments of levity during my post-op recovery is when Hannah knocked on my bedroom door and tearfully asked if she could talk to me. I was convinced the gig was up and that she had seen through the flu ruse. My kids are sensitive, intuitive and attuned to their mother's wellbeing. Wrong. Hannah was distraught over the appearance of a new and oh so unwelcome pimple. If ever there was a time to embrace the blissful self- indulgence of 15-year-old girls, this was it!

The 5-hour surgery, which was also laparoscopic, really beat me up. My recovery has been tough and I have suffered numerous post-op complications. I have also been told by my new team of doctors and by my fabulous friends and family members who are members of the medical profession that my expectations need to be scaled back. If I had a penny for everyone who has said to me, "You just had major surgery!" I would not have to worry about Noah's college fund. I am now focused on regaining my strength and preparing my body for chemo, which will start shortly.

My cancer was classified as IIB, which is actually quite rare. Ovarian cancer is either caught extremely early (Stage I) or after symptoms appear, when it has often invaded other organs and lymph nodes (Stage III or IV). My lymph nodes came back clean – a huge relief! – and the chemo will hopefully eradicate any microscopic traces of it left behind after surgery. I will receive the chemo both intravenously and through a port (that was surgically implanted during my surgery) in my abdomen. I am scheduled for six cycles, each of which is approximately 3 weeks in duration (full day of infusion on Day One, half day of infusion on Day Eight, and nothing on Day Fifteen). Dr. Naumann, who has encouraged me to live my life as much as possible (that's when I knew we would get along just fine) is flexible with the scheduling so that I can work in a few of the trips I had planned for this summer, such as looking at colleges on the East coast with Noah. And I explained to him that Scrabble tournaments are essential to my recovery as well.

The pathologist who found my cancer also noted markers of the BRCA-1 gene, a genetic mutation that is carried by people of Ashkenazi Jewish descent. I had a genetics test and confirmed that I do, in fact, carry that gene. We just met with a breast oncologist at the Blumenthal Cancer Center to discuss a plan of attack since the gene gives me a significantly increased chance (a whopping 85%) of developing breast cancer. But that will have to wait until I emerge, victorious, from my battle with ovarian cancer. One cancer at a time, that's my motto. I may even have t-shirts printed up.

If I sound brave and resolute in this email, know that I have had plenty of moments of despair and fear. There were a few very dark days following the surgery, when I faced unrelenting nausea that was impervious to whatever drugs were used to try to curb it, that had me questioning my ability to face more of the same this summer. But I also know that, in the realm of folks who are dealt this kind of blow, I am incredibly lucky. David has been a loving and patient partner and friend through all of this and he is blessed with a job – and years of accumulated sick leave – that allow him to be by my side whenever needed. My kids are mature enough to process this difficult news and old enough to be of help to me when I will no doubt need to rely on them during my chemo. My friends and family have showered me with support and bolstered me with the care and good thoughts. I have said on more than one occasion, when being treated to a meal or a pedicure or receiving a heartfelt card or hug, "This isn't all bad."

So if you see me without my trademark energy (or hair) in the months ahead, you now know why. I have no idea how I will fare with the chemo, but I will hope for the best and keep you posted. Know that I have every intention of beating this thing and I look forward to sharing that news with you – albeit down the road a bit – too.

Fondly,
Katya

     I choose to send out emails, adding names to my list as warranted or requested, even though there are certainly several other options available to people in my situation who want to chronicle what they are going through and keep friends and family apprised of any developments. I know quite a few people who have posted updates about their own illness or that of a loved one on a patient website called Caring- Bridge. Having been a recipient of updates on it, I decide that it isn't a good fit for me as a vehicle for sending out my own updates because I don't like that the ensuing messages and discussion prompted by my postings would be up there for all to see. It is bad enough that my well- intentioned but totally off-base tennis ladder proselytizer is sending *me* a religious reading list; I would be even angrier and more put off if I were not the only one to see it, and if I were not able to simply hit the delete button.

I opt against writing a blog, even though many people encourage me to do so, especially after the first few Ovarian Odyssey missives go out, because I don't want the pressure of writing daily or even regularly. There are some weeks when I send out several missives, and there are others when I simply have nothing to report. There are also days when I am simply too ill to write or process what I am going through, or when my limited energy and time are better spent in real time with David and the kids. And I like being in control of who receives my OOs. I keep them all on a group email, that grows as word gets out or as folks ask to be added to it, and I blind-copy the group each time I send out an OO update.

I do not write the OO's with an overarching goal or theme, but it appears that several emerge over the course of my sending them out.

Some of these are unintentional and are, frankly, what the readers bring to the table rather than any lesson I am trying to impart about what I am going through. For instance, many people respond to missives that detail particularly grueling physical issues I am having with apologies for whining about their own miniscule problems (their words, not mine) and thanks for putting their own seemingly incon- sequential worries in perspective. That is never what I have in mind. We all have our own stuff to slog through, our own lives to live. My shit, no matter how awful it is, is not *your* shit. Therefore, even if my stuff is objectively worse, your hangnail is going to hurt you more than my 13-hour surgery is going to hurt you because *you* are experiencing the pain of *your* hangnail, you are not – no matter how empathetic or angelically concerned you are – experiencing the pain of *my* surgery. And that is as it should be and is nothing about which you need to be ashamed or apologetic. And who's to say what's worse on a given day? I complain more about a cold I get after all of my chemo is over than I ever do about any of my chemo.

I am so happy you are more than half way through and canNOT wait for you to be done!! I am so sorry for all of your suffering and so glad you can see some light at the end of the tunnel and some silver linings in a really difficult time!
I had a root canal today and thought, "suck it up, this is nothing

compared to what Katya and Rosanne are going through!" Thanks
for helping us all through your difficult journey and the necessary
life reminders to keep things in perspective!
Thinking of you!
XO, Jen
(Jennifer Haber, a long-time friend from when we lived in
Maryland.)

Many people also comment on my sense of humor and my
ability to find the lighter side of what I am going through. That, too,
is unintentional, in that I do not set out to write a funny chronicle of
cancer. I don't think, "Oh, I can't write today because nothing funny
has happened," nor do I try to always strike a humorous tone in how
I write about my cancer journey. But I will say this. I am a generally
happy person. I love to laugh and I do find humor or inject humor
into most of my days and experiences. Sometimes that's because I'm
a clod or a klutz or someone whose filter is either nonexistent or set
on very, very low, so that I say and do things that are embarrassing
to my children but make for funny moments when they are
recounted. And I'm also someone who, given the choice, will choose
to laugh about something and will then want to share that laugh-
worthy moment or experience with others, even if it's at my
expense. There are, in turns out, a surprising number of moments of
levity in my cancer diagnosis and treatment. There are also a lot of
moments where I have to make a conscious choice to find the
humor, to laugh rather than cry, and I think that is what resonates
with people.

I appreciate the kudos I receive for my good sense of humor,
both in my approach and in my writing, but I again want to point out
that this is far more readily achieved when you are given the
diagnosis that you are going to live. Yes, I have days that are not
remotely funny and elicit not a single smile or giggle, but overall, I
can find the humor and I can laugh at myself and my predicament
because I knew that all of this is merely a bump in the road. If I were
told I only had a limited time to live, if I truly had to confront saying
goodbye to my kids, I can assure you I would not have been funny.
Not one bit. So again, the compliments need to come with a caveat,
and people who aren't able to see the humor – for whatever reason,

whether it's because they're sicker than I am or that's simply not in their DNA – are no less worthy.

Another thread that soon emerges and runs through almost all of my OO missives is the phenomenal love and support that surrounds me. I honestly don't feel like I do it justice, but what I am able to chronicle blows people away.

My friends and family are so amazingly supportive and I am really happy to be able to document and highlight just a fraction of what they do for me. I also enjoy highlighting the many gestures of kindness from people I didn't know well, all of which reinforce my worldview – often mocked or doubted prior to my cancer – that people are generally good.

But perhaps my favorite theme to emerge from my cancer journey and my OO emails is the portrait of David and the kids. With- out trying to paint them all in a "aren't they just the best?" kind of light, a year's glimpse into my life and the way my husband and children rally around me does just that. Just as I receive almost daily confirmation that I have, in fact, married a wonderful man and we have raised three loving, grounded and giving kids, so, too, does everyone who reads about my journey. I feel especially happy with this development, this championing of the other, often unsung heroes in all of this, because of how it highlights David's strengths. I brag about my kids all the time and, frankly, they don't need any help convincing folks that they are fabulous. But David is another matter. He runs the risk of being over- looked or overshadowed in this family of extroverts, getting the shortest paragraph in the holiday letter and being okay with the fact that many of our friends have no idea what he does in his down time other than chasing the kids around and supporting me and my causes and activities. I have always known that David is a great guy and that his love for me is pretty special. Now everyone's in on it... or at least everyone on the OO distribution list.

When I attend an after-school event at Randolph Middle School in the spring following my chemo and surgeries, Gwen Aldridge, Eliza's PE teacher who was also Noah's and Hannah's PE teacher so I have known her, albeit peripherally, for over seven years, pulls me aside to tell me how much she enjoys my OO missives.

"You know what I think?" she asks, looking at me earnestly. "What really came through for me is the love you and David have.

Your cancer story is really a love story."

Just as the OO missives take on a tone and arc of their own, so, too, do the way they elicit responses. Some people write back every single time, some people never do, and some do so intermittently, but I always receive a slew of replies. These emails from cyberspace are my salvation. They do more to lift my spirits and reinforce my will and strengthen and sustain me than anything else that is said or done during my many difficult days. I receive them while I am stuck in the infusion room, tethered to an IV pole, or at the JCC, trying to get through a workout, or at the grocery store, wondering if I'll have the strength to cook dinner that night. They often begin with something along the lines of, "You probably get sick of hearing this, but..." and I'm here to say, for the record, I *never* tire of hearing nice things. These kindnesses are sometimes the one thing I need to hear in order to get through something or get back to being the me that is being championed, and they always make me feel tethered, connected, and less alone.

With my first OO missive, news of my cancer goes from a small circle of people to a wide array of acquaintances, friends and family. It makes it suddenly very real, forcing me to confront it and deal with it as my new normal, rather than a whispered tangential to my life. Those first responses, as varied as the people included in my OO distribution list, set the tone for the exchange that will flow for the next year.

From Bill Snoddy, a competitive Scrabble player in Asheville, NC:

What an amazing woman you are, but then you must be told that so often. Such entertaining writing about such a difficult subject. I am flattered to be included in the group that gets this piece of work, and as a physician I will offer the unsolicited opinion that you will live a long life and play ONAGERS against me when I am an old man. Sounds like you are already getting the very best, and yet I will still wish you the very best!
Bill-

From Stacey Koval, a local friend and tennis player:

HOLY $^%#& ! That's what ran through my head when I read this email. I was floored by this news. I was very aware of your *conspicuous absence from the tennis ladder when I saw the list on Friday. I had been out of the loop as I did not play in the spring due to my achilles problems. I was going to email you just to see why you weren't on the tennis ladder. This is certainly not what I expected to hear. Busy schedule, too many vacations, worst case scenario - a bad case of tennis elbow. Never would I have dreamed of this! Of course I will bring you dinner one night and I will be more than happy to run errands or assist you and the family in any way that I can. Thank you for including me in this email distribution and please continue to send me updates. I will call you in the next couple of days. I would offer to come play scrabble with you but you probably would not find me a worthy adversary :-)*

From Sue Udelson, whose daughter was in preschool with Hannah and whom I have seen only sporadically over the last few years.

Katya,
I appreciate receiving this email very much. Of course my initial reaction was something like, "What? Shit! Damn it! *&%^ #*%&$&###(*&%#", but upon further reflection I quickly determined that if there is any person that has the ability to kick cancer flat on it's ASS it is you, Katya. You are an incredibly strong woman in every way, and by every definition, and I know that you will absolutely return to complete health. It would be an honor for me to help you and your family with whatever is needed, so please let me know who the contact person is for this. I am qualified to serve as a domestic engineer as well as a staunch advocate for lousy service in an infusion clinic. Just name it. Oh, and let me know who you feel is the second-best caterer in the area so that we can line them up for your "Clean Bill of Health Celebration" in the near future. You have so many chapters left to write Katya.
With love and friendship,
Susan

From Britnee, a girl I met when volunteering at a homeless shelter the previous Christmas and whom I have been mentoring and taking out with us on occasion.

Im sooo sorry to hear that mrs Katya. And i hope you ghet bettah

*and everything.please i dnt want you to stress ur self out. I hope you
have a great summer and im on ur tyme kk..you are a very very good
person over all. You will ghet through this and GOD is with you
every second of tha day..i jus wanna thank uu for helping me with
everything and being their for support....if you every need anything
that i can do for you jus call or email me ii will make my day
available even if itz not...I PROMISE. I pray that you get better mrs
Katya..and dnt ever stop believn or being strong..you can over
come any obsticle possible because you have a BIG heart and GOD
sees that in you..please keep in touch and tell ur kids i said hey..and
remember to stay strong......Thanx for helping when i had no one
else too..have a great summer and DO NOT stress ur self kk*

From Tom Tozer, my editor at The Charlotte Observer:

*Dear Katya,
I am on vacation at the beach and am slow to respond to my email.
Your email shows all your strengths, your ability to write, love your
children, face life straight up, and always going forward with spunk
and courage.
Thanks for sharing your journey. Know that my prayers are with
you.
Your friend, Tom -*

From Valerie Preston, one of our neighbors:

*Katya,
I have to say that yours was the most entertaining and surprisingly
uplifting cancer communication that I have ever read! Nevertheless,
the news is very disturbing and my heart goes out to you and your
family. I'm sure you've heard it all and I won't blather on about the
unfairness and how someone like you will knock cancer on its ass,
but I have to think that this will be just one more thing to put on your
incredible resume.
I know you have a great support network, but if you need any help at
all, please don't hesitate to ask. I'd be happy to help get your kids
where they need to go, run to the grocery, do your laundry, anything.
Please let David know that we're on call as well. Send the kids over
the fence for dinner if you need some time to yourself. Just get well!
Lots of love- Valerie*

From another neighbor, Kim Companion:

June 13, 2011
Well, you're certainly going into this with just the right attitude and that speaks volumes of your strength and fortitude.
Trust me when I say that a positive attitude makes all the difference in the world and I know you're going to do incredible throughout this process!
The great thing about the hair loss is that you're beautiful no matter what and you know you're doing great things by donating what you have--what a generous gift you're able to give.
I always think it's better to beat this disease and treatment to the punch before it punches you first.
You have so much to look forward to in the midst of your treatment so just look at the fun, family time ahead of you and muscle through the rough patches with your always "CAN DO ATTITUDE" and tell this to disease to F OFF!!!!! Knowing you, you'll be the new role model for how to look cancer in the face and KICK IT'S ASS!!!!!
Much love goes out to you all!
Kim

I know it sounds crazy, but I really do think of cancer as my foe. We aren't exactly facing off in the boxing ring, but it is me against cancer in some sort of battle, sometimes physical, sometimes mental and emotional, some days theoretical while others truly do feel like a war zone or boxing ring, but always, it is Katya versus Cancer. What these emails do, these lovely and poignant and touching and empowering responses to the OO updates I send out, is make me feel like cancer doesn't stand a chance. It hovers there, cowering and alone, friendless, while I am backed by a veritable army of support. I am not well versed in military matters, but I do know that one's arsenal is an important part of the equation. Those emails are my stealth bombers and flak jackets. Whether it is bolstering my self-confidence, reinforcing my strength, or promising to care for me and my family, they leave me feeling that I can do this.

Cancer doesn't stand a chance. Really, it isn't a fair fight.

CHAPTER TWELVE

Subject: Ovarian Odyssey
Date: June 9, 3011

Hi folks,

I had my post-op meeting today, where I was pronounced to be doing great – until Dr. Naumann ascertained as much with a physical exam – ouch! I was also pronounced ready for chemo. Ready physically, that is. I'm working on the mental/emotional readiness.

As promised, Dr. Naumann has worked my chemo schedule around my summer plans, leaving the three trips I most wanted to take intact (the 4th of July Scrabble Tournament in Albany, Noah's college visits up the East coast, and the Scrabble Nationals in Dallas). The downside is that I have to start right away so that I get a full cycle in before leaving for New York with Noah and Hannah, so my first cycle will start this Tuesday. Yikes! Day 1 will be a full day, starting with an IV of Amifostine, which was described as a "chemo protector" to help fight off nausea. I will then get Paclitaxel (Taxol) intra- venously and Cisplatin via my peritoneal port. (This is mainly for all the medical folks out there; the rest of us – and I include myself in that category – just know that I'm getting a bunch of drugs that will kill good stuff as well as bad; and will hurt me in the short run in order to help me in the long run.) On Day 8 I will go in for half a day and will only get the Taxol via IP.

Continuing the good news/bad news theme, the good news is that I will have a private room rather than sitting in one of the chairs lined up one next to each other in the infusion room. The bad news is that the need for the room stems from my having to lie in a bed for my day-long infusion because of the way the IP is administered. As it was described to us by the lovely chemo coordinator (and she must be really good at her job to be deemed lovely despite the most ominous of job titles), my abdomen will be infused with 2 liters of drugs which will puff it out to pregnancy proportions (somewhat ironic, given that all the parts needed for an actual pregnancy are now missing). It will apparently take several days for my stomach to flatten again (or, to be more accurate, to return to its original size/shape) so I'm off to buy what she referred to as "Thanksgiving pants."

Aside from the nausea, which varies from person to person and I simply won't know how I fare with it until I'm several cycles in, I can also look forward to fatigue, numbness and tingling (which is permanent in some patients, so I was warned not to ignore it if it becomes debilitating) and chemo brain. My kids are already concerned that I am suffering from early onset Alzheimer's, so I can only imagine what they'll think of my diminished capacity with my newfound chemo brain. I actually consider that particular side effect one of the aforementioned silver linings to all of this because I now have a built-in excuse for anything I forget or misstate. I wonder if there's a special dispensation for chemo brain at Scrabble tournaments...

Again, at the risk of giving most of you far more information that you need or want, here is my newly minted chemo schedule:

Cycle 1 – Tues., Jun. 14; Tues., Jun. 21
Cycle 2 – Tues., Jul. 19; Tues., Jul. 26
Cycle 3 – Mon., Aug. 15; Mon., Aug. 22
Cycle 4 – Mon., Sept. 5; Mon., Sept. 12
Cycle 5 – Mon., Sept. 26; Mon., Oct. 3
Cycle 6 – Mon., Oct. 17; Mon., Oct. 24

David and I will celebrate our 20th wedding anniversary during Cycle 3, and I plan to distract myself from the more unpleasant aspects of chemo by planning our celebratory trip when this is all over. David looked at me, when he could tell -- as people married to each other for 2 decades tend to be able to do – that the chemo schedule, with its stretch way beyond summer into the fall and its many possible side effects that are no longer theoretical but imminent realities that lurk right around the corner, had me down, and he said, "First chemo, then Italy." I plan to have that as my mantra from now on.

I have been told that my particular chemo regimen is very aggressive and makes losing one's hair a certainty. I found out that my hair is actually long enough to donate for a wig so I plan to proactively shave my head to ensure my imminent hair loss at least serves a purpose, because I will not be able to donate it once it starts falling out. So my "Thanksgiving pants" shopping spree will also include some hat shopping because I'll be rocking the bald look as of next Monday. I plan to bring the girls with me and make it a celebratory event and I'll be back in touch then to send out photos. I know it pales in comparison to some of the other injustices of this disease, but I just have to once again lament that I JUST GREW OUT MY BANGS! Arghhh. And wouldn't you know that I've been having one great hair day after another... sigh.

Okay, that's it for now. Many thanks for all of the wonderful messages of support and love... I truly appreciate all of the encouragement, advice (okay, maybe not all the advice) and concern.

Fondly,
Katya

My OO missive doesn't capture the frustration of my post-op visit with Dr. Naumann. As usual, he is running egregiously behind. I grant him this transgression because it is true of almost everyone in his profession and I figure every appointment with an oncologist has an additional time-consuming emotional component. I am sure Dr. Naumann's patient interactions rarely translate into a simple *let me write you a prescription for that and I'll see you next time.* This is heavy stuff we're dealing with, difficult questions need to be asked, major decisions made. I don't mind because I know my turn will come, and I have my own slew of questions stored up.

The first time I saw Dr. Naumann, I was a shell-shocked mess. David and I rattled off a few timid queries, but for the most part we just tried to take in and process all of the new and unwelcome information Naumann was rattling off. The next few times I saw Dr. Naumann were when I was in post-surgical hell. I cared only about getting through the trauma of that moment, focused solely on having him do what he needed to do to make the world stop spinning. This post-op visit, the only time I will be able to see him for quite a while because from now on I'll go directly to the infusion room and be in the hands of his nurse practitioner, Trish Sullivan, is also the first time I am feeling relatively okay physically, as close to my pre-surgery, pre-cancer self as I am going to get. I feel physically and mentally ready to face the next part of my journey and I have a bunch of questions about how to go about doing that.

Dr. Naumann gives me five minutes, tops. He comes in the room, his stress palpable, and lays out a brief overview of what chemo will entail. He then turns and appears to be *leaving!*

"Wait, wait," I say, dismayed that he is apparently done with me. "I have a bunch of stuff I need to ask you."

Dr. Naumann looks at his watch. "Make it quick," he says, "I'm running behind."

Dr. Naumann is not a bad guy. He's a very good guy, in fact, just one who has many demands on his time. It is upsetting to me that I am not one of those demands.

"I *know* you're running behind," I want to yell at him. "I've been waiting for you for an hour. Now it's my damn turn!"

But instead I speed-talk my way through the most salient of my questions – can we work the chemo schedule around my summer plans, what are the most likely side effects and how will I manage them – before he pats me on the knee, tells me I am going to get through this just fine, and leaves.

The demands placed on doctors to see more patients, to give those they do see the short shrift in order to do all of the other things now required of them, from filling out forms to documenting everything to appeasing insurance companies, boards, and a schedule that puts them behind from the moment they start their day (this is not hyperbole – I find out later that some of my doctors are double-booked for the few days they are actually in the office and not in surgery. They literally start off the day behind and the length of the delay grows with each hour, and double-booked patient, that passes. I quickly learn to schedule my own appointments early in the morning, before the inevitable delays have a chance to build too much) is fodder for another book. What I will say now is that it is a frowns-all-around dynamic. Nobody benefits. The doctors are stressed and understandably resentful of things that are asked or done in a visit that don't *have* to happen right then, putting them even further behind schedule. As a patient, I pick up on that stress or resentment, and I, in turn, resent *it*. I've waited too, buddy, and now all I get is a hurried physical examination and a doctor who's already looking ahead to the patient behind the next closed door. Not okay.

Fortunately, the morning is salvaged by Nichole Filyaw, the Blumenthal Cancer Center's Chemo Coordinator. After I am dressed, I traipse down the hall to her office where she sits with me and David, her sweet and calm demeanor just what we need to diffuse the anxiety and frustration we're both feeling. She takes out a calendar and actually maps out my entire chemo schedule, assuring me it is no problem to accommodate the trips I have already planned for the summer. This is such a relief because I have been really looking forward to taking Noah on his college visitation trip. It is a right of passage and one I want to share with him, and one that all sorts of people told me I could kiss goodbye once I found out I had cancer.

It's not all good news, though. I learn that my chemo will not be administered in one of the reclining chairs that line the perimeter of the infusion room, but instead I'll get a private room with a bed because I will have to lie down thanks to my peritoneal port. Nichole warns me that the liters of fluids and drugs they pump into my stomach, including two liters of chemo poisons, will swell it up. She suggests wearing what she calls "Thanksgiving pants" that have room for the inevitable expansion. She also gently points out to me that the expansion will probably not be temporary. The steroids I'll be on throughout chemotherapy will puff me up and have a tendency to make patients gain weight. Great. What happened to the silver lining of at least getting to lose some weight during all of this? I learn that gaunt and emaciated chemo patients are a thing of the past. Seriously?

We agree that I will start chemo on the following Tuesday, June 14th. It is no longer a hazy future event. It is real and right around the corner. I have a tremendous amount of anxiety about the chemo and I am very conflicted about it. I am dreading it and, in that sense, I would like to delay it as long as possible. I can't quite get my head around the fact that I'll be pumping huge quantities of poison into my body. I fear the treatment will be worse than the disease and cause just as much damage. But I also know that I cannot move on with my life and proclaim myself cancer-free until I complete this necessary evil, so in that sense I am eager to get started.

CHAPTER THIRTEEN

My veins don't seem to realize that this is the *first* day of chemo, not the last. They have already had it, and the worst part of my day is the very beginning of it, when they refuse to cooperate. Maggie Hield, the chemo navigator who is also my nurse for the day, has tears in her eyes as she unsuccessfully tries to start a line. "I am so sorry," she says to me, in what will become a familiar refrain as pretty much every nurse who is assigned to me fails to start a line on the first, second or even third try.

You couldn't order up a more perfect first day of chemo nurse than Maggie. She is fun and perky, but also exudes empathy and con- cern. We instantly hit it off and she is also a hit with all of my friends, who traipse in at regular intervals according to the chemo buddy schedule Lisa Zerkle has set up. Maggie explains what she is doing each time she adds something to my regimen, so that I feel a little less bewildered about what is going on.

We begin the day with fluids, once the vein is blown, flushed, and a new one is located. The fluids take about 2 hours, including the vein fiascos, and I am in pretty good form. I lie back on the bed and hold court as David and my friends keep me company and take it all in with me. Before long, I will know all of the nurses' names. I will become adept at unplugging my IV pole and electronic monitor and pulling it along with me to the bathroom. I will know not to freak out when my machine starts beeping, indicating that an IV cycle is completed or, the more likely scenario, that I have jostled the needle somehow and interrupted the flow. I will know how each drug, each bag that is hung, will feel as it enters my veins and bloodstream, and how it will effect me, both in the immediate aftermath of its coursing through my body and hours and even days later. I will come to recognize the looks of pity and support from my visitors, the looks of bravery and shared pain and

discomfort from my fellow infusion room patients, and the looks of kindness and compassion from all of the nurses. But on that first day, when it is all new and bewildering but, in a bizarre way, also somewhat exciting, the way the first day of school is full of the promise of new relationships and experiences, I am trying to process it all.

Following the fluids, I get a series of drugs, all to offset some of the side effects of the poisons to come. I get Pepcid to help with the inevitable heartburn, Decadron and Zofran for the nausea. I also get Benadryl, which is not your over the counter, I've-got-the-sniffles Benadryl, let me tell you. When it is administered intravenously, it is a far more potent drug and makes me instantly woozy. I can feel my eyes getting heavy and my mind turning to mush. Next comes Ativan, which relaxes me even further and has an amnesiac effect as well. The two chemo drugs will follow the Ativan, so that I am feeling no pain by the time they hit me. Maggie explains that she will give me the Taxol intravenously on my long days, Day One of the three-week cycle, because I'll get Cisplatin through my port in my abdomen. On Day Eight, what my team refers to as my half day even though it ends up running just a few hours shy of my long day, I will get the Taxol through my port because I won't get Cisplatin on those days.

Maggie has been flitting in and out of my room all day, oohing and aahing at the phenomenal network of friends I have and the goodies they bring me in a steady stream throughout the day. I have the plush robe and blanket that Marni presented me, as a group gift, the moment she and my other friends heard of my diagnosis. I complain to Jen that my feet are cold and she texts Lisa Zerkle, up next on the chemo buddy schedule, who comes bearing fuzzy socks for me. And on it goes, with Maggie maneuvering around the constant stream of friends (and saying nothing about how they exceed the limit of one visitor per patient) with ease and good cheer. When it's time to give me my first chemo drug, however, there is a major change in both her appearance and demeanor, so much so that I do a double take when she enters the room. True, I am in my Benadryl and Ativan haze. I say things that don't seem silly to me but I see David and my friends exchanging smiles and winks at my expense. I comment that Colin Firth is due for a visit any minute. (I don't actually remember saying this, but I am told that Colin Firth – a longtime crush – figures prominently in my post-Ativan ramblings.)

But even taking my loopiness into account, Maggie's transformation is jarring. She is wearing a long-sleeved blue apron-like covering that, true to its name, covers her arms and torso, down to mid-calf. Her reassuring smile is hidden behind a surgical mask and both of her hands are gloved. She comes in carrying the Taxol in a bag in front of her, at arms' length, and I can feel my pulse quickening.

It's more than all the protective gear she's wearing, though. It's her suddenly somber mood and the careful and deliberate way she carries in the Taxol that looks dark and menacing enough without her obvious treatment of it as hazardous material. I hazily ask about all of her precautions and she explains that the next two drugs she will be giving me – Taxol and Cisplatin – are immensely toxic. She and the other nurses must take great care so that they are not exposed to even one inadvertent drop of this poison. I look back at her, my eyes conveying my consternation and bewilderment. Maggie is hooking up a bag the size of a small infant, pulling a switch so that its entire contents will now seep slowly but surely into me. I am trying to understand how something so toxic, requiring my nurse to go to great lengths to protect herself against it, can enter my body in such a huge quantity. Surely, if even a drop is to be avoided at all costs by a medical professional, it cannot be right to put hundreds and hundreds of drops directly into my bloodstream.

Intellectually, I get it. The cancer is a poison and the only way to kill it is to hit it with an even more odious poison. I am lucky that I live in a time when they have these drugs and there is a treatment option for my cancer, versus just waiting for it to fester within me and slowly kill me. But there is something so upsetting and just wrong about seeing your nurse don all sorts of protective gear to shield her from this thing that is being purposefully injected into you in huge quantities.

I am very anxious about the Cisplatin because I have heard that it is the big daddy of all chemo drugs. I am also apprehensive about how it is going to be administered. The IV needle, although problematic, is now routine. I get it. The port, not so much. Several weeks later, when I again wonder about how the port works, I am shown a prototype of it. Being able to visualize it helps a lot, in that I understand why it is so difficult for the nurses to get the needle into the right spot. The peritoneal port is made of flexible white plastic and is about an inch in diameter. In the middle of it is a small circular mesh that the needle must locate and pierce. This would not be a daunting feat if the port were both stationary and visible, but neither applies. It is untethered in my abdomen and has a tendency to move around. The nurses have to feel for it through my skin and then do their best to push the needle through my stomach and through the mesh. The mere thought of it is nauseating and painful, and the sight of the needle – a huge, menacing thing – gives me even more heebie-jeebies.

Luckily, the Ativan they give me to relax me does a masterful job. Even though my port is a constant struggle for my nurses, some- times requiring three of them to both hold me down and several painful attempts to locate the port and pierce it correctly, I have no recollection of any of it. My friends are often traumatized from witnessing my port complications and my apparent discomfort, but I never remember any of it. I show up at the infusion room the next day for fluids and I am invariably approached by one of the nurses apologizing to me. "Oh Katya, I'm so sorry about your port. Do you hate me?" I just look at the contrite offender blankly, "I have no idea what you're talking about."

The Ativan haze extends past the port debacle and into the rest of the day. Noah comes over after his internship at Mayor Anthony Foxx's reelection headquarters. I introduce him to everyone but the next time he visits me in the infusion room, I show him around and try introducing him again, convinced it's his first time there. When he tells me that he visited me at the end of my first day of chemo, that he was, in fact, the one who pushed me out in a wheelchair, I have absolutely no recollection of his being there. What is interesting and reassuring is that, even though I'm not conscious of what I am saying and I don't remember it afterwards, my personality and sense of humor remain intact. When the nurses insist on my leaving in a wheelchair, the only one available is an extra large one. I apparently joke about my new girth (not knowing how prophetic that will actually be) and how offended I am that they picked out such a large wheelchair for me. I find it fascinating that certain aspects of my personality and, frankly, my parenting (trying to make the situation less daunting and sad for Noah by injecting fun and teasing into it) are able to surface, despite the drugs and the fact that I'm not conscious of or in control of what I'm saying and how I'm behaving.

The Ativan haze continues when I get home. The girls greet us as I'm going in the house to announce that our neighbor, Joy Boyce, has offered to pick us up dinner at Mario's, an Italian restaurant around the corner. David tells the girls to thank Joy but to tell her that we are all set. I apparently disagree, insisting not only that we should let her get us dinner, but placing the order – down to my mesclun salad with grilled chicken and the house Italian dressing, not the balsamic one that ordinarily comes with the salad– in minute detail. When they return with the food, I demur and say that I have no appetite and couldn't possibly eat anything. My family looks back at me incredulously. Was I not the one who insisted on ordering this very food? I do not remember doing so.

I do not yet feel nauseated, just worn out. I find this encouraging and I am hopeful that my lack of morning sickness with my pregnancies (that Brenda, Dr. Naumann's nurse, promised me is a good prognosticator of chemo-induced nausea) will carry me through the next few months. Perhaps the worst of the nausea is behind me and this chemo ride won't be so bad.

Subject: Ovarian Odyssey
Date: June 15, 2011

Thanks to all of you who sent good thoughts my way for my first day of chemo yesterday. It turns out neither my phone nor my internet worked all morning (service is intermittent at best) in my lovely private room at the Blumenthal Cancer Center, so I'm assuming that's why all that good karma didn't kick in right way — it was all gathered at some cyber holding cell waiting to reach me. In the interim, I was off to an auspicious beginning. Within five minutes of getting settled (it still feels so bizarre and surreal to know my way around there), I was crying and writhing in pain. Nurse Maggie took one look at my veins, which have been through the ringer lately, and called in reinforcements. They decided to try to start my IV in my wrist vein. Bad idea. They hit a nerve, it turns out, and flushing it out only exacerbated what was already an excruciating situation. They mercifully concluded that it wasn't going to work and moved up to my beleaguered but much less finicky vein in the bend of my elbow. Much better. I turned to David, with tears in my eyes, and wondered aloud what they would have done to me if I hadn't brought in a big platter of cookies for them to share.

We all crossed our fingers that the botched IV episode would prove to be the worst part of the day ... and I'm happy to report that it was, mainly because I was knocked out and loopy for some of the other indignities I suffered. Nurse Maggie was really great about telling me exactly what she was doing and how it would likely impact me and what was coming next. (I did warn her, however, that she'd make a terrible poker player. If I asked her if something was going to hurt or if I'd be experiencing one of the odious side effects, she'd wince and say, "We'll see." The wince is her tell. She tries to mask it with a lovely smile and a very sweet bedside manner, but that wince pretty much says it all.) She was also sympathetic to my small bladder, especially since she was the one pumping me full of liters upon liters of fluids, so my private room did not end up being quite as isolating as I had feared because I was able to make some friends on my many trips to the bathroom. Among my new acquaintances was a woman from the Congo, formerly Zaire, who was beyond delighted to hear me speak French and have some familiarity with both Lingala and Tshiluba (the dialect of Mbuji-Mayi, where she grew up). I told her my friend Mbuyi's name for me in Tshiluba, Mukanakamomu, which roughly translates to "the mouth that never closes." My nurses were all quick to agree that it was a fitting nickname for me.

I was given several anti-nausea drugs and then it was time for the Taxol, which was daunting enough without having it administered by Maggie, clad! in full-on protective gear, including a big blue surgical robe, blue gloves and a blue facemask. Nothing like knowing this toxic, toxic drug is entering your body in large quantities when the medical professionals administering it to you take such precautions to avoid contact with it. She gave it to me slowly for the first half hour to make sure I didn't experience any of the side effects that often occur when it enters the bloodstream — back pains, metallic taste in one's mouth, sweats — but I was good to go, so in went the rest. She then numbed the area in my abdomen where my port is located and gave me some sedatives.

Good thing, since the sight of the needle alone was down- right scary. Lisa, one of my chemo buddies, told me that I began discussing Sesame Street with her during this time — so interesting where one's mind goes! David arrived in time to see them experience several complications with my port (it had apparently moved, which is no surprise to me since it has been bothering me all week) and he says they really struggled with it, but I was off in my own world by then and I have, blissfully, no recollection of any of that. I apparently implored Nurse Maggie to tell the director of my play that I knew my lines and then asked for my coach to let me in. Hmmm ... do you think being side- lined this summer is impacting my psyche?

When they woke me up to go home at 6:15 pm — I was the last patient left! — Noah says that I was able to joke with Nurse Maggie about the wheelchair she brought in for me. Apparently she could only find an extra-large one so I teased her about how the steroids (which are supposed to make me puffy) must have already kicked in.

I will pause here to note that I find it a huge medical travesty that they cannot find another way of curbing nausea other than giving you steroids to increase your appetite and make you gain weight. Really?!? I'm going to lose my hair and have to deal with cancer and chemo and I can't even lose weight? Arghhhh. Noah is making me a sign for my hospital room that reads, "Bald, bloated and boob- less, you will still be beautiful." Nothing like unconditional love.

I drove Noah to his internship at the Mayor's Reelection Campaign headquarters this morning and then Eliza and I met a friend for breakfast. I made it two bites in before realizing that today, ostensibly my good day before every- thing that is coursing through my bloodstream really kicks in, is actually not so good. I left Eliza there to enjoy both her breakfast and mine and headed home, where I am now ensconced in bed for the foreseeable future. Nausea (not nearly as bad as I experienced post-surgery, but nausea nonetheless) and assorted aches and pains are my companions, but I just keep reminding myself that all this discomfort translates into getting better in the long run. It is mighty depressing to look over at my dresser and see eleven prescription drugs all lined up and awaiting their designated time with me. Many are supposed to be taken with food that, under normal circumstances, would not be a problem at all, but most food makes me gag right now. I have found that the Lance peanut butter and honey crackers are about the only thing I can stomach right now so they are my new best friends. And I have to say that everyone who is bed-ridden should have two pure-bred mutts as companions. It is difficult to succumb to a big ol' pity party when Darcy is nibbling your ear and Molly is licking your foot.

I continue to feel so touched by the outpouring of love and support. I entered chemo yesterday with a blanket that was the envy of the floor along with a new iPod and headphones, so thanks to all the family and friends responsible for those goodies. I told Lisa M., who visited me in the morning, that I would have to remember fuzzy socks for next week's chemo session, and she promptly got word to Liza Z, my next visitor, who arrived with them in hand. I'm going to see how well this system of expressing desires and having them immediately acted upon works, so next week I plan to lament the fact that I'm not getting these treatments in, say, Hawaii. I'll keep you posted... And many thanks to those of you who have already delivered frozen meals and other goodies —my family's appetite remains intact, so it's good they are not reliant on me to decide what should be on the menu these days!

Many of you have asked what you can do for us and I truly appreciate all of! the offers of assistance. My dear friend, Lorrina Eastman, has volunteered to coordinate our support and serve as the point person for us. She can be reached at.... Another dear friend, Lisa Zerkle, is coordinating chemo buddies for me. She can be reached at....

There appears to have been some confusion as to when I am losing my hair, so let me clear that up now. I am going to shave my head next Monday,! June 20th, which follows my first round of chemo but precedes my second. After that point, I would no longer be able to donate it for a wig because the chemicals would have kicked in. I plan on taking the girls with me and we will be sure to take some photos to send out with my next update... I'm not sure if that's a promise or a threat, so anyone who wants to be spared the sight of my newly shorn head can opt to skip my next missive.

Hugs to you all,
Katya

CHAPTER FOURTEEN

The day after my first round of chemo, I wake up thinking, "This isn't so bad." The room does not appear to be strapped to an amusement park ride. I am somewhat bloated and sore from all the poking and prodding, but, all things considered, not too bad. Eliza and I drive Noah uptown for his internship and we then head over to Terrace Café, a favorite breakfast spot of ours, to meet my friend Carrie Nagle and her baby, Fiona. I am taking full advantage of feeling good, knowing that the chemo side effects sometimes take a few days to kick in. It reminds me of being a new mom and being told to go out and do things while my infant is portable and spends most of his time slumbering. This is my window of opportunity, and it is also my shot at showing Eliza, who is watching me intently, that I am fine. That we can do this. That it won't be that bad.

Midway through breakfast, I feel as if the restaurant is suddenly on the ocean, and the wave on which we are perched is cresting. The nausea hits so suddenly and violently that I can't even process what is happening at first. I throw some money at Carrie and ask her to please take Eliza home and I hurry out the door, knowing that my time to get myself home is limited. I grip the wheel and feel my spirits plummet with each wave of nausea. So much for the lull before the storm.

I get under the covers with Molly and Darcy, who are delighted at this strange, middle of the day behavior, and hope that lying down keeps the nausea at bay. It does not. Wave after wave hits me, unrelenting in both its ferocity and its tenacity. I feel the need to throw up, but I can't. I have the occasional dry heave, probably because I haven't eaten enough to warrant emptying my stomach, but I mainly just lie in bed, feeling utterly miserable. As if the nausea weren't tough enough, it decides to partner with pain, knocking me out with a one two punch. First the wave of nausea, then shots of pain, radiating from my vagina and shooting up my abdomen. Then the cycle starts again. Nausea, pain, nausea, pain. Lest I get bored or complacent, the nausea and pain team shake things up, appearing in tandem or switching their order. The pain, I am told, is due to the fact that the Cisplatin, the more potent of my two chemo drugs, was administered through my peritoneal port directly into my gut, where all of my internal surgical sites are still raw and vulnerable. It is akin to pouring lemon juice on open wounds, only these are inside of me and cannot be assuaged.

David tries to entice me with various offerings of food, but I can't even stand the mention of them without gagging. The only exceptions are Tang (a blast from the past) and Lance peanut butter and honey crackers. A neighbor, Rick Clark, gets several crates of them from the Lance factory, blowing us away with his kindness. Neighbors and friends stop by with meals and treats, and it is comforting that my own food boycott is not impacting David and the kids.

Jun 15, 2011

Hi Katya,

Sounds like the chemo was really awful, which does not surprise me. I'm glad you made it through the first day though. I hope you're up to more than peanut butter crackers in a few days. I also hope all of our good thoughts for your next chemo session will make it through the ether, so it goes better next time.
I just wanted to let you know your new Red Sox hat is on its way and should arrive in time for the disappearance of your hair. And, since my birthday is on Sunday, I will wish myself a happy birthday on your account, so you won't need to!

Love, Nikki

June 15, 2011

Oh Nikki,

I feel just awful today. My bones hurt. My stomach is cramping up all over -- probably in protest of the $(@%9 peanut butter and honey crackers. And the nausea. The worst part is that this is supposed to be my good day! I am so fearful of what comes next, *especially once the drugs they gave me to ward all of this off wear out because I am extremely leery of putting anything more into my body given my track record with that.*

Sorry to vent -- I'm just sitting here having a pity party for myself. I am just so miserable and I find it hard to imagine enduring this until the end of October. I can only hope this first week is the worst.

And I appreciate your excusing me from wishing you a happy birthday but I do not accept being replaced by the birthday girl herself, so plan on hearing from me again, and hopefully I will be in much better shape physically and emotionally when it comes time to wish my dear, dear friend a happy birthday.

Love, Katya

On the third day post-chemo, David takes me back to the hospital. Trish Sullivan, Dr. Naumann's nurse practitioner whom I have not yet met because she was on vacation but who will be my primary care provider moving forward, suggests I come in to get fluids and some intravenous doses of the anti-nausea drugs I am taking. I sit in one of the chairs against the far wall and try to keep the room from sliding out from under me. Maggie and Nichole come over to visit me and I must look terrible because they both kneel down, one clasping my hand and the other patting my knee. They both have tears in their eyes, which touches me.

"Oh baby," Maggie assures me. "Poor baby."

She exudes sympathy.

"We will figure this out," Nichole assures me, and I believe her. They seem as intent on ending my misery as I am.

Trish informs me that it is crucial, moving forward, to stay ahead of the nausea. Once it kicks in, it is much, much harder to knock out. The plan from now on is to have me come in for the two to three days following each day of chemo to get fluids and IV drugs. "It is important to stay on top of the nausea," Trish tells me, as if I need convincing. She could have told me to strip off all my clothes and sing Happy Birthday in Polish and, if she decreed it to be a way to stave off the nausea, I would have done it without a moment's hesitation. The nausea just colors my world, making me feel sidelined and sad on top of the physical misery it inflicts. I do not shy away from expressing just how miserable I am to Lisa Miller and Jen in this e-mail exchange:

June 16, 2011

Hi Katya –

How are you doing? Jen and I are having an early lunch tomorrow before we go to Waxhaw for an end-of-camp horse show from Audrey, Claire and the others. We'll be dining at Ilios Noche starting at 11:30. I don't know if you'll be up for an outing but we'd love to have you along.

Hugs, Lisa –

Lisa and Jen,

I would like nothing better than to join you tomorrow but there is no way I will be there. I have had a truly miserable day with everything that could possibly hurt or make me ill working in tandem. Sore bones, cramping stomach, unrelenting nausea, migraine headaches, and -- the kicker – a vagina that feels like it's on fire because the pubic hair is starting to fall out. I can't eat and I am horrible company (the sight of any family member who comes to inquire how I'm doing makes me instantly weepy) so I will be a no show tomorrow but I appreciate the optimism in thinking I could make it. Needless to say, I cancelled my trip with Noah and Hannah for this weekend. Sigh. This cancer/chemo thing just SUCKS.
Okay, I probably should have just politely declined and left it at that. Sorry about the vent...

Hugs to you both, Katya

------
katya-

i'm SO sorry to hear that today and the past couple days have been so miserable. i'm not planning to shave my head, but i wish my pubes would fall out instead of yours. aka never feel like you can't vent or share what you're going through and should just politely decline.

xoxo
jen

Katya,

That completely SUCKS! I am so very sorry. And you can vent all you want. I suspect it's a healthy outlet. I'm sorry to miss you tomorrow. We're away for the next week (beach), but will be in touch via email. May the angels of mercy be good to you (or FUCK the cancer and chemo!)

Cyber hugs – L

On Day Five, a Saturday, I turn the corner and start to improve. I head in to the hospital for fluids and drugs and, for the first time, feel revived afterwards. I am like a plant that is so parched and dry that the first few times it is watered, in an effort to nurse it back to health, appear to have little effect. But finally, the soil is damp, the roots and leaves suck up some of the moisture, and it starts coming back to life. Saturday's watering appears to do the trick for me.

When we get home, we see that Rick is again vying for the honor of nicest neighbor on the planet by coming over, while we are at the hospital, with his chainsaw. Now that might actually strike you as alarming behavior in a neighbor, well, in anyone, considering that we aren't home and the kids are all in the house, alone. But that's because I haven't shared with you that the backdrop to this whole week of hell, when I am bed-ridden and miserable, is that our front yard looks like a tornado has hit. David has hired some tree cutters to prune our two big trees out front and cut down a third that was in danger of falling on our house. The cut-rate deal he negotiates includes having them cut the branches and trunk into small sections and move everything to the curb for pickup. There was obviously a communication breakdown because what we find, when we come home from the hospital several days earlier, is a yard literally covered in huge, unwieldy pieces of wood, of all shapes and sizes. Neighbors gawk as they walk by and it is clear it will take a Herculean effort to get it all cut up into more manageable pieces and hauled to the curb for pick up. Enter Rick and his chainsaw. He rings the doorbell and tells Noah to get his shoes on and meet him outside. Good thing Noah does not move at his usual snail-like pace because he joins Rick outside just in time to stop him from cutting down our remaining trees. Rick had not understood what the mission was (cut up the trees on the ground, not those still standing) but, once clear on that, works all morning to make it so that I see a green lawn by the time I get home from the hospital. A Reuben sandwich from Katz's Deli, where we stop on our way home to get me some chicken soup, is all he accepts as payment.

I try to walk every day, even when I feel like shit, because I want to get outside at least once a day. I am convinced that I will sink into a deep depression if I stay in my bed, even though my physical symptoms are dictating that I do just that. I also walk because my doctors assure me it will help with my healing. Some days I lean on David, trying not to be discouraged by the fact that I have to stop every few houses to catch my breath. Other days I venture out alone, assuring David that I have my phone and that I know someone in almost every house I pass, so really, there is no need to worry.

I know he is struggling with just how much of a mensch to be, how many restrictions to impose without really pissing me off. It is a balancing act we both navigate, out of love for each other. I try hard to interpret his patronizing limitations as the concern and love I know them to reflect. He does a masterful job of biting his tongue and understanding that some things need to happen for my emotional well being even if they end up costing me physically.

We both continue to marvel at some of the physiological changes that are starting to happen. I shower and look down to see a discernible thinning of my pubic hair. And I learn that hair doesn't just silently and painlessly fall out. It actually hurts, almost like a burning sensation, when it is pushed out. I keep thinking, as I will throughout my entire cancer journey, that this would be utterly fascinating if it were happening to someone other than me.

CHAPTER FIFTEEN

"Wouldn't you know?" I say to Lorrina, who is busy snapping pictures of me perched in the salon chair, about to have my head shorn, "that I am having a fabulous hair day today?"

Lorrina laughs and agrees that my hair does look particularly nice. The bangs that I have spent the past year growing out now fall just below my ears, and the haircut I got in Philadelphia (on the day I got the Big C call, when I was walking around the city, numb and alone, trying to find a way to make myself feel better) has given my hair a healthy wave and glow. My long layers fall around my shoulders and look exactly as I'd always wished they would on this, the day that I am cut- ting them all off. You just have to laugh at the irony.

We are at the Ballanyne Spa again. I'm treating the girls, including Margot, Lorrina's youngest child, to pedicures while I get my head shaved. I figure it will make what is clearly causing the girls a great deal of anxiety more fun and festive. And Lorrina and I found out, when she treated me to my pedicure the week before, that the haircut is free since I'm donating the hair to charity. If that's the case, I might as well go to a swanky salon. I originally fear that I don't have enough hair to donate (letting out an audible Homer Simpson-like D'OH the moment it dawns on me that it was idiotic to get my hair cut on the heels of my cancer diagnosis since that same diagnosis will engender losing it all). I would definitely have had the requisite 8 inches to donate prior to the 3 inches I trimmed in Philly, but now I am not so sure. Luckily, I haven't taken into account the fact that I don't need to measure from just below my ears, the way most people do who are donating hair but still want to have some semblance of a hairdo left behind. Since *all* of mine is being shorn, I can measure from the top of my scalp, and that does, just barely, make the cut.

The hairdresser pins all of my hair up in various clips and clamps and it all feels like any old haircut. I am chatting with both her and Lorrina, enjoying the fact that I am feeling only twinges of nausea, the best I have felt since my hysterectomy and first round of chemo.

"Okay, here we go," the hairdresser says, and before I can

even process what that means, she takes the scissors and cuts an entire ponytail away. My reflection is a lopsided look of shock. There is no going back now. She continues to cut until my hair is just a series of clumps and spikes, like a poorly mown lawn. Lorrina snaps away and tears are welling in my eyes with each clump that falls to the floor, which we notice later in the photographs. In the scope of the tragedies that are befalling me, in the realm of life changes that my cancer will engender, this one is minor and relatively shallow. In the long run, my bald head will be of little consequence to me and I will wear it around town with minimal self-consciousness, foregoing bandanas, wigs and hats. But now, staring at my drastically transformed mirror mate, some- one who seems to be entirely separate from me and catapulting me into a stage of this journey I'm not ready to take, someone who is gazing back at me, a bemused but somewhat frightened expression on her face, it is a shock.

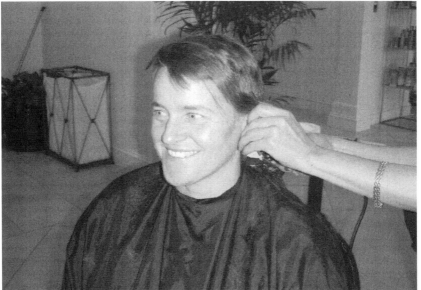

Getting my hair cut off at the Ballantyne Spa. She is clipping my hair and it feels like any other hair cut.

The hairdresser takes out the razor and finishes the job, leaving a thin but discernible layer of hair across my scalp. The girls are summoned from their separate room and giggle nervously at this radically different mom smiling encouragingly at them. We all then go sit in the plush waiting area, sipping fruit-infused water, while we wait for David to show up. He is meeting us there because he has to take Hannah to the Temple for a tutoring gig.

An elegantly-coiffed woman sitting next to me is summoned for her appointment. Her hairdresser is the same one who just took care of me. I can't help myself.

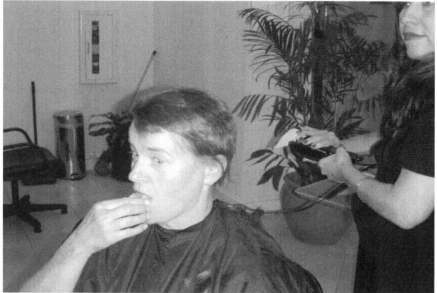

Wait! Wait! What? She just cut off that entire ponytail! Okay, now this feels real.

"Watch out," I say, looking up at her with my newly shorn head. "I asked for just a little trim and look what she did to me." The woman looks horrified as my hairdresser leads her away, no doubt explaining the situation.

"You're so bad," Lorrina says, and we all laugh. It is a good laugh. It is a "that's the Katya we all know" laugh, a laugh of relief that only my hair fell away in the last hour. It is reassuring, even to me, especially to me, that my personality, my sense of self, is intact.

When David arrives, I can see the nanosecond of shock register in his eyes, but he recovers quickly.

"It looks *good*," he says, hugging me.

On the way home, Lorrina and I stop at her hair salon,

Carmen Carmen, to drop off my ponytail. They will then ship it to Pantene Beautiful Lengths, a partnership between Pantene and the American Cancer Society which makes wigs for women with cancer. The ponytail looks much darker than how I perceive my hair. It is pronounced extremely healthy hair (I have never colored it; I have barely even used a hairdryer on it) and will make someone a nice wig. It feels good to do this, to have something positive come out of this cruel chemo twist. And it is particularly satisfying to be in control, to let cancer know that I'll be the one decreeing when I lose my hair, thank you very much.

That night, I hear David's end of a conversation with his mom, and I am glad he is the one taking the call.

"But why did she cut it all off?" Susanne asks. "She didn't *know* she was going to go bald."

"Yes, Mom, she did," David says. "The doctor told us she would definitely lose her hair between the first and second chemo treatments. They have this down to a science."

"But Carol Ann…" Susanne counters.

David is turning red.

"Carol Ann? Who had *breast cancer* seventeen years ago?"

Susanne is not the only one. Everyone seems to want to equate my cancer to their own cancer experience, whether it's a spouse's esophageal cancer or a neighbor's lung cancer or, as in Susanne's case, a friend's breast cancer. Setting aside the fact that Carol Ann didn't have my type of cancer, the fact that she'd been treated so many years ago makes her experience radically different than my own. Not to mention that the staging of your cancer, the type and duration of your chemo, and what you bring to the table – your own physical fitness and stamina, your pain and nausea thresholds, your support system, your prognosis — can all impact one's cancer experience. It is just ludicrous to assume that you know what I'm going through, that you can predict what will happen to me, or that any one cancer experience has any bearing on another.

This is a button-pushing experience for me. I find myself wondering if I did that in my pre-cancer days. Did I equate all cancers? Did I naively and erroneously assume that all chemo is the same? I don't think so, but one thing I know, I certainly never said so to someone with cancer. I didn't presume that I knew what Cancer Friend A was feeling or experiencing or what was in store for her because of Cancer Friend B's experience.

Another way this universal cancer approach irritates me is when folks try to warn me of the horrors that await me. I know their intentions are noble and that you are awarded a certain latitude when you have suffered these indignities yourself or you've watched a loved one suffer. I try to be forgiving because I figure they truly mean well – they were blind-sided and are trying to keep me from suffering at least that part of the inevitable hardship. And, consciously or not, they are probably trying to salvage some sort of sense from it all, a purpose to their pain. If they can share it with me, articulate exactly what I'll be feeling, then it has not been entirely in vain.

But I am having enough trouble dealing with my post-surgical issues. I want to enjoy the few days I have left of feeling relatively restored to my former self before embarking on chemo. A hazy dread of what is to come, a general but low-lying sense of foreboding, is good enough for me. I don't need the specifics. But that, alas, is what I get.

"I just want you to know what's coming up for you," an acquaintance who had breast cancer two years earlier, calls to say, "because *I* would have liked to know."

Had she stopped to ask if, in fact, *I* would like to know, I would have thanked her for her gesture, but unequivocally said no. But I am not asked. She just plows ahead.

"You're going to have pains shooting out of your ass. You're going to wake up at 3 o'clock in the morning and not know who you are or where you are. Your mouth will be filled with sores that make even swallowing unbearable. You won't be able to leave the house..."

David comes downstairs to find me holding the phone at a distance, as if I can somehow mitigate the litany of woes that will befall me by sending them out into the expanse of our living room rather than into my ear.

When she finally stops and I have extricated myself from the call, thanking her for her advice even though I want to scream, "You had *breast* cancer. You didn't even have the same chemo I'm going to have. You are ten years older than I am. Seriously?!?" I turn to David and say, "Well, that was thoroughly unhelpful."

I am feeling particularly irritable about some of the cancer no- no's that folks seem to be committing left and right. What ever happened to tiptoeing around a delicate subject? To treating someone who is dealing with a catastrophic disease gingerly and with the utmost respect? I am finding myself expending energy I don't have to spare trying to meet people on their terms, letting them dictate how this experience will unfold rather than their taking their cues from me. It is pissing me off.

I fire off an Ovarian Odyssey with a list of my grievances, a sort of *what not to do* guide for the uninitiated. I will later feel somewhat contrite about the tone of my email – people are, after all, well- intentioned – but the fact is that getting annoyed and offended is part of my cancer experience too. If I am going to chronicle it frankly, my short fuse moments shouldn't be whitewashed.

Subject: Ovarian Odyssey
Date: June 19, 20111

At the risk of sounding like a broken record (does that idiom even apply in these days of CDs and iTunes?), I am sorry to report that these last few days have been really rough. The chemo did a number on me, both because it is a particularly brutal regimen (since it involves both Taxol and Cisplatin) and because I had a particularly bad reaction to it. I went back in to the hospital for two days of IV fluids and anti-nausea drugs and I seem to finally be rebounding today.

Here are some insights I have gained in the last few days:

Chemotherapy sucks.

Taxol is evil, but Cisplatin (administered directly into my abdominal port and thereby longer-lasting) is even worse. Cisplatin and I do not get along. At all.

My husband is a loving, caring, patient and wonderful man.

The nurses and chemo coordinators and nurse practitioners at the Blumenthal Cancer Center are amazingand I am lucky to have the health insurance I! do to afford me such excellent care. Both Nichole and Maggie (my chemo coordinators/nurses) came to check on me when I returned to the hospital for post-chemo help and they both had tears in their eyes to see me so miserable. Tricia, my nurse practitioner, spent a long time with us explaining what was happening and how we were going to combat this type of hell in the future. (The plan going forward is to go in for fluids and IV meds for the two days following the chemo, plus we're looking into getting me an anti-nausea patch for future rounds.) She also pointed out that the next round should be better because it won't be on the heels of major surgery.

Hair loss hurts. It burns.

It is possible to feel full of despair while simultaneously feeling overwhelmed with gratitude.

Neighbors we rarely see have stepped forward in extraordinary ways, friends and family members write or call and offer the perfect insight or just strengthen me with their good thoughts, and my kids floor me with their resilience and caring. (Okay, sometimes I do wonder if their resilience doesn't actually mask a self-indulgence that is both mind-boggling and amusing. Their ability to return to their usual bickering and whining, with no "Gee, maybe we should step it up a notch because Mom has cancer" reboot, is refreshing but also somewhat distressing.)

This is my own journey. I appreciate folks who get that. Most do. Please note that you do not know exactly what I'm feeling because Uncle Floyd had prostate cancer 8 years ago or your neighbor had an easy time with chemo when she had breast cancer last year. It is not helpful to know what horrors await me. It is helpful to know that I will get through this, even when there are moments, hours and days when that seems unlikely.

Some of my close friends, whom I valued plenty pre- cancer, have shown themselves to be the most selfless and supportive friends anyone could possibly have at a time like this. You don't pick your friends with cancer in mind — at least I don't — but talk about a litmus test. Mine have truly lifted me, anticipated my needs, given me space when I need it and coddling when I don't, and have made me oh so grateful to have them in my life.

This is not just happening to me. I know how hard this has been on David and my parents, who are pained to see me hurting. I hate that. My kids have seen me weep more in the last week than they had in their entire lives prior to that. I hate that. (Okay, for the record, I am distinguishing between crying and weeping. They have seen me cry plenty of times —at a sappy movie or commercial, an old man eating alone in a restaurant, you name it — but never out of pain or dis-

tress.) I summoned up all of my energy — a short walk around the block exhausts me these days — and made dinner for my family tonight. We sat around the table, eating the food that I prepared (I hadn't even set foot in the kitchen since my chemo) and enjoyed our first family dinner together in quite a while. Let's hear it for life's simple pleasures.

Fondly,
Katya

CHAPTER SIXTEEN

I have often heard my friends complaining about what babies their husbands are when they are sick. For the record, David is not one of those guys. He pretty much goes about his business and doesn't whine or whimper or complain that he is about to die from what turns out to be the common cold. It is true, though, that the response folks have to the same set of symptoms or circumstances can vary widely. I learned this first-hand when I was the Community Coordinator at Providence Spring Elementary School, a position I initiated after I was PTA President during a year when we suffered a slew of tragedies – the death of two kindergartners and two parents, all in separate incidents. The entire school community wanted to express its support to each of these families during their time of crisis and loss, but each family had very different needs. The way they each grieved was very different, with one bereaved mother wanting complete and total privacy while another welcomed the public outpouring.

For the mother who wanted to be left alone, respecting her wishes was the best way we could show our support. This was a hard sell to some folks, who insisted on showing up unannounced with casseroles. And even if I had been able to convince everyone to back off, decreeing that this approach is best for everyone grieving the death of a child, it would have backfired because it would have left the next mom who had to face this kind of unthinkable loss feeling alone and ignored. The Community Coordinator position was my way of channeling and managing the support, so that well-meaning gestures could be tailored to each grieving family's needs.

A point person is a good idea, I think, someone who can serve as the gatekeeper or the organizer of all that well-meaning but often chaotic and overwhelming support. My point person extraordinaire is Lorrina. Within days of my diagnosis, she sets up email groups, coordinates gifts and meal drives, and runs constant interference with everyone. How she manages to do what pretty much amounts to a full-time job on top of her actual full-time job, not to mention being a mother of three, is beyond me. Lorrina is perfect because instead of plowing ahead with what she thinks is right for me, she always checks in with me and asks me how I want her to handle things. She is doing the heavy lifting and the coordinating, but I am still involved and in the loop.

Lisa Zerkle takes on another point person role as the coordinator of my chemo buddy schedule. She arranges to have someone drive me in, someone drive me home, and other buddies take on 2-hour shifts so that I am never alone. David actually gets upset when he sees the first schedule because he is not on it. I explain that my friends are just trying to spare him the obligation to come, so that he can get work done or ferry the kids to and fro, but that he doesn't need to be on the schedule in order to come hang out with his wife. It is funny, though, what set us each off. I didn't like the emails going around about me behind my back and David feels like his role as my number one caretaker is being usurped. And in each instance, the intentions could not be nobler.

I have to learn how to take well-meaning advice and expressions of concern better. On most days, reminding myself that folks mean well is enough to take the edge off, but there are times when I just want to scream, "You are not being helpful right now. You are being the opposite of helpful!"

A perfect example is the woman at Panera Bread who is responsible for cleaning off tables and straightening up. When she gets to me, she stands in front of my table and simply asks, "What kind?"

I look up from my computer and smile at her. "Excuse me?"

"What kind you got?"

I'm still not getting it.

"Breast? Lung? What kind of cancer?"

"Oh, um, ovarian," I reply.

Her face lights up. "Oh, that's what this other customer had. Yup, ovarian. She came in here all the time. Just as bald as you."

"And how is she doing now?" I ask, more to keep up my end of this decidedly awkward conversation than out of any real curiosity.

"Oh, she died," the woman responds. "She fought it for a long time but it got her in the end."

And off she goes to wipe down another table, while I am left sitting there, mouth agape, wondering why on earth she felt a need to share any of that with me.

Another time, my mom (a yoga enthusiast who once expressed incredulity that my girls couldn't lift their legs behind their necks the way she could) calls to tell me that she is arranging for a private yoga instructor for me since I can no longer do aerobics. Wait! What? First of all, who says I can't do aerobics? My doctors certainly didn't put any such restrictions on my level of activity. And I hate yoga. It holds zero appeal to me. If I didn't like it before cancer, I'm not about to change my mind. I know Mom is just trying to do whatever she can from afar to care for me and show her support. I tell her as much and that I know she and Dad are totally there for me; they do not have to prove it with private yoga instructors.

Another day, Susanne, my mother-in-law, calls to see how I'm doing. She and Norman, my father-in-law, are always asking what they can do and offering to help. This time, though, the call rubs me the wrong way. I am in considerable pain, both from the constipation and the vaginal scars, which seem like they will never, ever heal. I hear more of the maternal advice we have tried to nip in the bud, how I have to take it easy and not overdo it, and then she asks, "How's David?"

I know this is hard on David too. And it's natural for her to inquire about her son, who is hurting in different ways. But on a day when my physical pain is at its peak, I feel nothing but envy for David's ability to eat, poop, and do things with the kids. How's David? He's fine because he's not the one who's sick.

On the heels of this phone call, I head outside for a walk. My docs told me to walk as much as possible because it will help get things going again in my body and I am desperate to put an end to my constipation. I must look a sight because I feel as if my vagina is going to tear open with every step and I still feel as if I'm carrying around a 10- lb. bowling ball on my ass.

A neighbor in the cul-de-sac near me comes down her driveway to intercept me, a look of concern and pity transforming her face.

I am prepared to tell her that my doctors want me to walk. Yes, it is difficult, but I am a trooper and I am trying to just get through this one footstep at a time. No, I don't need to rest. I'd prefer to just keep going.

But she does not ask about me. When she reaches me, her lower lip trembling with sympathy, her question is, "How's David?"

I have had it. David is fucking fine.

"Well, given that he didn't have his vagina sliced open," I reply. "He's doing pretty well."

That neighbor has never again intercepted me on my walk.

The most common bone-headed thing that is said to me, though, is inquiring about my prognosis. Really, when is that ever going to go well? If my prognosis is not good, it should be up to me to share that news with you. If you don't know me well enough to know my prognosis, you shouldn't be asking. The fact that some people have the added chutzpah to ask me in front of the kids just gets me going. This is one query I cannot cloak in good intentions or forgive because it is well- meaning. It's just plain nosy and rude. Later, after we've told the kids about the cancer diagnosis, Eliza confides that she finds the prognosis query particularly upsetting because, as she puts it, "I didn't even know you could die until people started asking you about your prognosis."

Eliza and I are out walking the neighborhood once, in the midst of my chemo, when another neighbor approaches me. After complimenting me about how strong I am and how well I am pulling off the bald look, she leans in and asks, in a conspiratorial whisper, "So do you mind my asking what your prognosis is?"
Eliza looks up at me with her big, blue eyes. I squeeze her hand, letting her know I've got this.

"Well, I've only got a week or so left, but I'm trying to make the most of it, " I reply.

CHAPTER SEVENTEEN

Subject: Ovarian Odyssey
Date: June 20, 2011

      The responses to my newly shorn head fly in fast and furious. Most are funny, all are uplifting, and I think they have a lot to do with my ability to "rock the bald" all summer and fall. I walk around town bald and proud, and I am convinced I have the confidence to do so thanks to all the compliments I receive on the nice size of my head or how being bald makes my blue eyes pop or just that I look good.

Lorrina and Jen buy out the hat and scarf inventory at Nordstrom's and Target, respectively, but I just can't carry the look. I occasionally wear hats but the scarves just don't work for me, so it's a good thing everyone makes me feel so comfortable and confident going without.

From Gail Johnson, a Department of Justice attorney whom I knew in Washington, DC:

Wow! You look like a (1) Punker; (2) A Women with likely lots of "tats; and (3) a remarkably generous person who thinks of others while going through one of the most challenging times of her life. Love 'em all.
Thanks for sharing, Katya! You look fab, Dah-lin!

From Kelly Simmons:

You're actually quite beautiful with the short do. Bill thinks you're hot. Bill, as you know never says anything like this. :)

From David Klionsky, a Scrabble buddy:

That is such a kick-ass look for you...love it!

From Rob Carter, my former brother-in-law:

Love the new do!!!Short, long, no hair...you'll always be beautiful!!!
XO, *Rob*

From Donna Gaskin, a former Providence Spring Elementary PTA Board Member:

You look great!!!!! I know you don't think so but you do!
The most beautiful part of you is still there honey....it is the person you are inside that shines through in all situations. I watched you this morning with the children and others you encountered. You still have the twinkle in your eye, the laughter in your voice and the welcoming smile that lights up your face when greeting others. Cancer will take many things but it will not take the person you are inside.

From Mary Rhoades, a competitive Scrabble player in Texas:

You'd make a cute boy if not for the boobs!

From Pat Hardwick, a competitive Scrabble player in Ohio:

Sexy!

From Jim Crawford, one of my closest friends whom I've known since high school, now living in Texas. Jim spent a summer in Zaire with me while we were both students at Brown University.

Excellent look!!

What was it you used to get your driver to say to you every morning in Kinshasa: "You look very beautiful today" And I mean it. Love ya.

From Lorrina, whose parents and sisters become regular email buddies of mine.

Thought you'd appreciate my Mom's comment about your "new do." "Please tell Katya that she has a most gorgeous cowlick in the front which was hidden by her bangs before-she looks just beautiful and more radiant than you would ever expect someone who has just gone through such a week as last!"

From Sarah Wheeler, Noah's former teacher at Randolph Middle School:

Katya,
Truly, you were meant to be rock n' roller. Look out Annie Lennox and Sinead O'Connor. :)
Larry and I are sending you LOTS of love!!

From Uncle Carl, David's paternal uncle, who lives in New York and whom I visit regularly on my way to the Albany Scrabble tournaments.

Katya,
Your new "do" made me think of competitive swimmers who closely cut their hair to reduce water drag and possibly knock a second or two off of their event times. So the next time you jump in a pool, let

me know if you think your time for a 25 meter lap has improved.
Love, Carl

From Strat Story, my friend Diane's husband:

They say women with that point in their hairline are really 'hot'

From Jeff Klein, one of David's college buddies:

One last thing. Love the new do. You look kinda punky. I think David always wanted to date a "bad" girl so thanks for making his wish come true. –Jeff

When I show up for the second day of chemo on June 21st, the nurses exclaim over my new look. I look around the infusion room and realize with a start that I now look like I belong there. I am a cancer patient – no getting around it. I am lying in bed, awaiting my litany of pre-chemo meds, when I see Trish, my nurse practitioner, show up. She looks through the glass partition in my door but then walks away without saying anything or coming in. I see her talking to the nurses and gesturing in my direction, shaking her head, then returning, more cautiously, to my room. When she pops her head in the door, she looks at me closely and then says, "Oh, it *is* you! I didn't recognize you! I told the nurses, 'No, she has long hair. I just saw her last week.'"

When I complain about how rough my week has been, Trish explains to me how she will try to improve things moving forward. I'll come in for fluids and meds for the three days following my chemo and she is also going to order an anti-nausea patch for me to wear starting the day before my chemo. It will last for up to a week and will slowly release the anti-nausea drugs into my bloodstream and that should help also. She also says it won't be as bad next time because I won't be fresh out of surgery and my wounds will have had time to heal. But Trish makes it very clear it will be better, but not easy. I should expect a rough ride. She says that Cisplatin is old school and just awful in terms of its side effects. There will be more tough times ahead, but somehow she turns that inevitability into a *good* thing.

"We are going to beat you up," Trish tells me, in her no-nonsense, direct way I have come to appreciate. "You are young and strong and your cancer is curable. So we are going after it with everything we've got and yes, you will feel beat up. But it's because we can cure you and we don't have that option with a lot of our patients."

Her pep talk does me good. There is a purpose to my pain, a reason for my suffering. And I cling on to the *we can cure you* core of her message. Even though I am doing my best to emerge from the *cancer = death* mindset I had prior to getting cancer myself, I am not quite there yet. Every assurance I can get that I am not going to die – especially from medical professionals and not just well-meaning friends and family members – is immensely comforting.

Jen is the first of my chemo buddies to show up, getting there shortly after I do. She's there for the Trish pep talk, note- book in hand, taking notes. She then asks Trish some questions on my behalf and it is clear she is taking on the Mother Hen role. Jen has been very concerned about my overdoing it so she makes a point of repeating the responses from Trish to which she wants me to pay particular attention.

"So what kind of aerobic activity should she be doing?" Jen asks.

Trish says that most things are fine, but it'd be best if I stick with low-impact aerobic activity.

"Low *impact* aerobic activity," Jen repeats. "Interesting. Could you specify what that entails?"

Trish rattles off a list and Jen is nodding and taking notes.

"So no running. Interesting. Katya, isn't it interesting that running is *not* low-impact?"

I point out that I have actually been a good patient and that Jen does not need to worry.

"Uh no," Jen is quick to point out. "Doing a catering job four days after major surgery is ˆnot being a good patient."

It wasn't exactly four days later, more like six days after I got released from the hospital, but I decide not to quibble. Her concern feels a little patronizing and stifling, but I know it comes from a really good place. She is not doing it for any reason other than that she cares about me and wants me to get well.

I am hungry for the first time in a long time and I have a bizarre hankering for egg salad. Gabi Culpepper is on the lunch shift and word gets to her that egg salad would be a happy thing. She decides that buying me an egg salad sandwich is risky because you never know what funky things a restaurant is going to put in their egg salad, so she decides to make it for me herself. This involves buying some fresh bread at Amelie's, where she also picks up two boxes of pastries, some for me and some for my nurses. It turns out they do not need to be bribed to be nice to me, but they certainly appreciate the gesture. I also bring them in goodies (homemade cinnamon rolls) so they are quickly learning to eat a light breakfast on the days I am scheduled for chemo.

Gabi brings the lunch in a wicker picnic basket, complete with a tablecloth, a vase of flowers, and real cutlery. It makes my sterile hospital room seem instantly more dignified and pleasant. Several friends bring in what become their trademark offerings, and while their company alone would be gift enough, these thoughtful gestures enhance my hospital stays. Lisa Zerkle always brings in fresh wildflowers from her garden, in little glass bottles that serve as a vase. I'm not big on store-bought flowers (David learned early in our marriage that purchasing them for me was a waste) but these flowers instantly cheer me – and my room – up every time Lisa shows up with them. Marni, who is also a Brown University grad and a recovering attorney yet shares my guilty pleasure of *People* magazine and celebrity gossip, often comes in bearing a slew of trashy magazines. When your mind is filled with drugs and your days consist of a million interruptions, *War and Peace* is not going to cut it. That is not to say that books don't make for good chemo companions. Jen's husband, Bill, orders me several books that he thinks I will like, and given that their kindergartener enjoyed them too, they are at just the right level for a day of chemo. They are big hits with my kids too and strike just the right note as far as focusing on the positives of life when it would be easy to get sucked into a pity party of negativity. Entitled *The Book of Awesome, I and II* (Bill heard about them on NPR one day and thought of me, which is touching since it means I have made it onto the radar of not just my friend but also her spouse), they chronicle the little moments in life, from the silly and minute to the grandiose, which are truly awesome.

And speaking of awesome, I have a brand new iPad to accompany me to chemo, thanks to a widespread gift-giving campaign coordinated by Lorrina, and a set of spiffy headphones contributed by my parents, brother and sister. It is ironic that the iPad is deemed an ideal chemo gift so that I can wile away the many hours I'll be tethered to an IV pole watching DVDs or playing online Scrabble, when, in fact, I never get a chance to use it during chemo because I have round the clock visitors! Whenever Iris, who works at the hospital, pops in, she offers to take the kids (on the days they are there) with her to the doctors' lounge, where they stuff their pockets with all of the unhealthy treats that are, ironically, a staple of the place medical professionals go to relax and refuel. My friend Amy, who is often on lunch duty, goes absolutely anywhere to pick me up the lunch of my choosing, no matter what part of town it is in. "What do you *really* want?" she asks. "What are you craving?" And no matter what I say, a Greek salad from Akropolis café at the Arboretum shopping center near our house, or the Latin Wedge Salad from Fran's Filling Station across town, she always acts like that is exactly what she is hankering for as well and I am doing her a big favor by providing her with an excuse to go get it.

In fact, everyone is so eager to please and to make my chemo days more palatable that it becomes downright amusing. Laura Lewin texts Gabi, whose chemo buddy shift precedes hers, asking if there is anything she can bring me. Unbeknownst to her, I text her back – as Gabi – and put together a truly ridiculous list, including a

Gabi delivering lunch to me in the hospital.

velour sweat suit, fresh guava juice, 40 milkshakes, and I can't remember what else. Laura's reply text reads as follows: *I can only handle the milkshakes on my way in but I'll get the rest later. What kind does she want?* We set her straight, and when I tease her about how she didn't hesitate, despite the absurd- ity of my requests, she says, "I was just so happy that you wanted something and that I was able to do something for you."

But for anyone who is reading this book as a primer for how to proceed with a friend or loved one who has cancer, here are my final two cents as far as the gifts go. They are wonderful, they brighten your day and make you feel loved and spoiled, but they pale in comparison to the real gift of friendship. Just offer up your time and companionship and you will do more for your loved one than anything you purchase could ever do.

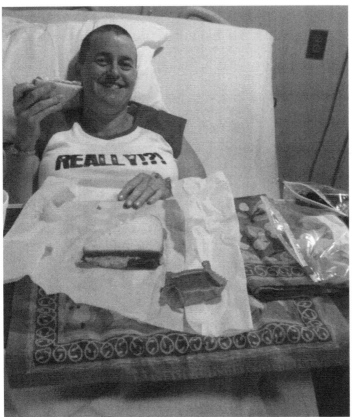

Enjoying the egg salad sandwich Gabi brings me for lunch (and wearing the Really?!? t-shirt my sister sent me).

CHAPTER EIGHTEEN

It is a glorious day. I am done with chemo until I get back from my trip up the East Coast, so I will have a good, long respite and can look forward to feeling better each day. I am on my way to the airport to pick up my sister, Nicole, who is coming in for a weekend visit before flying home to California after a work trip to DC. I haven't seen her since my diagnosis and she is the first family member to see me in my newly-shorn, post-hysterectomy, chemo and cancer state. (Not, I should add, for lack of trying. Mom tried valiantly to come out for my surgery, but I demurred.)

Nicole and I head straight to Terrace Café, where we are meeting a bunch of my friends for breakfast. I am so happy to be surrounded by such a fabulous group of women and I feel so loved and supported. I am also excited for the food. I haven't had much of an appetite and things have tasted funky to me but this morning I am hungry and hankering for a good cup of coffee (Terrace Café has its own barista) and the fruit and yogurt plate that mercifully comes with a big hunk of coffee cake as well. Gabi is up for sharing that and the spinach eggs benedict, which suits me just fine since this way I'll get both sweet and savory and we happily place our orders.

First to come is the coffee. I sip mine and I look around to see if everyone else is finding it bitter and nasty. No one else appears to be unhappy with her cup. In fact, several people at the table ask for refills while I'm still trying to figure out if I should switch to something else or just give a freshly brewed pot a try. Then our food comes and I can't wait to dig in. Gabi is oohing and aahing about what great selections we made while I'm finding it totally inedible. And then it hits me, in the kind of Mack truck way a realization that one's taste buds are out of whack hits a foodie like me, everything tastes *metallic!* It's not the food, it's *me,* or, rather, it's the chemo. I am so distraught because I thought I had dodged this bullet, and it makes no sense that it is hitting me like this *now,* almost a week after Day Two of chemo and almost two weeks following my first round of chemo.

Nicole and I go from breakfast to the hospital, where I am due to get what Trish calls a Happy Meal – fluids and anti-nausea drugs intravenously. She wants me to get all of that in my system

At Terrace Café with, clockwise to my left, Nicole, Marni, Amy, Gabi and Laura.

before my big weekend and my trip. While we are there, I complain about the metallic taste and she says, without a moment's hesitation, "Oh, that's the Cisplatin peaking." The *Cisplatin?* That I had way back on Day One of Chemo almost two weeks ago? Yup. It peaks on Day 10. It is amazing to me that it stays in my system that long and actually becomes more potent, rather than less, as the days go by.

Trish also gives me a pep talk, which could also be interpreted as a lecture, about managing my expectations. "You are going to crash next week. It is coming and there is nothing you can do about it. I don't want you to be upset or concerned and I want you to adjust your activity level accordingly."

Nicole looks at me knowingly. We both realize Trish has my number.

It takes the nurses several tries to get the needle in and it is quite painful. I am used to it at this point but Nicole winces and looks away. We meet a man and his wife seated next to us. The tubes going into him are red and we learn that he is getting a blood transfusion because he has lung cancer. Talk about putting your own problems in perspective. I am very glad to not be getting a blood transfusion.

We decide to go home and spend some time with the kids before heading out again to see Hannah's Possibility Project (a city-wide theatre troupe she has been in all year) performance. Jen, Lorrina and Melissa are seeing the show as well and we are all going to go out together beforehand. David, who has been away on a work trip, will meet us in time for the show. I am feeling increasingly shitty as the day progresses, which has me down because I was so looking forward to this weekend and to feeling well enough to enjoy it. I have been constipated all week and the pressure is unbelievable. I am in quite a bit of pain and discomfort and the worst part is that I feel a need to go, almost the way diarrhea sends you running to the bathroom, but each trip to the toilet yields nothing but frustration.

We meet at a restaurant that I've been longing to try, a tapas restaurant uptown near Hannah's theatre, but I spend most of the night in its tiny bathroom. When we get to the show, we take our seats and I squirm and shift in discomfort until I can stand it no longer. I make my way out of the darkened theatre and to the bath-room, where I am again treated to nothing but frustration. No relief. I am near tears as it is, and they flow freely once I learn, back in my seat, that I have missed Hannah's solo.

On Saturday, we meet some other friends for lunch (using the incredibly generous gift card I received to a restaurant near my home) and we meet Iris and her husband, Dan Uri, for dinner at Fran's Filling Station. Both meals are exercises in frustration for me because the reality falls so far below my expectations. I have looked forward to this visit from my sister immensely and each gathering with friends was marked on my calendar with great anticipation. My focus during each meal was supposed to be on the wonderful company, the joy of weaving my sister into my life in Charlotte, and the great food, but instead most of my thoughts during the remainder of her visit are on the agony inside my body.

I have been taking laxatives and over the counter stool softeners around the clock, but by Sunday morning, I am ready to cry uncle. I can barely walk and I know I am dangerously plugged up. Dr. Naumann, who happens to be the doctor on call, confirms as much. He tells me that the longer the stool stays in the colon, the harder it gets because all of the water leaves it. I am, as he puts it, in dire straits. He suggests an enema and Miralax, a stool softening powder you mix with water. If that fails, surgery will be in order. I am still recovering from my last surgery; this is not welcome news.

I am also eager to resolve my situation because, aside from my physical discomfort, this is no way to greet and entertain the 147 guests we will have arriving at our house that afternoon. We had volunteered to host the Charlotte-area social for NCSSM (Noah's school) back in early May, before I knew I had cancer, and while we could have backed out (and the Zerkles, whose son has been admitted to the school for the following year, had offered to host it in our stead), I wanted to make it work. Noah was psyched to have it at our house and, even though the numbers were far greater than we'd anticipated (it turns out the Charlotte *area* covers quite a few outlying towns), I figured an afternoon event wouldn't ask too much of me. I made a bunch of brownies, cookies and fruit salad and asked the invitees to bring their own beverages. We are all set to go, but for the fact that I am constipated beyond comprehension and can barely move.

When we get back from bagels, having picked up an enema on the way home, we have exactly five minutes to administer it before taking Nicole to the airport. David undoes the packaging and studies the diagram and directions while I drop my pants to my ankles and get on all fours. As if that position were not humiliating enough, David instructs me to drop to my forearms and lift my butt in the air. The enema apparently needs gravity's help to do its thing. I follow his utterly ridiculous, *Saturday Night Live-* like directions, and implore David to get on with it.

David has already loosened the lid of the enema and measured the contents, knowing he has to insert half of it into me at one time. I am certainly hoping the other half won't be necessary. I feel him fiddling around but nothing happens. I am extremely uncomfortable, I am eager for the enema to take effect, and I know we are cutting it close with Nicole's flight, so I cannot for the life of me understand what on earth is taking David so long.

"DO IT!" I finally yell at him in exasperation, trying to sound as authoritative as one can with one's cheek pressed to the bedspread and one's naked butt high up in the air. "What the hell is taking so long?"

"Umm," David replies sheepishly, "I can't, um, I can't find it."

"You can't find *what?*" I demand. He has the enema in his hands. What else could he possibly need?

"I can't find your asshole," David says, desperation lining his voice. "I can't find your asshole."

It turns out I am so riddled with hemorrhoids, from my week of straining to poop, that my butt is hemorrhoid city. Finding the opening for the enema, my asshole among all those hemorrhoids, is like a really gross version of *Where's Waldo*.

On the one hand, this is a new low. Every indignity I have suffered until now pales in comparison to this butt in the air, hemorrhoid nightmare. The fact that David has to give me an enema is bad enough, without there being *complications* to this humiliating ordeal. But on the other hand, and this is the route we choose to take, there is great humor in that sad, pathetic moment; a situation so absurd and ridiculous that you couldn't script it any funnier. We look at each other, understanding that this is the kind of marital bonding no one could ever predict or prepare you for, and we laugh. We laugh and laugh and laugh. We laugh so hard and long and loudly that Nicole actually taps on the door and asks if everything is okay in there.

When David finally does locate my asshole, after some very painful probing, he administers the enema and then leaves to take Nicole to the airport. I have already said my goodbyes be- cause I have to remain in that butt in the air position for as long as possible before rushing to the bathroom to hopefully unload what the enema set in motion. Unfortunately, it is yet another failure in the long list of products designed to soften my stool and move it along. I feel things gurgling and grumbling and that I am about to explode, but nothing happens.

I make myself a glass of Miralax and when the Zerkles arrive for the party, Andy encourages me to drink another glass. "That stuff is a miracle drug," he says, "and there is no harm in drinking more than the recommended dosage." So off I go, yet another glass of make-you-shit concoction in hand, while guests are arriving and milling around outside. The good news about Miralax is that, as potent as it is (and I am not the only person who swears by it), it really is flavorless. As far as medicines go, and I've had my share of late, this one is pretty innocuous. I find a little relief that afternoon and I am able to enjoy the party and the guests, without looking as constipated as I feel. We take Lorrina and her husband, Jim Pegram, and Lisa and Andy out for dinner, leaving all the kids behind at our house, to thank them for all they are doing to help us out. It's a fun evening, especially since we regale them with the hemorrhoid fiasco, but I am still quite uncomfortable. When we get home, I go to the bathroom, not expecting much, but the Miralax (fully earning its name, if it is, indeed, sup- posed to be a play on the word miracle) has finally kicked in. Hallelujah! I lose six pounds overnight! Miralax becomes a staple of my chemo diet; I start each day with a glass and will happily do an infomercial for them if they come calling.

Subject: Ovarian Odyssey
Date: June 27, 2011

Greetings from the gay, punk rock biker chick ... and that's just a few of the comments my new do elicited. I'm toying with getting a tattoo or nose ring to complete the look, although David tells me a mere snarl of the lip does the trick. Rubbing my head has become a favorite neighborhood pastime — my new policy going forward is that the first rub is on the house but I charge for any additional ones. Thanks to the generosity of my phenomenal support system, I need never show my bald head if I don't want to do so. I have a hat or scarf for any occasion, including hand-knit caps, hats that announce the different roles I play in my life (writer, walker, altruist, etc.), scarves of every color and size, several Red Sox hats (that I plan to wear at Fenway — more on that later!), a big white cowboy hat, and the two hats Hannah and Eliza made for me. One reads CHEMO SUCKS (no arguing with that) and the other CANCER CONQUERER (hopefully no arguing with that either).

We have also been overwhelmed with meals and other goodies. Not a day goes by that someone doesn't bring us flowers or something to eat. I know my culinary skills have some folks intimidated, but I'm here to tell you that everything we have received thus far has been deemed the best ever by my appreciative family (somewhat to my chagrin since I, too, make some of the dishes we have consumed!). And while I do enjoy cooking and expressing my love for my family through food, I have to say I have learned to enjoy having someone else cook for me as well ... definitely some- thing I could get used to. And while I am thanking you all for the embarrassment of riches, I have to say that you have distinguished yourselves with your creativity. Today I opened the front door to find my Hawaii wish (expressed in a previous e-mail) granted. There sat a very tropical flower arrangement, a CD of Hawaiian music, a box of macadamia nut cookies, and a container of pineapple lychee tea! Another family made me a chemo bag that reads "Katya, a woman of many hats" and filled it with the personalized hats mentioned above. Tonight at dinner we went around the table and discussed some of the highs and lows of this whole ordeal and the kids were big on all of the treats that have come our way thanks to the cancer card. I look around at the infusion room at some of the folks who appear to have no support system, while I am already negotiating to have more people visit me than are allowed, and I feel such a sense of gratitude for how loved and supported we are. Whether it's a meal, a book or CD, or just a call or email letting us know we're in your thoughts, we want you to know you have all made this so much more palatable... and, to be frank, downright enjoyable at times ... than it would be trying to do this solo. We feel very spoiled and blessed, which is saying something since cancer and chemo are not what one traditionally associates with those sentiments.

I am happy to report that Day 2 of chemo was much kinder to me than Day 1. I followed up my day of chemo with two rounds of IV fluids and anti- nausea drugs (what my medical team refers to as a "happy meal") and we were able to keep the nausea at bay. Unfortunately, I did experience some other side effects that once again confirmed that modern medicine still hasn't mastered how to cure me without simultaneously hurting me. The very drugs that are offsetting the nausea are extremely constipating, so I have endured days of extreme discomfort and jolts of pain thanks to the still raw (and, in my mind, pissed off!) nerve endings and surgical sights. I have also developed a metallic taste in my mouth that makes some of my favorite foods taste awful. For anyone who knows me, this is the saddest development to date. You can do a lot to me and I'll take it like a trooper, but please don't get between me and my food! My doctors told me that several of my new symptoms were actually a result of the Cisplatin peaking in my body, which would be fascinating if it weren't actually happening to me. The fact that this drug is so potent that it can have new and unwelcome manifestations of its potency nearly two weeks after it was administered is mind-boggling.

Fatigue is probably the biggest constant and I suspect I will need to continue to adjust my expectations. I have, however, tried to continue to live my life! as much as possible. This week had me resuming some of my work duties (conducting interviews for my

Charlotte Observer column and meeting with students for my college advising business) and we hosted the Charlotte area social for the North Carolina School of Science and Math yesterday afternoon. We saw Hannah's show, enjoyed a visit from my sister, and dined out with friends. Did I feel in top form for these activities? I'd be lying if I said I did. But is it important to me to try to muddle through and get back to life as normal, albeit a new normal? You bet. And that is why I am so grateful that my doctors scheduled my chemo around my trip up the East Coast, which seemed like a pipe dream when I was bed-ridden and in the throes of nausea hell, but that is now just around the corner.

Noah and Hannah and I leave on Weds. for the Albany 4th of July Scrabble Tournament ... surely this is an event that looms as large in your lives as ours. We then meet up with David and Eliza in Maryland, where we will enjoy a visit with David's folks before putting the girls on a plane to Seattle. They will enjoy a week in British Columbia at Stratchona Park Lodge with my parents while David, Noah and I head out on college visits. Two highlights of our trip promise to be the tickets I scored (without even playing the cancer card!) to see Book of Mormon in New York and the Red Sox game we will be seeing at Fenway in the players' families' section. Whoohoo!

So those of you who are picturing me ill and distraught in bed, please readjust your mental image to that of a happy and healthy (relatively speaking) woman — albeit a bald one, but really, in the scope of the indignities I've suffered, that's just not a big deal — headed off to enjoy a wonderful vacation with her family.

Fondly,
Katya

CHAPTER NINETEEN

The light fuzz that lines my head could be mistaken for a super short haircut. One does not necessarily look at me and think *cancer patient*. But I can tell my ability to pass, to stave off the looks of pity and concern that will routinely greet me once people know, will be short-lived. When I towel off after my shower, I see hair on the towel and in the sink. When I get up in the morning, there is hair on my pillow. I am glad I preemptively cut it because these stray hairs are disconcerting enough; I imagine it would be far more traumatic if huge clumps were falling out.

I'm generally okay with all of these changes that are happening to my body. It's just hair, after all. It will grow back. It's pretty low on the list of indignities that I am suffering as a result of this cancer. But sometimes I am just blown away by something seemingly small and insignificant, and I feel the full force of the loss and the outward changes that mirror the turmoil going on inside.

I go to David's office, which I visit infrequently, to get the forms notarized that give my parents permission to travel out of the country with the girls. While I am there, I see an enlarged photo of the two of us on his windowsill. It was taken while we were in Switzerland two years earlier, a trip we took with my parents and the kids to introduce them to all of their Swiss relatives. David and I are on a boat on the lake in Luzerne. Gorgeous snow-packed mountains form the background of the picture, as does crystal-clear water below us. We are on the deck and the wind is blowing, which makes my long hair blow away from my face. We both look happy and carefree and healthy, but what I focus on is my hair. I miss it in a way one would mourn something far more valuable, and it is the first time I feel a real pang of regret for the me that was.

The second hair loss angst moment comes when I am trying on these fun and creative scarf hats that Nicole's friend's mom made especially for me. They look like scarves tied around my head, but instead of my having to struggle with tying them, they come pre-tied, with elastic that fits snugly around my ears. I think they look pretty good and are a welcome change from the hats I've been wearing, but Eliza disagrees. Wholeheartedly. She surprises me by bursting into tears and imploring me to take them off.

In Switzerland with David on a better hair day.

"Honey, what's the matter?" I ask, taking off the offending headwear.

"They make you look... ," Eliza tearfully explains, trying to find the right words to capture the source of her distress, "like you have *cancer!*"

I point out to her, oh so gently, that I *do* have cancer. But I get what she means. It's easy to forget or to move along with life without cancer rearing its ugly head, and yet, sometimes, it does not allow us to forget.

Hannah seems the most adept at forgetting. It's partly her age, and it's also the fact that David and I do our best to insulate the kids. She seems the least inclined to pierce the insulation.

When we are at bagels with my sister, the morning that I'm in agony and still reeling from my first two chemo treatments, Eliza mentions that she would really like to accompany me to chemo one day, since both Noah and Hannah have been able to go along.

"Oh, you *should* go," Hannah tells her. "It's *really* fun."

I stare at Hannah in disbelief.

"Not for me, it isn't," I shoot back.

David chastises her for her insensitivity and she apologizes. She has inherited my extrovert gene and she enjoyed meeting the nurses and the other patients, plus my friends brought in all sorts of delectable food and she got to play Angry Birds with Gabi. I get that, from her perspective, it made for a fun day. And it's pretty age-appropriate that *her* day is all that registers for her. I'd much rather err on that side than have her walking on eggshells, consumed with thoughts of my cancer or impending death. But at the time, it feels like a dagger to my heart. To be so chipper about something that is so truly awful to me, to declare one of the worst experiences of my life as *fun,* just comes across as betrayal.

That Sunday night, after we go out to eat with the Zerkles and Lorrina and Jim, we return home to find the kitchen a mess. Hannah reports that Eliza is driving her crazy. I ask her to bring some of the leftovers down to our friends and neighbors Alex and Melissa Papazanakis and she gives me attitude – why can't Eliza do it instead ? – because she wants to return to the show she and Ivy are watching. While I am putting together a Tupperware full of goodies for the Zerkles to bring home, Lisa pulls Hannah aside to express her disappointment at how little Hannah is helping out and rising to the occasion. She essentially tells Hannah, with a sternness Hannah has never seen from sweet, gentle Lisa, that she needs to step it up.

After Lisa leaves, Hannah breaks down. She is very distraught, but I get the sense that she is more mortified than contrite. She asks me several times the next day, "Was I really that bad?" I know she wants me to mollify her, but I cannot offer the reassurances she needs. It would be easier to take that route, but I want this to be a learning experience, and it is from these painful and

165

embarrassing scenarios that we grow and mature. So I tell her that I do expect more of her, and that these very conversations are indicative of a self-centeredness that proves the point. This isn't how I should be expending my energy right now, at a time when I have so little of it and I need to direct it to getting well. It seems to sink in. She does an about-face and makes a concerted effort to help around the house and be more patient with Eliza.

Noah seems to be doing fine. He is busy with his internships and is looking forward to having his parents all to himself for our college visits trip up the East Coast. When my parents offered to take the girls with them on a Road Scholar trip (excursions all around the world for active elders and their grandchildren) to British Columbia, they worried that Noah would feel left out. "We will do something nice for you," Oma (what the kids call my mom) assured him. Noah, in turn, assured her that she already had by removing his sisters from the family dynamic for a few weeks. Smiles all around.

Eliza really struggles at first, needing extra time with me and lots of assurances that I am going to be okay. More worrisome than her questions and teary vulnerability are her silences, when she stares out the window or up at the ceiling and her eyes get big and wide. It is clear she is processing things because invariably she'll come up with a question that has been lurking for days. "So if the chemo kills the cancer, what keeps it from killing the rest of the stuff in you, the stuff you need?" Excellent question, and one I've had myself. I explain how administering it through a peritoneal port allows the doctors to blast it directly onto my cancerous sites, much more so than administering it through my veins and bloodstream would allow them to do. But I, too, picture it killing off good stuff as well as bad. As it has, in fact, done. My eyebrows are now completely gone, as are my eyelashes.

Or Eliza will ask, "If your cancer is genetic, does that mean I'll have to get tested too?" I explain to her, as I did to Hannah early on because she grasped the significance of the positive BRCA-1 gene right away, whereas Eliza needed time to mull over it and process it, that there is a 50 percent chance she will have the gene but she doesn't need to worry about it until she is much older. She will be tested when she is 18 and, worst case scenario, she'll have to monitor herself more rigorously than other women her age, opt for having kids earlier rather than later, and then have prophylactic surgery to minimize her risk.

166

I know Eliza is doing better, though, when I call David's grand-mother and great aunt Margie, both in their 90s and living in a retirement community in Florida, to tell them the news. Susanne wasn't going to tell them but it feels wrong to me to keep them in the dark for so long, and I hope that my upbeat voice and attitude will assure them that I am okay. Margie takes it pretty well but Grammy falls apart, sobbing on the phone about how it's so unfair and how she wants to kill herself. Whoa. So maybe Susanne's instinct was right. Eliza and I are walking at the time and I finally hand the phone to Eliza, having failed to appease Grammy and hoping the distraction of talking to her great granddaughter will help. Eliza is a champ. She tells Grammy that she, too, was very upset when she first heard the news but she thinks the worst is over and that it will all be okay. She sounds so mature and articulate and I get the sense she is assuring me as well as Grammy.

That newfound maturity crumbles when it's time to drop her and Hannah off at BWI airport for their cross-country flight to Seattle, where Oma and Papa will pick them up. David and Eliza are waiting for us at his parents' house when Noah, Hannah and I come back from the 4th of July tournament in Albany, and we enjoy a few days' overlap before separating from the girls. They will visit with my brother and get to meet his wife, their new Aunt Celine, for the first time, and will then head to British Columbia with my parents. It is a trip they have eagerly anticipated but it is now looming large in Eliza's mind as a forced separation from her bald and ailing mother. I fear that the lies I initially told so seemingly effortlessly to hide my hysterectomy and the cancer diagnosis now have Eliza convinced she is being shipped away so that more bad things can befall me in her absence. Never mind that this trip with my parents was planned long before I found out I had cancer. My assurances fall flat because she is scared and, frankly, my word is mud. Hannah seems fine and resolute and I implore her to dig deep and be extra patient with her admittedly whiny little sister.

Noah and David, who await me in the airport lobby since only one of us can accompany the girls past the security checkpoint, mock my red-rimmed eyes when I reemerge from seeing them off. The tears are not what they think. I will miss the girls, but it's only two weeks and I know they will have a great time. I am also excited for our upcoming college trip, rendered much more doable without the girls in tow. No, my tears stem from relief and gratitude.

167

Watching Hannah and Eliza disappear from sight has me overwhelmed with the enormity of what could have been. Leave it to melodramatic me to transform a simple airport farewell into a permanent deathbed farewell, but that is where my mind goes. I am so very grateful that I am simply saying goodbye as they head off to enjoy quality time with their grandparents, and not the kind of goodbye I had mulled over, in those dark days following both my diagnosis and the surgery, when I seriously considered how they would fare without me, not for two weeks, but for the rest of their lives.

Our first stop after sending the girls on their way is New York, where we visit with a bunch of David's relatives, including his brother, Daniel, his Uncles Kenny and Woody, and Uncle Carl, Aunt Beth, and Grandpa Joe before heading off to visit the East Coast colleges Noah wants to see. The timing of our arrival at Carl and Beth's house falls exactly six weeks from the date of my hysterectomy, which is significant in that it coincides with a date I have marked on my calendar with a huge smiley-face and the word BATH taking up the entire square of blank space reserved for appointments and activities. Yet another cancer side effect, admittedly way down on the totem pole as far as traumatic life events go, but significant to me nonetheless, is the fact that my surgery came with several precautionary restrictions. Some mattered not at all to me. I was not allowed to lift anything above six pounds. None of my children were babies or toddlers at the time, so this was easy to accommodate. I was not allowed to drink alcohol while on certain narcotics and pain relievers. No problem. My drink of choice is diet Coke, so going without booze is not a deprivation. No sex for six weeks. *Huh?* My vagina was sliced open. My hysterectomy catapulted me into instant menopause. No libido plus internal wounds *down there* plus the decidedly unsexy feel and look of bloating and baldness... let's just say a prohibition on getting it on with David was not necessary. But no *baths?* That stung! Seeing my dismay, the nurse who was explaining these post-op dos and don'ts to me thought I'd misunderstood the extent of the restriction. "Oh, you can still *bathe,*" she explained, as if speaking to a dim-witted child. "You just have to stick to showers. No baths." Dagger to my heart. No baths! I pouted while David explained that my daily bath is one of the highlights of my day. It felt particularly cruel to be deprived of soothing baths when I was convinced they were a likely source of pain relief during my nausea-filled days following the surgery and first two rounds of chemo.

But I arrive at Carl and Beth's house on the day that is prominently marked in my calendar, in red sharpie, all in caps, as the one when I am finally allowed to resume taking baths. Hallelujah! And what opportune timing it is because Carl and Beth bequeath to me their opulent master bathroom, complete with a Jacuzzi tub that is large enough for me to fully stretch out and barely reach the sides. (Yes, that is both a function of the tub's grandiosity and my own diminutive height, but let's just focus on the tub.) I lie in the Jacuzzi tub and reflect on all that has happened and all that lies ahead. I let the warm water soothe me and I think that all will be well, now that I can take baths again.

When I towel off, I have that momentary shock that seems to accompany every time I see my reflection in the mirror. My remaining hair fell out in patches while Noah and Hannah and I were in Albany, New York (for the July 4th tournament that has become as much a staple of our vacation plans as the New Year's tournament) and I am now completely bald. Just as my doctors predicted, the chemo peaked within my body and my hair fell out in patches (if the buzz cut I had can qualify as yielding patches) over a period of a few days. You could literally run your finger in a line across my scalp and remove a line of hair, as if a plane were skywriting across my shorn head. Hannah and I marveled at this phenomenon and decided to have fun with it. Hannah played a game of tic-tac-toe on the back of my head, both of us giggling at the absurdity of it.

My short crop of hair is all that stood between Katya-with-a-decidedly-short-summer-'do and Katya-the-cancer-patient. I now look the part, and both David and Eliza (who saw me but a week earlier looking decidedly different) were shocked at the difference the loss of my remaining hair made when we reunited in Maryland. I have two go- to hats – the Red Sox baseball cap Nikki sent me and a blue straw hat that David Klionsky, a Scrabble buddy, presented to me at the Albany tournament. "I'm not much of a shopper," he sheepishly told me as he held out the fancy box, "but I saw this in New York and thought of you and your blue eyes." I find it amusing and endearing that my female friends, all good shoppers, have tried in vain to find hats that suit me, as I have, to no avail. Hats, it turns out, are not made for bald women. They don't fit properly because they need hair to hold them in place and to make them look right. But here's my friend David, who picked out just one hat, who simply wanted me to know he was thinking of me, and somehow stumbles upon a hat that fits perfectly.

I wear the Red Sox hat to the Red Sox game that we are able to attend in Boston thanks to another Scrabble buddy, Judy Cole, who procured the tickets through a work connection of hers. Sitting in the ballpark section reserved for the players' family members with a fabulous view of the game, I think, not for the first or last time, that there are definite perks to this cancer ride. It is not all bad. We go to see The Book of Mormon while in New York and the Red Sox game while in Boston and we combine the college visits with visiting several good friends, like Allison and Carter Wilkie in Boston (Allison and I met while we were both working for the Harvard Kennedy School of Government right out of college) and Nikki Levin and her parents (both of whom served as surrogate parents for me when I was in college) and David's former colleague, Abby Roth, who now works at Yale Law School. We get lots of quality time with our son and we enjoy the excitement that mounts with each school he visits, because we know he will be happy at any one of them and we think it is likely he will have his pick of schools.

Both David and Noah are so sweet and solicitous of me and I am filled with gratitude that we are on this trip, one that seemed so unlikely just a few short weeks ago. David seems to feel a need to touch me constantly, as if he needs to reassure himself that I am still here, that cancer has not robbed him of his wife. I have always been a demonstrative, physically affectionate person, hugging my kids, holding hands with my husband, but now, for the first time in my life, I want my space. I do not want to be touched. It is all I can do to quell the daily physical assault on my body and any additional physical stimuli, no matter how well-intentioned and loving, is unwanted.

And even though David is the embodiment of patience, he does make several references to the fact that the lifting of the bath embargo also means that the prohibition against sex has ended. He says he is worried about hurting me so we agree to hold off until I see Trish again when I return from the trip. When Trish examines me, she finds that several of my internal sutures have not yet healed and suggests holding off on intercourse for a few more weeks. I try to keep my relief hidden when I convey this news to an understanding but disappointed David.

Visiting Nikki (her big heart shirt says it all) in Boston.

Noah and I are driving home a day ahead of David because we both have to be back in Charlotte by the start of the week, so David will wait behind in Maryland for the girls to fly back from British Columbia. Noah and I both have obligations that await us bright and early Monday morning.. Noah is due to start his second summer internship, this one with Care Ring, a nonprofit organization that provides health care to the under-and uninsured. (Marni and Gabi, two friends who are very well connected in local politics and social service organizations, lined up both of the internships for Noah on very short notice. It is something they offered to do when I got sick and it is a fine example of something that helped me immensely, even if it didn't involve me directly, because it gave me peace of mind as a mother who let nagging her son about following up on internship opportunities fall by the wayside once cancer took over my priority list.)

My own need to be back in town is due to a chemo schedule I have to maintain. Dr. Naumann was fine with my taking this trip, and he worked around it as far as stretching out the break between the end of my first cycle and the start of my second, but now it is time to start the next cycle and it is important to stay on schedule. Even a day's delay will throw the whole, carefully orchestrated schedule off, because while there is some leeway with the length of time between each cycle, Day One and Day Two of each cycle must be exactly one week apart. On the drive home, I try to enjoy the time with Noah, but I can feel myself tensing up about the horrors that await me as soon as we get back to Charlotte. I have had a nice, long respite from chemo and all things cancer, but it is now time to go home and face the music. Just as Noah is starting a job, I, too, must get back to work.

It is time for me to clock back in as a cancer patient.

Subject: Ovarian Odyssey
Date: July 14, 2011

I used to find it amusing and endearing that my grandmother, whenever she was asked how she was feeling, would always answer, "A little better." It was never good or bad, just a little better. I can relate... so much so that I am now tempted to borrow her trademark line every time I'm asked how I'm faring. In my pre- cancer world, I would no doubt have complained about my assorted aches and pains and what can best be described as flu-like symptoms, but now, having truly suffered post-surgery and with my first round of chemo, I would describe those same aches, pains and flu-like symptoms as feeling great! It's all relative, I guess, but I have generally felt fine (albeit a new definition of fine) on my trip. Some fatigue, some frustration with continued digestive issues (I will leave that intentionally vague) and I am now completely bald except for a tiny, stubborn patch on the back of my head that looks like a botched Mohawk. But what I have felt most consistently on this trip is gratitude that I am on it. My traveling for such an extended period — let alone leaving my bedroom — seemed in serious jeopardy a few weeks ago, so I truly appreciated being well enough to be able to travel, enjoy good food, and visits with friends and family.

The Albany 4th of July Scrabble Tournament tested my ability to enjoy this game I love to play even when I play it extremely poorly. Despite my poor performance, however, I was so happy to be among my Scrabble buddies and enjoying quality time with Noah and Hannah, especially since it had seemed so likely I'd have to cancel our travel plans when I was first diagnosed and the long and daunting chemo schedule was laid out for us. One highlight from the tournament: my opening rack of my second game had the tiles Y A V R E! F O on it. I stared at it for a moment, then chuckled at the irony as I played OVARY for 30 points! The other highlight – at least for Noah – is that he fared slightly better than I did and surpassed me in both rating and ranking. I will have to wait until the Nationals in Dallas in August to show him who's boss. After the Albany tournament, we headed back to Maryland where we met! up with David and Eliza for a few days before putting the girls on a plane to Seattle. Eliza had a hard time at first with my newfound baldness — I suspect because it makes it impossible to deny that I am sick — but she took to calling me "her little rat" and parted ways with minimal tears. Props to Hannah for stepping up as a big sister and making both Eliza and me feel better about the separation. They are having a great time with Oma and Papa in British Columbia and will return next week.

David and Noah and I enjoyed what we have come to refer to as the I-95 college tour. We visited MIT, Harvard, Brown, Yale and Princeton. I battled fatigue on some days but then, so did David and Noah. We also thoroughly enjoyed seeing Book of Mormon in New York (irreverent and hilarious) and our fabulous seats behind home plate at Fenway from which we watched my Beloved Red Sox beat the Orioles in an action-packed game. As the week has progressed, my trepidation about my next round of chemo and the dreaded Cisplatin and Taxol has heightened, but I'm trying to keep it at bay. I have a new patch that I'll be wearing that will hopefully help offset the nausea and I'll be getting fluids and IV drugs following each chemo from now on so hopefully I'll bounce back faster and better (I sound like an ad for a new laundry detergent!) this time.

Many of you have had me in your thoughts and have suffered along with me. I so appreciate your concern and support but I do worry that this is sometimes harder on those who care about me than it is on me. If I have a rough time again, please know that I will not be as despondent as I was last time because I will know that it is of limited duration. I can take whatever nastiness Cisplatin and Taxol have in store for me because I just had a wonderful vacation, and here are some photos to prove it...

Love, Katya

CHAPTER TWENTY

Subject: Ovarian Odyssey
Date: July 20, 2011

I am happy to report that the anti-nausea patch is working wonders so far and seems to be keeping the nausea at bay, or at least minimizing it dramatically. My second round of Day 1 chemo (the Taxol coupled with the Cisplatin) went as well as can be expected. I started off with IV/vein issues — seems to be my routine beginning — which was disappointing since my veins had enjoyed a nice vacation and should have been more cooperative. Other than that, things went swimmingly, including the port infusion. Ativan again worked its wonders, making me both loopy and forgetful. Several of the nurses were comparing notes today on some of my more humorous Ativan- induced commentaries. Yesterday's included several Colin Firth references — I was apparently frustrated that he was not playing a starring role in my dreams, as promised! I'm just glad I'm not a woman of many secrets because I'd surely spill them all in the course of my chemo.

I am attaching a column that ran today about my cancer journey, for those of you who missed it ... which I assume is anyone not living in South Charlotte, since I don't think it was picked up by the AP wire.

Cheers,
Katya

Wednesday, Jul. 20, 2011

Finding the positives in a bad situation

Cancer diagnosis has shown me ways I am lucky

Katya Lezin

In early May, I was diagnosed with Stage II ovarian cancer and had a hysterectomy at the end of the month.

I decided to cut my hair after my first round of chemotherapy so that I could donate it to Locks for Love, since my doctors told me I'd start losing it in patches shortly thereafter.

The haircut was one small way I could take back control from this disease - the big scary "C" that has always loomed in my mind as the worst thing you ever want to hear your doctor tell you - and have something good come out of one of the many indignities my diagnosis has inflicted upon me.

I was out of town at a conference when I got the call from my OB/GYN (the one that starts with, "There's no good way to tell you this...") and so I had several days to process my diagnosis away from my family.

By the time I returned to Charlotte on Mother's Day, I had realized that once I accept that I have been dealt this blow, I am actually quite lucky.

It is not always easy to see the silver lining or find the good in a particular moment or day, but there have been a plethora of positives in this huge negative.

I am lucky my cancer was spotted when it was, through the removal of a twisted ovary that appears to have been a fortuitous coincidence. Ovarian cancer is a particularly insidious cancer because it is often very advanced by the time symptoms appear; mine is Stage II B.

I am fortunate that my husband's job allows him to be by my side whenever needed and affords us the kind of health insurance that makes my excellent medical care affordable. The Blumenthal Cancer Center, where I am being treated, combines state of the art technology and treatment with

Southern charm and compassion, and I can't imagine receiving better care anywhere else.

But most of all I'm lucky to be surrounded by friends and family who have overwhelmed me with their love and support.

My husband has made the wedding vow about being there in sickness and in health (I can't say I really gave that any serious thought on my wedding day 20 years ago), something that confirms I married the right guy.

Neighbors and friends have shown themselves to be generous and compassionate, from making meals for our family to buying me fun hats to wear atop my bald head to dropping off books or flowers or any number of distractions for my long days of chemo.

This cancer, such a scary and bad thing, has engendered many good things in my life. Don't get me wrong. I would much rather not travel this road. The surgery was brutal and the chemo even more so.

Some things - the unrelenting nausea that lingers for days following my chemo, my diminished energy and ability to do the things I want to do - are just plain bad and there is no spinning them into a positive.

But many aspects of my diagnosis do have silver linings. It is just a question of finding them.

I will profile some of the people I'm encountering on this journey in subsequent columns, beginning with the two nurses who serve as my chemo navigator and coordinator.

Katya Lezin is a freelance writer for South Charlotte News. Have a story idea for Katya? Email her at bowserwoof@mindspring.com.

Reprinted with permission of South Charlotte News, a Charlotte Observer publication.

Lisa Z's chemo buddy system is a well-oiled machine. Lorrina brings me in for my second cycle of infusion, with Marni covering the lunch shift and Amy bringing me home. On the following day, for my happy meal of fluids and meds, Lisa Z. brings me in and then David and Noah come to pick me up. Maggie and Nichole and Trish also pop in to say hello to me throughout the day, as do Boris and Iris (who do not count as exceeding my visitor limit since they are wearing their white doctor coats and they actually work at the hospital). We also share a laugh with Rachel Burns, the cancer center's dietician, because I look at her blankly and ask if we've met. It's a running joke because I truly did forget meeting her the first time, when she spent over half an hour discussing the dietary issues that often accompany chemo, since I was high on Ativan and woozy from Benadryl at the time. Now I pretend I don't know who she is each time I see her and ask if she can do her spiel again.

An older man getting infusion has been watching my parade of visitors over the course of the day and the preceding one and my rapport with the nurses. "Who *is* she?" he loudly inquires of his nurse. We all crack up.

Noah puts his arm around me. "I knew you'd be the mayor of the infusion room," he says.

The new regimen of prophylactic fluids and the patch do lessen the nausea, so that's encouraging. But I realize with dismay that the nausea is not my only foe. Removing it from the equation, or at least diminishing it, does not magically transform me into a happy camper. As the chemo settles in and begins to work its magic – both fairytale pixie dust magic and black, voodoo magic – I suffer a host of new and unwelcome symptoms that all combine to leave me feeling like shit.

As the week progresses, I feel worse and worse. I am really swollen from the fluids and the chemo, which results in horrible heart- burn. I am hungry but I really can't eat because there doesn't seem to be any room. My stomach spasms with fairly regular jolts of pain, no doubt from the poison that is attacking it from within. It was, after all, directly blasted there. The menopause that my hysterectomy catapulted me into, full-throttle, adds a slew of additional joys like profuse sweating, hot flashes, and vaginal dryness. And to top it all off, my hands are bruised and sore from all of the failed attempts to start lines on me all week.

I find it hard to hide my misery from the kids. I am lying in my bed, cursing my body and the many ways it is betraying me, when the girls come in to try to snuggle with me and watch TV. I try to make it work, wanting to do at least that with them, but I just can't take it. I am too miserable, too much in pain, and I'd rather not have them see me like that. I tell them they will have to leave, trying to pass it off as fatigue rather than the misery I am feeling. I don't fool anyone. Eliza turns to me, on her way out of the room, and her face is wet with tears. "You don't deserve this," she says. It breaks my heart that I can't shield her from seeing me like this.

The kids often find themselves in situations where they have to disclose that their mother has cancer, and I hate that too. I can tell that the kindness and pity that such pronouncements usually engender are harder for them to take than the cancer pronouncement itself. I drop the girls off at our local *Great Clips,* prepaying for their haircuts so that I can scoot into Harris Teeter for some groceries wile they are getting clipped. After I leave, one of the hairdressers turns to the girls and asks, full of astonishment, as if I had opted to shake things up in suburbia with a radical new haircut, "Did your mama cut off all her hair?" When the girls tell her no, I'm bald because I have cancer, she says, "Oh, bless her heart." It is a common refrain, one we will hear so much that it becomes a staple of my cancer experience.

My body continues to be a freak show. Every other day a new symptom appears, a new *Gotcha!* moment piercing the "So you thought you had a handle on this?" veneer. I develop a horrible rash across my butt and lower back. David thinks it is because I am taking frequent baths (they are one of the few sources of comfort for my bloated and painful stomach) and I am not drying off well enough afterwards, probably because many of them are occurring in the middle of the night. He digs around the kids' bathroom and finds the industrial-size Desitin we'd bought when Eliza was a baby. That unmistakable Desitin smell takes me right back to the days of diaper-changing, and it is a new low that I am now having to lather it on my 46-year old ass.

Another new and most unwelcome symptom, one for which menopause gets to win the round in its constant battle with cancer/chemo as far as what can cause me the most pain and discomfort, is insomnia. I have always been a good sleeper. It has actually amused me that people who marvel at how much I get done in a day assume that it is sleep that I sacrifice. "You must never sleep," they say, when the opposite is true. I don't sleep a ton (an average of six or seven hours each night) and I tend to be an early riser, but I do sleep. Well and regularly. When I decree that it is bedtime (after reading or watching a show or two with David or playing a few games of online Scrabble), it's bedtime. It's as simple as that.

No longer.

I struggle to fall asleep and then, when I do, I wake up a few hours later, fully alert. My body is exhausted and I crave the sleep, but my mind simply won't let it happen. Or perhaps it's the other way around. All I know is that I spend more of each night awake than asleep, a sad turn of events in anyone's life, but particularly in mine where sleep provides one of the few respites from my pain and dis- comfort. (The other being my soothing baths, and we know how *they've* turned on me.) I wake up, drenched in sweat. trying to get comfortable, and I just curse the injustice of having to deal with menopause on top of all this. That, more than the cancer itself, strikes me as really unfair.

I've also been robbed of my regularity. That is another cruel dose of cancer irony, another round of being forced to appreciate some- thing I took for granted until it was unceremoniously yanked from me. To me, constipation meant not going first thing in the morning. Or not going twice in one day. Now I fully appreciate what constipation is, why there are so many products and advertisements directed at its sufferers.

It is an impolite thing to discuss, I know, but I can't describe my cancer journey without talking about poop. Like so many things in life, one's regularity is something that is totally taken for granted, like the fact that skin covers our muscles and bones. Is skin necessary? Does it provide a useful function? You betcha. Do I ever give it a moment's thought? Nope. But I bet burn victims do. Okay, so that's an extreme analogy, but the point is that there is much about my body and the way it works that is suddenly new to me, with most of the lessons being of the hard knocks variety because I

am confronted with examples of it *not* working. I used to poop every morning, no problem. That's how I started my day. Until I didn't. The chemo drugs and the painkillers are all known constipators, and they do a number on me. I get totally plugged up and it just colors my world. Even when my other symptoms die down or seem to give me a break for a day or two, the constipation is a constant irritant, an annoyance that has to be addressed on a daily, and sometime bi-daily, basis.

We find the generic version of Miralax at Costco and buy in in enormous quantities. Just looking at it, one 17.9 oz. jar of LaxaClear on the counter, two more, still sealed in plastic, awaiting me in the medi- cine cabinet by the sink, depresses the hell out of me. But I also sing its praises because it really does work. And once Andy Zerkle assured me that you cannot OD on the stuff, I find that, on the occasions when my constipation seems impervious to my morning glass of LaxaClear, a second glass usually does the trick. While it is tasteless, which is such a relief after that nasty contrast solution I had to gulp down for my CT scans, it is not without side effects. It leaves me feeling even more bloated, a state of being I am achieving just fine on my own. No help needed in that department, thank you very much. I remember Noah telling me, "Bald, bloated and boobless, you'll still be beautiful." Well, I'm two for three at this point (I still have my boobs, for the time being) but I sure don't feel very beautiful.

Most days, I feel incredibly unattractive. I've never fancied myself a real looker, but I've also never been distraught about my physical appearance or hyper critical of myself. Now, though, I look in the mirror and see little to like. My body is bloated, my hair is gone, and my eyes have big bags under them from the lack of sleep. I think about the way pregnant women have that special glow and I realize I have the opposite thing going on, a cancer suck. And I look *old*. Over- night, I have aged considerably. No one is going to mistake me for younger than my 46 years, whereas pre-cancer that was not uncommon.

David and I have plans to meet Laura and Marc Lewin and Marni and David Eisner for dinner uptown for Queen's Feast (when upscale Charlotte restaurants offer a $30 3-course menu for a week) and I don a dress for the occasion, mainly because I'm struggling to fit into most of my pants. The combination of my bald head and my bloating has me looking totally ridiculous. I tell David as much but he disagrees.

"No you don't," he says, shaking his head. "I think you look *hot*.

"If that's not love, I don't know what is.

CHAPTER TWENTY-ONE

Eliza's essay for Mommy School (what I call the periodic assignments I dole out over the summer to ensure the kids' minds don't turn to mush – I suspect they have another name for it) is about cancer. It essentially says that she used to associate the word cancer with death but now the words that come to mind are courage and conquer. It warms my heart because I think that ultimately the kids see me as strong and resilient, and that has to be reassuring to them. I am so thankful that my chemo, as rough as it is, doesn't knock me out or have me hunched over the toilet all day. I am pretty much able to live my life, albeit with some adjustments made for my aches and pains, and for that I am grateful.

You wouldn't know that gratitude and an appreciation for how much worse things could be are my overriding emotions when reading some of my diary entries. Here's one on the morning of the start of my second chemo cycle.

7/26/11

Going in today for more chemo. Fuck. I hate the puffing up of my stomach the worst. Just impacts everything else. Digestion. Heartburn. Breathing. And nothing fits.

It is so ironic, and I mean that in the *that's so @#))&%$#@ ironic!* way, that I am unable to fit in any of my clothes. I always imagined that would be a problem, but because they'd be sliding off of me, not because I'd be unable to button or zip them. Trish assures me it's the bloating, but Dr. Naumann tells me bluntly, when I complain about the weight gain to him on one of my few visits with him, that the odds are stacked against me and that the weight gain is probably permanent. In addition to the fact that my stomach is getting pumped full of chemo and fluids, I'm also in full-on menopause. That means my metabolism slows way down and, to complete the one-two punch, the steroids I'm on as part of my chemo regimen make me ravenous and are designed to *keep* the weight on me. From the doc's perspective, weight gain is a good thing. Emaciated cancer patients are those who aren't doing well.

I get that. I get that it's far more important to be alive than thin. I get that many of these factors are out of my control. But still, it bothers the hell out of me. It just seems so patently unfair to have to struggle with weight gain on top of all the other shit I'm facing. Seriously? I continue to hit the gym and I try to watch what kind of calories I'm consuming, but I also go out and invest in leggings, big tops, and lots of elastic waist bands. Sigh.

Subject: Ovarian Odyssey
Date: July 29, 2011

I am happy to report that I have now completed two of the six rounds of chemo (Day 1 and Day 8) and I get a much-needed break before the next one. Yay! Overall, I fared much better with this second cycle of chemo — I was not bed-ridden, and that is a huge improvement — but there are a few aspects of it that are cumulative and were consequently tougher to handle than the first cycle. We were able to keep the nausea at bay and that was a huge improvement, but a few other symptoms opted to compete with the nausea for what can most elicit the "Chemo sucks" reaction from me.

It turns out that all of that poison hanging out in your stomach — both the Cisplatin and the Taxol are administered through my abdominal port — make for one huge, never-ending stomach ache. I try to console myself with the fact that all of that pain means they're doing what they're supposed to do, but I'd actually be just fine with the chemo working its magic a little less obviously. My incision sites are deep purple and I am convinced they look pissed off, as if they are representing the beleaguered organs within who are wondering what the hell I am doing to them. (Not to worry, the chemo has not yet fried all of my brain cells. I do understand that my liver and spleen are not actually conversing with me.)

I'm also suffering from eye problems — reduced vision and irritation — that I was dismayed to learn also stem from the chemo and will be with me for the duration of my treatment. It is easy to become somewhat hypochondriacal and assume that the chemo is the culprit for any new ailment. The other night I awoke with a numb arm and I worried that it was a sign of the tingling and numbness I'd been warned about feeling in my hands and feet, some of which can be permanent. This was a tingling and numb- ness across my entire arm and I was already trying to figure out how incapacitating it would be when I noticed pillow lines across it and realized it had simply fallen asleep. Full feeling was restored in short order and I had to laugh at my initial panic about what was no doubt a case of Darcy (aka bed-hog dog extraordinaire) lying atop it during the night.

My last ailment — and this concludes the whiny portion of this update — promise! — is insomnia. My sleep deprivation is due to a variety of factors — the anti-nausea drugs I take, my full-on menopause, and my stomach issues — but having always slept well prior to cancer, it is a most unwelcome addition to my life. It seems particularly unfair to struggle with sleep since this is a time my body most needs it. Let's hear it for laptops and the Internet, though, which make 3 a.m. restlessness so much more bearable.

The good news is that there continue to be a plethora of positive and funny moments in my cancer journey and they far outweigh the negatives. I am finding that my bald do has distinct advantages in this record heat wave we're experiencing. I am enjoying getting to know my medical team and fellow patients at the Blumenthal Cancer Center. My friends, neighbors and family continue to support us in ways both big and small. I have been able to exercise, socialize, and work — all things that seemed in jeopardy when I was first diagnosed.

As for the funny, I'll spare you some of my medical complications that David and I choose to find humorous (because, really, some of these indignities are s! o outrageous that they really are comical) and instead I'll share with you the unique way I befriended one of my fellow patients in the infusion room. When you need to use the restroom during treatment, you have to unplug your IV pole and take it with you to the bathroom. When I am in the private room, my IV pole has two plugs and I am accustomed to unplugging them both for my oh-so frequent (some things never change!) bathroom visits. The other day I was out in the main room, in one of the many chairs lined up against the wall, and I unplugged both plugs for my bathroom visit. Luckily, I noticed two things — some resistance in my journey, and the fact that my neighbor, a nice, older man who *was minding his own business — appeared to be accompanying me on my bathroom visit. Turns out I only had one plug and by unplugging both I was unwittingly but quite forcefully bringing the IV pole belonging to the poor guy next to me — and, therefore, him as well! — along with me to the bathroom. We both had a good laugh about it and he told me he hadn't laughed like that in quite a while.*

So I leave you with that image — who knows whom I'll drag in there with me next time! — while I sign off for now. We have a lovely family from France visiting us right now and we are planning to take them to Asheville this weekend for some fun in the NC mountains. (I asked my nurse practitioner for permission to go down a waterfall and ziplining — both of which we have planned — and she smiled and shook her head and said I was the first cancer patient to request such things.) Next week, Noah and Hannah and I head to Texas for the National Scrabble Championship where I am hoping the Tile Gods reward me with blanks and power tiles aplenty.

Love,
Katya

      I usually don't have an appetite on my chemo days and the following day or two, probably because I'm so bloated that there simply isn't room. Ironically, even though I'm not eating much on those days, that is when my constipation is at its worst. During week two of my second cycle, I am really blocked up and thinking about augmenting my LaxaClear intake. I return from the hospital feeling surprisingly hungry, and it happens to be a day that a meal was delivered to us. It is also a night when all three kids are home and we don't have anything planned; a rare opportunity to sit down together as a family for dinner, with Mom actually joining the rest of the family at the table and partaking in the meal.

      A quick side note about the meals that are delivered to us. Most, as I said, I don't eat, but it gives me peace of mind to know my family is eating well. Most people go all out, providing salad, bread and dessert as well as a main course. They also go all out in terms of what they make. For some reason, my own culinary skills intimidate some folks and have them scrambling to make unusual

One of the many all-out meals that were delivered to us during my illness. This is a Persian feast made by my Iranian neighbor Fallen Shahnizadeh.

dishes, bizarre dishes, sometimes, I suspect, trying recipes that are and effort to make, and it does not need to be fancy or new to them, all in an effort to impress us. But we are truly happy with just about everything. You are, after all, bringing us sustenance, something you have taken time

It is one of these new, somewhat unusual dinners from a well- meaning neighbor that awaits us on the night I choose to join my family for dinner. The entrée is a shrimp quesadilla casserole, which we've never had or heard of before, but we're game to try it. Noah and I both have seconds. Later that night, we also both have food poisoning. I'm thinking the shrimp were bad, or maybe just the ones in our servings (since neither David or the girls suffer any ill effects), but we are, let's just say, the opposite of constipated.

The next day, when I go in for my happy meal of fluids and meds, I tell Trish that I have a new cure for the constipation that afflicts so many of us on this chemo diet. It is better than Miralax, better than laxatives, and is extremely fast-acting and effective. From now on, I tell her, just prescribe two slices of shrimp quesadilla casserole.

Subject: Ovarian Odyssey
Date: August 14, 2011

On the eve of heading back to the hospital for my third round of the dreaded Cisplatin, I find myself filled with trepidation and dread for what I know lies ahead this week. More toxins filling my gut and swelling it to uncomfortable and unsightly proportions. Another cycle of indiscriminately killing off good things, like my hair and eyelashes (almost all gone) and who knows what else unseen within me. And more fatigue, which is proving to be a cumulative foe I must fight and conquer each day.

But I also find myself reflecting on all that I've been able to do this summer, much of which seemed destined to fall under the "I-can't-because-I-have- cancer" column when I was struggling with nausea and other indignities post-surgery. Since I last wrote, I traveled to Asheville and enjoyed hiking, swimming and sliding down waterfalls in the Pisgah National Forest. We also went ziplining in the Blue Ridge Mountains and I yelled out "Chemo sucks!" while shooting across an 1100-foot line 200 feet high, above a canopy of trees. Very cathartic. I heartily recommend it to all chemo patients.

We also hosted a family from France! for a week (thus the trip to Asheville) whom we met in San Francisco five years ago. While we were waiting for them at the airport, and I admitted that I could barely remember what they looked like, Noah told me that this trait of mine of inviting folks we hardly know to stay with us is endearing but is, in his words, aging him prematurely. I told him I have a good sense about people and most folks are kind and good ... but I hastened to add that if I was wrong and they ended up murdering us all in our sleep, I was truly sorry.

All kidding aside, my cancer has actually helped reinforce this belief of mine that there is far more kindness and goodness in the world than the evil that is so often featured in the news. People just continue to astound me with their generosity and love. I have received mementos from trips this summer, including an Elvis potholder and a Red Sox shirt that reads, "Peace, Love, Sox." I have laughed as I unpacked a Mr. Bill doll that yells out, "Oh Nooooo!" when you press his stomach (although Noah has commandeered that for his room at NCSSM) and wondered about the identity of the anonymous and stealthy friend who has been dropping off a slew of stuffed animals in my mailbox. I have enjoyed cards aplenty, in-cluding one from an artist who makes and sends me one for each day of chemo. Equally appreciated are the more traditional gifts of meals, rides, and chemo companion- ship... all daily reminders that I am not fighting this battle alone.

This embarrassment of riches continued in Dallas, where Noah and Hannah and I competed in the National Scrabble Championship. On the first day, my friends from the National Scrabble Assoc. presented me with a t-shirt (the only one of its kind) that proclaims, in Scrabble tiles, "This is one challenge I will win!" The next day, I arrived back from the lunch break to discover that the giant, oversized Scrabble board had a message, using all 100 tiles (no easy feat!) that read, "Quite vivacious Katya Lezin and her two protégé children are up in Texas to develop words in a frabjous big family game." And on the last day, I was presented with the Rose Award, which is given to the player who best embodies a "sense of fairness and con- geniality as well as competitiveness." I think it was essentially the prize for traveling to 107-degree Texas in August to play 31 games of Scrabble while battling cancer, which I suspect would earn me another kind of prize (Biggest lunatic? Most Obsessed Player?) in other circles, but at the Nationals it earned me a lovely crystal paper- weight. Oh, and let the record reflect that I beat Noah not once but twice and restored my standing as the highest rated player in the family.

So here's hoping my finicky veins and uncooperative port behave themselves tomorrow...and, if they don't, here's hoping Colin Firth is there to console me!

Fondly,
Katya

Ziplining in Asheville with Hannah and Eliza.

At the National Scrabble Championship in Dallas with Noah and Hannah and the board that was customized for us.

There are days when I have got this. I get into a rhythm. The aches and pains are now familiar aches and pains, and I know how to ride things out, how to manage most of my symptoms. The management part is a big time suck, consuming most of every day with the 30 to 45 minute drive to the hospital, the inevitable delays, and the hours of fluids (and that's for the non-chemo days, when the entire day is shot) but it is a small price to pay if I can keep the nausea at bay.

When our French friends arrive for a visit, I don't think twice about dropping them off uptown so that they can walk around, swinging by the hospital for my happy meal, and then picking them back up again before meeting David and the kids for dinner. They keep thinking it is a language barrier problem. "You are going *where* after you drop us off? You can just go to the hospital, just like that, and then leave again? *Ce n'est pas possible.*"

I know I am worthless on my chemo days, so I continue to let Lisa Z. work her magic and line up rides and meals and round-the-clock companionship. But I cancel the buddy assignments for my fluids days. I learn that I can actually be productive on those days. I bring my laptop and I write columns or interview folks by phone for my *Charlotte Observer* columnist job or I review and edit college essays for my Perfect Fit College job. I find myself far less resentful of the infusion room captivity if I can leave there with things accomplished.

In fact, in the lulls between chemo cycles, I sometimes forget I have cancer. I'll notice someone staring at me or casting a pitying glance my way and I'll wonder about it until I realize, with a start, *Oh yeah, I'm bald and I have cancer.* When we show up in Asheville to visit my friend Joann Goddard (who gets a gold star for hospitality since she opens up her magnificent mountain home to not only me and the girls, but my French guests, whom she has never met), she is startled by my appearance. "Now it feels real," she says. Joann also compliments me on my attitude, saying I remind her of her neighbor up the street who is also plowing ahead with her life despite a diagnosis of Stage 4 breast cancer. (A few months later, when I ask about her neighbor, Joann tells me she has died. It is yet another reminder that, within this unlucky realm of getting cancer, I am very lucky. I am still here.) Many folks echo Joann's kudos, applauding my humor and overall can-do attitude.

Dear Katya,

What good news that the patch is working and all went better this time around! I enjoyed your article in the paper this morning - what a writer you are, but more than that, what a special person you are! I have been in wonder of you for many years with all that you do, accomplish, enjoy, and create. And now, with your Odyssey and all that it brings, my jaw drops even further towards my kneecaps!
Jill
(Jill Fung, our neighbor and the kids' piano teacher) ------

Dear Katya,

You are amazing. I am awed by your strength, sincerity, honesty, and eloquence. I carry your story with me in my mind and heart. I'd love to be there more for Noah, Hannah, and Eliza. Can I have their emails so I can keep in touch?
With prayers for a complete healing.
L'shalom, Judy
(Judy Schindler, Senior Rabbi at Temple Beth El) ------

Katya,

As part of my usual Wednesday morning routine I always search the South Charlotte News to see if there is an article written by you. It's always a highlight of my week to read one of your enlightening commentaries. Needless to say - I was shocked and saddened to learn of your recent diagnosis and subsequent treatment. It's not surprising to know that you're fighting back with such strength and positive energy. Please know that my thoughts are with you dear Katya and if anyone can turn a difficult situation into encouragement for others it's you.
Take care ~ Julie
(a Charlotte Observer reader)

Katya:

Granted, it's just one (elderly) man's opinion, but in my private view you are among the most amazing people in Scrabble, if not in actual first place, for all that you do and the way you do it! I admire you more than words can express for your courage, your relentless good cheer, your concern for others, and your willingness to take the blows dealt by outrageous bad fortune and come up smiling (at least on the outside) every time! Having spent several hours with you and your bright, friendly, and fascinating children last week in various contexts, I am persuaded more than ever that you deserve all the gifts and benefits that life has to bestow, and I predict with great confidence that you will not only endure the chemo, the baldness, the abdominal problems, and sundry other indignities requisite to restoring you to full health, but that you will PREVAIL! Trust me; you WILL!

Bruce

(Bruce Shuman, a fellow Scrabble player

Howdy

Here's the conversation at the lunch table (at Cowfish!) today:

Eli (sighs deeply): Well, I guess there will be no Katya clubs this year.

Me: I think Miss Katya is planning on doing her clubs.

Eli: Really? I though treatment for ovarian cancer was more debilitating than that.

Me: It is for most people, but Miss Katya is still playing tennis. Ivy: Eli, this is Miss Katya we're talking about!

Lisa

(Lisa Zerkle, whose son Eli was in both the Drama Club and the Scrabble Club that I ran at Randolph Middle School)

I appreciate the props for not letting cancer slow me down, but really, what's the alternative? On the days when I feel like shit but I show up at the JCC to work out and everyone marvels at my tenacity, *Weren't you just in the hospital yesterday?*, I explain that I could feel like shit lying in my bed at home, or on the elliptical. The

------
193

choice seems clear to me.

I know my pushing of the boundaries that most chemo patients seem content to stay well within can be a source of consternation and frustration for my medical team. Before leaving for Asheville, I ask Trish if I can go down Sliding Rock while in Asheville. I love water and I know it will be exceedingly hard on me to escort our French friends and the girls to this waterfall that also serves as a natural waterslide without getting to ride down it myself. Trish, who is relatively new to North Carolina, asks me to describe it and I tell her about the smooth rocks that propel you down, never the same way twice, and land you in an 8-foot pool of icy water at the bottom.

Trish mulls it over and looks as if she's going to forbid it, saying she's concerned about my port (which isn't tethered to anything and has a tendency to move around a bit) and the bacteria in the water, but decides it will be okay if I promise to get out immediately. I clap my hands in delight and then ask her about ziplining.

"You're kidding me, right?" Trish asks, laughing. "You do understand that you have cancer, right?"

She does, however, agree to let me do that as well since she does not see how that can harm me. Provided, she says, that I am feeling up to it. She reminds me that the chemo's side effects are cumulative and I will continue to feel worse and worse.

She is right. On the day that we are supposed to go ziplining, I feel downright awful. My stomach hurts, I have been battling low-grade nausea for days, and I have some new, unwelcome symptoms. My eyes are suddenly killing me, and there is a ringing in my ears. I call Trish and she confirms that both are Cisplatin's calling card, letting me know it is continuing to kill the good with the bad. When I return from the trip, Trish asks whether I did, in fact, go down Sliding Rock.

"I did," I tell her. "And I made sure to check for my port each time after I landed."

"Each time? " Trish replies, practically yelling. "Each *time?* I recall giving you permission very reluctantly. I certainly don't recall giving you permission to go down more than once."

"But," I say, employing the technique every kid perfects, "you never said I couldn't."

The Asheville trip and its waterfall and ziplining excursions were fun and exhilarating. They allowed me to once again let cancer know that it did not get to dictate everything. That I had some say in my life as well. But even more importantly, it allowed me to stick with the plans the girls and I had made, with great enthusiasm, back before I had cancer. It allowed me to once again salvage this summer for the kids, so that it is not defined solely by my cancer.

CHAPTER TWENTY-TWO

Subject: Ovarian Odyssey
Date: August 25, 2011

Several milestones have been reached since I last wrote. David and I celebrated our 20th wedding anniversary. We're looking forward to many more together, with this serving as the test our relationship passed on its way to Italy. Noah headed back to NCSSM for his last year of high school. He had a tough time leaving while I'm still sick and is checking in more regularly, but he seems to be off to an exciting and jam-packed year. The girls started school today (7th grade for Eliza and 10th grade for Hannah), and we spent yesterday baking together and reminiscing about all that we were able to cram into our summer. Oh, and bickering. There was lots of that too.

And I had my first Queasy Pop. The fact that it was all I could stomach on the day I miserably sucked on it in lieu of breakfast — or that I've now got a ready supply in my chemo bag — pretty much sums up how my last cycle went down. I wish I could report that Cycle 3 went as well as Cycle 2, but that was definitely not the case. The patch — for which I was ready to do testimonials and infomercials after the second cycle — was not quite as magical this time around. It didn't so much keep the nausea at bay as keep it at a low, barely manageable constant — kind of like being on a boat (not a big luxury yacht, but a little beat up dingy) in the middle of the ocean. The seas weren't storm- worthy turbulent, but they sure weren't calm. I also experienced some new symptoms which I understand will be my new companions from here on in, such as a shortness of breath (diminished red blood cells) and cramping and pulling intestinal pain.

So I've reached the halfway point — yay — but it doesn't quite feel like the celebratory milestone it should since it does not represent a peak but rather a midway point on the way to more discomfort and pain. That sounds more bleak and pessimistic than I intend, because it is gratifying to know that I've knocked out three of the six chemo cycles, but the fact that all of the sucky parts of chemo are cumulative is frustrating and, at times, down- right demoralizing. I feel like I've had the flu for so long that I've forgotten what it feels like to feel normal. When folks ask me how I'm doing on a particular day, it's hard to know how to answer. Do you mean within the realm *of feeling shitty all the time, or compared to my four tennis matches a day prior self? But I also know I have it so much better than a lot of my fellow patients at the Blumenthal Cancer Center, and for that, I continue to be grateful.*

And the cancer funnies continue too. The latest prize for creative gift giving goes to my sister, Nicole, who printed up my very own deck of cancer cards. These are cards I can whip out when the need arises that say things like, "I have cancer. You do not. Please do this for me." or simply have the word CANCER printed on them (in Scrabble tiles, no less) for the occasions that simply call for an all- purpose cancer card. Nicole hand-delivered the cards to me during a visit this past weekend with my parents, which was a real treat even though I think it was hard for Mom and Dad to see me getting my treatment. Maggie, chemo nurse extraordinaire, was off that day but she came in anyway just to meet my family. If that doesn't speak to what great care I'm getting, I don't know what does.

Another cancer funny — and this is simply because I'm choosing to laugh about it rather than cry — is the fabulous irony that the one part of my body that is small and delicate appears to be my veins. My veins continue to collapse and divert needles because they are, according to one nurse who said she's never seen any quite so bad, "so, so tiny," which is comical to me given that nothing on me has ever been described that way. Yet another "Really? Really??"moment in this whole weird, wild ride. Small veins. Go figure.

David and I are meeting with the breast surgeon tomorrow to discuss my double mastectomy that will follow on the heels of my chemo. (My motto of one cancer at a time does not apparently apply to the scheduling of treating each cancer, since that has to be done far in advance.) So who knows, at the end of all this, perhaps my veins won't be alone in the petite department!

Love, Katya

As I suspected, Noah's brave front crumbles when it's time to drop him back off at NCSSM. It is one thing to treat your mom's cancer as a clinical matter of science when you are with her, but it is something else entirely when you have to part ways for the school year. It doesn't help that I am feeling worse, rather than

198

I have cancer.
You do not.

Do you offer a
cancer discount,
by any chance?

I know it's not
your policy, but
please make an
exception.
I have cancer.

Please do this.
Why?
Because I have
cancer, that's why.

Kathleen Chasey, a graphic designer, worked with my sister to make these cancer cards.

better, so Noah knows I am suffering.

"I'm so glad I'm not heading off to college this year," he tells me. "I don't think I'd be able to go."

Eliza, too, is incredibly clingy. I try so hard to be patient, to remember that she's gone through a lot at a particularly vulnerable age, but it is grating. For one thing, she wants to be near me, touching me, on me, whenever possible, and I just do not want to be touched. She has also taken to calling me cute. All sorts of things I say and do are suddenly rendered adorable when accompanied by a bald head. I tell her it makes me feel weird to have my youngest child calling me cute all the time.

I am sure she does not find me cute when I see her first progress report for the year. In almost every class, she has failed to turn in multiple assignments. I blow up, she breaks down, and I am left feeling guilty about the limited way I am there for her this school year. Most nights, even on non-chemo days or weeks, I hit a wall right around dinnertime. I tend to lie down, either on the couch or, on particularly bad days, up in my room, away from everyone. I am not sitting with Eliza while she does her homework, following up on her progress on assignments and projects. I am not hands-on the way I usually am, and it shows.

Eliza is only 11. She skipped the first grade and, in a city where the norm seems to be to hold children back and to delay starting kindergarten, she is often a full year and a half to two years younger than her 7th grade peers. I am not the least bit concerned about her intellectually, but adjusting to the rigors of middle school has been a work in progress. Let's just say that her discipline and work ethic, unlike her intellect, are not beyond her years. She needs me to be on her, and I'm not. Cancer gets my attention this school year, not Eliza.

Making matters worse is Eliza's keen sense of how much I am suffering. She does not want to add to my troubles, to burden me any more than I am already burdened, so she uses the kind of short-term logic that is so prevalent among pre-pubescent kids and decides not to tell me about the subpar grades, the lost math book, the missing assignments.

"How did you think this was all going to work itself out?" I ask her, incredulous that she cannot see the big picture here.

"I thought I could fix it," she tearfully tells me.

It is a lesson with minimal learning curve. This pattern repeats itself throughout the year. Eliza will bounce back. Her grades will improve. She will succeed academically. But for me, it is the year that I dropped the ball. The year I didn't do my job as a mom.

There are reminders of this intrusion into my mom duties, this compromising of the way I would ordinarily do things, all the time. Hannah is given a long gown for her chamber choir performances and it needs to be hemmed. I'm not going to pretend that is something I would ordinarily have done (button sewing is pretty much the limit of my skills with a needle and thread) but I would certainly have been the one to take care of it. As it is, it falls to David to do (because, of course, Hannah tells us about it at the last minute and it needs to be done with minimal time to spare) and David takes it, at my suggestion, to our neighborhood dry cleaner who also does alterations. David arranges to have it done and it falls to me to pick it up on the day of her concert. I call David *en route* to ask him if he already paid or if I need to pay when picking it up.

Eliza held the camera for this shot of the two of us.

"No, you'll need to pay," he tells me.

"Okey dokey, how much?" I ask. "I have no idea," he replies.

"What do you mean you have no idea?" I demand. "You

didn't settle on a price? You didn't ask how much it's going to cost?"

David thinks I'm being ridiculous. These are not the kinds of things you settle on. I point out to him that they have our dress. A dress we need. We are basically going to be forced to pay whatever they demand. "When you arrange to have the guys come aerate the lawn," I remind him, "you establish what their fee is. You don't just tell them to come on over and do their thing and then bill you."

Sure enough, when I go to pick up the dress, the bill is $87! I go through the roof. $87? I don't spend that on purchasing a *new* dress! I am uncharacteristically and unjustifiably angry, both at the seamstress and, later, at David. I apologize later (to David, not the seamstress), saying that I think the fact that such an oversight wouldn't have happened on my watch has me feeling like I'm not doing my job. Like I'm less of a mother. There is no doubt David has had to step up his parenting game this school year, doing more of the carpooling, more of the dinner conversations, more of the tucking in at night. I hate it that I am not as present as a parent. That balls have been dropped. I know there are plenty of ways that I am still there, that I'm doing the best I can, but it still hurts.

Just as it hurts when I do make an effort, far more of an effort than I think the girls realize, and it goes unnoticed or unappreciated. Hannah's fall concert, the one that necessitated the hemming of the gown, falls on a day I have chemo. I nonetheless decide to go, because I know it is important to her and I do not want to miss yet another school event. (I had to miss her back-to-school night earlier in the school year, when you get to meet your child's teachers for the year, and it has me feeling lost and out of the loop.) I feel totally crummy, and David suggests I stay home, but no, I am doing this. It's important to Hannah that I'm there. We sit through the entire concert, one that involves several choirs, not just hers, and it is interminable. I struggle to find a comfortable position in the auditorium seats, I try to stave off the growing nausea, and I valiantly fight to keep my eyes open and a smile on my face. I am determined to stick it out, and I do. No acknowledgment from Hannah. Not a peep about how much she appreciates my being there. I should have gone to bed, I think to myself.

I give Hannah a pass on her failure to acknowledge my Herculean effort in attending her concert. Just as I don't let it get to me when Eliza asks for me to tuck her in and rolls her eyes when I say it'll have to be Dad because I just can't get out of bed. But there are times when I let them have it, when the frustrations of parenting with a cancer elephant strapped to your back and the dismay of your ungrateful children failing to acknowledge the elephant just get to you and you lose it.

Hugging Hannah (and wearing my beloved Red Sox hat)

On a drive somewhere, I don't even remember where, the girls are bickering over a piece of candy. We had bought a bag of penny candy at the Mast General Store in Asheville and only one piece remains of their favorite kind, each convinced it belongs to her.

I can take no more. All of their ungratefulness, all of my unappreciated effort, the full extent of my cancer fury is bound up into this one moment.

"It is JUST CANDY!" I yell like a crazy woman. "I have CANCER and you are fighting over CANDY!"

Silence from the back seat.

Nurses' care eases cancer pain

Treatment helped by supportive staff

Katya Lezin

Nicole Filyaw, 31, can trace her nursing roots to age 4, thanks to a photograph she has of herself at that age with her grandfather.

"I was pretending to be his nurse," she said. "I have always wanted to take care of something or somebody."

She earned her nursing degree in 2001 and first served as a floating nurse throughout the hospital.

"I fell in love with oncology," she said, citing the patients and the intimacy she is able to have with them as her reason for choosing to specialize in oncology.

Maggie Hield, 28, credits her mother with her interest in the medical field and her desire to become an oncology nurse. Her mother, who moved from the Bahamas to the United States with Hield and her siblings when Hield was 6, loved her job as a medical assistant. In 2001, Hield's mother was diagnosed with urethral carcinoma and became a cancer patient herself, ultimately succumbing to the disease. Hield

was by her mother's side for her surgery, chemo and infusions. She said she felt grateful to the "awesome nurses" who worked in oncology.

She knew she had found what she wanted to do with her life.

Both Filyaw and Hield are now nurses at the Blumenthal Cancer Center. Filyaw serves as gynecology/oncology chemo navigator; Hield serves as gynecology/oncology chemo coordinator.

Filyaw works with new patients to educate them about what treatment entails and serves as the liaison between the patient and the rest of the medical team. Hield works with patients to schedule appointments and oversees each patient's medication and symptom management.

"We are intertwined," Filyaw said. Hield added, "We talk about 100 times a day."

Both see their primary function as making sure patients do not fall through the cracks. "We are the somebody you can call who knows your situation," said Hield.

I can attest to how helpful it is to have a chemo coordinator and navigator to funnel what can seem like an avalanche of information and medical instructions to you and provide continuity in your care. The fact they are both compassionate women who exude empathy and comfort is a bonus.

The feeling is mutual: As much as their patients love and appreciate them, Filyaw and Hield say, they in turn value the relationship they develop with patients.

"We get to know them and their families," Hield said. "It's not a revolving door."

"We have a relationship with them," said Filyaw. "They become family."

The downside to this intimacy is that Filyaw and Hield feel the pain of losing a friend when patients lose their battle with cancer.

"We go to our fair share of funerals," Filyaw said.
"And we are often introduced as a member of the family," Hield said. She recalls one funeral when the deceased's spouse was comforting her. That role reversal is evident in the

Maggie Hield (l) and Nichole Filyaw (r), chemo navigator and coordinator extraordinaire.

infusion room, too, where Hield and Filyaw often are surprised by patients' queries as to how they are doing.

I can vouch for their empathy. When I struggled with nausea and despair after my ovarian cancer diagnosis and the first round of chemo, Hield and Filyaw were by my side, tears in their eyes, vowing to do everything in their power to make it better.

When they can't make it better, which fortunately for me was not the case, they do what they can to make the unbearable as bearable as possible.

"If it's curable, you go for the cure," Hield said. "But when it's not, you do what you can and try to make them as comfortable as possible."

It is hard to imagine anyone doing a better job at that than these two nurses.

Katya Lezin is a freelance writer for South Charlotte News. Have a story idea for Katya? Email her at bowserwoof@mindspring.com.

Reprinted with permission of South Charlotte News, a Charlotte Observer publication

CHAPTER TWENTY-THREE

Subject: Ovarian Odyssey
Date: September 19, 2011

It turns out that there is no cosmic balance between the Cancer Gods and! the Computer Gods, so facing my own mortality did not buy me a pass as! far as my computer's mortality was concerned. My hard drive died shortly after my last treatment and the Apple Store Genius (that is, in fact, his official title) told me nothing was recoverable. You are probably thinking this isn't such a calamity since obviously Katya knew enough to save everything onto an external hard drive — all her photos, columns, client lists, addresses, you name it — but you would be wrong. In a boneheaded display of both laziness and obstinacy that predates my cancer and so cannot be blamed on it, I had nothing saved and faced the truly terrifying prospect of total (files) loss. Fortunately, after a very long week that was taxing enough without the computer fiasco, I found a data recovery company that saved the day. That's a long- winded way of letting you all know that I am back in business and I appreciate all of the queries wondering how I was doing in the interim.

My medical team warned me that Cycles 4 and 5 of chemotherapy would be tough. I would have loved to prove them wrong but so far they have called it like it is. The cumulative effect of all that poison swirling within me is pretty brutal, but the good news is that it comes and goes. In the good stretches, I am continuing to live and enjoy my life. In the bad stretches, I console myself with the thought that I still have it so much better than most. The two most annoying symptoms this time around have been a ringing in my ears (that I am told will be with me until I am done with chemo) and really painful heartburn. I also continue to have a lot of stomach pain, which is no doubt a "What the hell?" shout out from my organs. (It might also have something to do with the fact that one of my nurses tripped on the IV line connected to my intraperitaneal port! Ouch!)
I have mixed feelings about the battle analogy for cancer, mainly because it implies that those who lose the battle didn't! fight hard enough when it is often an unfair fight, but I have to say that I do conceptualize it that way within my own body. The chemo to me is like the atomic bomb or some other horrible weapon of war that is a necessary evil but has all sorts of nasty consequences that undermine its worth. It is mind- boggling to me that we have made

such strides in medicine and technology but we are somehow unable to cure someone without hurting her a lot in the process.

But now for the good news ... I have completed four of my six cycles of chemo! The end is definitely in sight and I know I can do it. When I think back to the first few weeks after my surgery and the first few rounds of! chemo, when I truly didn't think I could suck it up for what seemed like an interminable stretch ahead of me, the knowledge that I am nearing the end and that I have made it this far bolsters me when I am struggling physically. Nothing has even come close to being as bad as those first few weeks so it is helpful to have that as a basis of comparison. I have also managed to get out on the tennis courts and have some good, competitive matches. I am by no means my old self as far as energy and stamina goes, but it feels great to be exhausted from something other than chemo. All you worriers (you know who you are) need to know that even if the tennis has exacerbated some of my symptoms, it is a trade off I am knowingly and willingly making.

Hannah and I just returned from West Virginia, where we competed in a Scrabble tournament in Charleston and enjoyed some quality time together. At one point, Hannah forgot the number of our hotel room and the front desk clerk wouldn't give it to her unless she could provide more than just her mother's name. When Hannah was describing me, she said, "She has shoulder- length dirty blonde hair. No wait! No she doesn't! She's bald!" She said the look on the clerk's face was priceless. Hannah also gets the prize this time around for coming up with this cycle's moment of mirth. She accompanied David and me to the breast cancer reconstruction symposium and was as surprised as we were with the many options available to women who undergo reconstruction following a double mastectomy. There are, for example, myriad choices when it comes to nipples. They can be surgically constructed or they can be tattooed on. This led to a family discussion of other tattoo options, with my favorite suggestion being Hannah's. She thinks I should have tattooed, in small print, "If you can read this, you are too close." So the ability to find the humor in all of this is clearly a family trait and know that we are laughing more than we're crying. But you'll have to wait until a future missive to find out which tattoo option I end up choosing!

Fondly,
Katya

9/20/11

Katya-

It is quite hard to admit that I have admiration for any Red Sox Fan as my self esteem really recoils at such wimpy ideation. Unfortunately, my self esteem must all be facade because I'm really so thrilled with your painful accomplishments thru cycles 1-4. Beth and I wish you good luck with 5 & 6. After they are completed, we hope you will always be disease free and you'll be able to talk to your former nemesis and say Adios Mutha Fucka.

XOXO, Carl
(Carl Lieberman, David's paternal uncle)

"How was your match?" David asks.

With my medical team's permission, I am back on the tennis courts, playing against other women across town on the 4.0 ladder. I get more easily winded and my strokes, never pretty to begin with, are a little rusty, but it feels great to be breaking a sweat and chasing a ball, to exert myself in a way I don't on the exercise equipment at the J.

"I won!" I exclaim with pride, but I then tell David that my opponent was a poor sport, barely talking to me after the match. I have long complained that some of the women I have encountered over the years on the tennis ladder seem to think there are great sums of prize money involved in how seriously they take each game, each point, with their questionable line calls and petty pouting when they lose. But this time, David sticks up for my poor-mannered opponent. "Hon, you have to give her a break," he says. "I think being beaten by a bald woman who's in the middle of chemo would test anyone's sportsmanship."

Another day, I am playing a woman I have played before, after assuring her that yes, I can handle it and yes, my doctors have approved my playing *with cancer*. It is uncharacteristically hot and we are both panting and sweating, but it feels great. With the score tied at 5 games all, a comeback for me, having won the last three games in a row, my opponent suddenly announces that she can no longer go on.

"I think I'm fighting a cold," she explains. "I just really don't have it in me today."

Really? *Really?*

Another time, I forget my hat. No problem, since I don't have hair to get in my way. Wrong. First off, I learn firsthand how much we sweat through our heads. I will spare you the details, but let's just say both my towel and the spare I keep in my tennis bag are put to good use. It is an unseasonably hot fall day, even for Charlotte, and I get home to discover that I have totally fried the top of my head. Ouch. As if being a bald lady isn't off putting enough, let's add to that a bald head that is now a bright red shade of *look at me!*

My parents get to see my shiny red head when they arrive for a visit, a long-overdue visit because I have not seen them since my diagnosis. Nicole is accompanying them and I have intentionally timed their visit for the weekend after my Day One, which is usually when I feel my best. They will then get to come with me for my Day Two, my easier day, and get to meet my medical team and see where I am getting such outstanding care. The plan backfires.

The weekend is wonderful. I feel as good as I could hope to feel, and we are able to do things like take a family walk at McAlpine Creek Park and go out to eat and go shopping at SouthPark Mall. While we are at the mall, I accompany my mom and I find a chair in each shop, since I am winded and I'm having a hard time getting my breath. Mom keeps asking me if I'm alright, if I need anything. I want to say to her, *This is me on a good day,* but I don't because that would only make her worry more. She tells everyone within earshot that I am fighting cancer, and I don't mind despite the inherent awkwardness of the pronouncements and the inevitable pity and "Bless her heart" they engender, because I can hear the pride in her voice and I know she is applauding my spirit and what a trooper I am. I know much of this can-do attitude can be attributed to her; it is something she has modeled my whole life. As for my Dad, I tell him that I have received an unwelcome lesson in what he has endured his whole life. My breathing difficulties, a new symptom that has me worried, give me an unwelcome dose of empathy for his asthma struggles.

On Monday, we head in to the Blumenthal Cancer Center, and I am eager for Mom and Dad to see for themselves how comfortable I am there and how well I am treated. What I do not take into account is that, as jarring as my bald head was for them, I seem relatively the same Katya they know and love. They both pronounce me the healthiest- looking sick person they know and I think, to a certain extent, they forget that I am sick. It fades to the background and this just feels like a fun family visit. But in the hospital, there is no ignoring my cancer.

I can feel my dad instantly recoil as soon as we enter the infusion room. I am so used to it, as are all of my chemo buddies, that I forget how disconcerting it is to first enter the room and see everyone hooked up to IV poles, a motley assortment of bald heads lining the perimeter of the room, getting their poison. And even though the poison is odorless, the room does have that unmistakable hospital, people-are-sick-here smell.

The whole day, as I'm poked and prodded and go through my Day Two regimen, my dad is eager to volunteer to go on coffee runs, go get water, anything to get the hell out of there. My mom seems to handle it better, being her usual perky and outgoing self, but I can see her looking at me when she thinks I'm asleep or out of it, and there is such sadness in her eyes. Another time she thinks I'm sleeping, after they've given me the Benadryl and Ativan that usually knocks me out and when I am lying back, eyes closed, my mom suggests asking the doctors about my diet.

In her efforts to help me, to do something from afar, Mom has been an active Internet researcher. She is convinced that I should be on a macrobiotic diet. She simply cannot understand how this has not been discussed with me or prescribed. When I tell her that I can eat whatever I want, and assure her that yes, I have checked with my doctors *and* the cancer center's dietician, and that there is no diet or food group that will enhance my treatment or lessen my side effects, she is incredulous.

"But I read..." she begins, for the umpteenth time.

I know it is well meaning. I have received quite a bit of unsolicited advice, not just from her, and all of it is well-intentioned. But I have a medical team. I have more doctors than I've ever had in my life. I really just want to go with them, not what the Internet says or somebody's Aunt Ethel who did this or that or what the latest break- through in Indonesia suggests. I'm good, and the advice gets annoying. Nicole had cautioned my mom that the dietary discussion is verboten, and Mom had promised that she wouldn't bring it up. When she mentions checking with the doctor about my diet, I sit bolt upright in bed.

"Mom!" I exclaim with indignation. "You promised!"

She looks at me with consternation and frustration. "You," she says, "were supposed to be asleep."

Subject: Ovarian Odyssey
Date: October 1, 2011

Another week confirming that this cancer journey is a wild ride of ups and downs. Every time I think I have it figured out — not mastered, but figured out — new symptoms and complications crop up that have me yelling out, "Seriously??"

On Monday, Day one of Cycle 5, we learned that my white blood cell count was below the threshold for continued treatment. They decided to proceed with my chemo, so that I could stay on schedule, but that I would need a shot of Neupogen to boost my bone marrow into producing more. So on Tuesday, when I came in for fluids and anti-nausea drugs, I also got a shot in my arm. Let's just say it's a good thing Eliza wasn't there, who hates shots and whose mom is always telling her it's just a quick prick and then it's done. One look at my face would have confirmed what she said when we first had the cancer talk with them, and she marveled over my keeping the diagnosis a secret until the end of the school year ..."Mom, you are such a good liar!" So yeah, the shot stung like the dickens and continued to sting for hours. It also produced bone pain and almost immediate flu-like symptoms. Looks like Neupogen is competing with Cisplatin for the dubious honor of helping only marginally more than it hurts me.

By Wednesday, I was fully convinced that Cycle 5 is the toughest yet. I returned to the hospital for fluids and meds and ended up in a room for half the day. Trish decided to hold off on any more Neupogen, seeing as it was decidedly not my friend, and instead gave me some IV drugs for my latest symptom, a migraine-like headache, along with my other chemical goodies.

So to complete the lows (and I do promise there are highs to follow), this week was also marked with some gastrointestinal issues that are basically my lot in life while both chemo and anti-chemo drugs swirl around my gut. And they unfortunately often result in major bouts of insomnia, which of course contribute to my feeling lousy. When I returned to the hospital on Friday, I was very short of breath so they

214

drew blood to see where things stood. (The fact that it took five tries to get a vein was not a good sign and has me looking like quite the junkie.) The good news is that my white blood cell count is back up. Neupogen is temporarily off of my most-hated drugs list. The bad news is that my hemoglobin count is the lowest it has been, explaining why I feel anemic and tired.

But I'm here to say that the human body is amazing in its ability to bounce back. Yesterday, I was struggling for breath, hooked up to an IV, wondering! if I would even get out of bed today. I asked DeLeslie, one of my nurse practitioners, if it was still okay to run the Race for the Cure this morning, given my week's ailments. She told me that in all her years of treating oncology patients, she had never been asked about running a race. DeLeslie is the one who reminded me that I was only one week out of major surgery when I was frustrated with my slow progress after my hysterectomy. She noted that Cycle 5 brings most patients to their knees and that I should feel good about just being out and about.

So with that in mind, I had decided to walk, rather than run, the race today. But I had a good night's sleep, first in a week, and woke up rejuvenated and energized, raring to go. So Lorrina and I ran it together (with frequent queries from Lorrina about my need to stop or slow down) and we only walked up the hill (which, in the interest of full disclosure, I am tempted to do every year, so it was actually nice to have cancer as an excuse to do so this year). We then met up with a bunch of other fabulous women, with whom we do the race every year, and walked the course together. We all sported the shirts Jen had made for us, which have a bunch of my cancer quotes on the back that were the source of many comments along the way. It was so empowering to share the crisp, beautiful morning with my wonderful friends, and show cancer once again that I have other plans, thank you very much.

Other highs this week included two close tennis matches, one of which I won (names of opponent left off by mutual consent), Noah's return home this weekend, and some good laughs in the infusion room, including a reclining chair that absolutely refused to release me from its grasp. Christine, another favorite nurse, and I were laughing so hard we were causing quite a distraction, leading Trish to assure the other patients that it was about to get a lot quieter as soon as Katya went on her merry way.

And the creative gifts just keep on coming! A Scrabble buddy sent a box full of individually wrapped presents, one to last through every day remaining of my chemo, and the girls have delighted in taking turns opening them up. My sister sent a bunch of water bottles that come adorned with the message, "Cancer sucks." Another friend sent a cancer voodoo doll. And that is not to say that the cards, emails and calls aren't equally comforting. I truly could not feel any more supported or loved, and at the risk of sounding hokey (although I think I probably crossed that bridge ages ago), the unwavering and truly humbling support is often what gets me through the lows.

I am attaching a photo of us at the Race this morning (including one of the back of the shirt) and an invitation to our annual dessert party. All you locals mark your calendars for November 12th, but any out-of-towners who want to join us are more than welcome as well. This year's party will be particularly celebratory as it marks the end of my chemo.

Day 8 of Round 5 is around the corner and then ... drumroll, please ... one more cycle to go. Whoohoo!

Love,
Katya

Juli, Lisa Z., Gabi, Lorrina, Baldy, Lisa M. and Jen after running Race for the Cure.

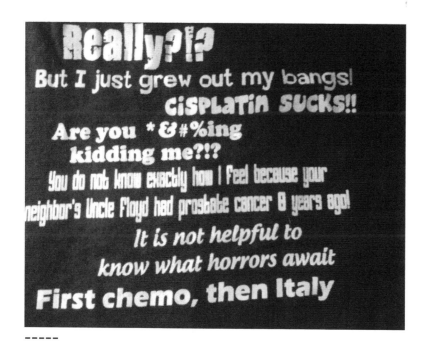

Really?!?
But I just grew out my bangs!
CiSPLATiN SUCKS!!
Are you *&#%ing
kidding me?!?
You do not know exactly how I feel because your
neighbor's Uncle Floyd had prostate cancer 8 years ago!
It is not helpful to
know what horrors await
First chemo, then Italy

Katya (aka the bravest woman I have ever known),

Hi! It seems like only yesterday I received news that you had been diagnosed with ovarian cancer, and here you are now completing cycle 5 of a 6- cycle chemo treatment! I am so glad for you that the end is in sight. Despite your complete disclosure and description of the treatment, it is hard to imagine how harrowing all this must have been for you on a daily basis. The word "chemotherapy" seems, somehow, a very innocuous word in its construct, since the therapy part of the word makes it seem almost benign, belying the fact that while it is, indeed, therapeutic, it is killing off not only the bad stuff in one's body, but very nearly finishing one off in the process! For the uninitiated, such as myself, it has been an eye opener to hear what a cancer patient must go through to fight off a virulent cancer. Thanks for the pic. I think that you look fab. You carry that rocker babe chick look really well, as you look very hip. You also look amazingly healthy for one who is undergoing such aggressive medical treatment. My hat is off to you. I think that your strong personal resolve to get through this experience is seeing you through this in a way that really takes one's breath away. You really should write a book about this experience. The emails that you have written throughout your ordeal are so descriptive and well-written that I see a book in there somewhere. You do not sugarcoat what the treatment itself has been like, sharing intimate information about what it is really like. Chemotherapy is not just about nausea but about so much more. More importantly, you illustrate with your writing and much charm, what the power of positive thinking and determination can do to get one through such a difficult journey back to good health.

I can't wait for this to be all over for you, and I am sure that you can't either! The new year is just around the corner and by then chemo will be behind you, as well as the double mastectomy (if it is still scheduled for December).

Looking forward to seeing you in Lake George!

Your scrabble bud,
Linda
(a fellow recovering attorney)(Linda Wancel, a Scrabble player and newly retired New York Assistant District Attorney
------

10/4

Hi Katya,

By the time you see this message, I hope that cycle of your chemo is over, though I realize the effects linger. When I looked at the schedule of your treatments, it seemed like you had the worst of both worlds. Four or five months seems entirely too long to have to deal with what you're dealing with, yet the individual cycles seem to come too close together for my taste. It seems like you don't have much time in between the recovering from one cycle and dreading the next cycle. But now thatthe fifth cycle is (almost) done, I'm sure that you're ready for cycle to come and go as quickly as possible.
Like everyone else, I'm sure, I continue to be impressed by all that you continue to be able to do, like tennis, racing/running/walking, etc. I also can't help but be reminded of the infinitely variable joke about "Doctor, will I be able to play the oboe during my treatment?" "Yes? That's funny I couldn't play it before."
But seriously, you continue to amaze.
Thanks for the dessert party invitation. Though we won't be there in person, I'm taking the invite as a license to chow down on dessert wherever we may be that day, as long as we're thinking of you!

Good luck with recovering from this chemo cycle and getting ready for the last one.
Brian (and Chris)
(Brian McLaughlin and Chris LeMaire, friends from Maryland.) ----
------

When I cross the finish line with Lorrina at Race for the Cure, running under the huge archway of pink balloons and past the crowd of cheering supporters, I am overcome with emotion. I have always heard that expression, *overcome with emotion,* and found it somewhat dramatic, as if it belongs in a Jane Austen novel along with heaving chests and beating hearts. But I now get it, because I am truly overcome, happily chatting with Lorrina one moment, relieved and excited to see the finish line, and the next I am in tears, literally weeping as I run past the clock with our time and into the chutes that signal that the race is mercifully over.

Part of it is the joy of finishing a race I didn't think I'd be able to participate in on any level. I truly pushed myself to my limit, both physically and emotionally, but in a good, cathartic way. To be hooked up to IVs one day and exerting myself at this level the next is truly gratifying. And the entire race is an emotional rollercoaster as Lorrina and I run by people wearing shirts emblazoned with the names of survivors, but also many who weren't as lucky, whose lives are being honored and whose photos are emblazoned on the backs we pass or, as is more likely the case, who pass us.

My own shirt elicits a lot of comments and thumbs up, as does my bald head. I am asked quite a few times if I'm a survivor, and I find it a difficult question to answer. Am I a survivor? I don't know. I'm here, I'm surviving, so in that sense I am. But I am still in the midst of chemo, still fighting, so is the jury still out? As we run the final stretch of the race, and we can hear the announcer calling out the names of women crossing the finish line and identifying them as survivors, I wonder how I will be classified. And then it hits me that nothing will be said about me because I didn't self-identify as someone with cancer when I registered for the race the preceding spring. That, more than anything, gets to me. It does not seem that long ago that I signed up for this race, and yet, in so many ways, it was a lifetime ago. I wasn't sick then, or I guess I was, but I wasn't aware of this sickness insidiously growing within me. Is it possible that it has been less than six months since my diagnosis? Since the day my world was rocked and changed forever? It feels like a lifetime ago...another cliché that now has added resonance for me.

Carolinas Medical Center Office/Clinic Visit Notes Office Visit

LEZIN, KATYA DATE OF SERVICE: 10/10/2011

HISTORY OF PRESENT ILLNESS: This is a 46---year old female with a stage IIB high---------grade papillary serous carcinoma of the ovary diagnosed in May 2011. She is status post laparoscopic surgical resection and staging. She then initiated chemotherapy consisting of IV/IP Cisplatin and Taxol and has now completed five cycles of therapy to date. She had a bit of a difficult time with her last cycle of therapy. She has been using the Sancuso patch for nausea and vomiting. However, she did not put this on until the morning of her chemotherapy. We did supplement her with some IV Zofran prior to her chemotherapy; however, she did have significantly more nausea associated with this cycle of therapy.

Additionally, her ANC was borderline on day one of her last cycle of therapy. As a result, I did plan on giving her several days of Neupogen. However, following the first injection of Neupogen, she had moderate to severe bone pain and flu-like symptoms that made her feel very poorly. As a result, we did not give her any additional doses of Neupogen. Her day 8 white blood cell count was adequate for administration of chemotherapy. Despite these symptoms, she has remained very active during the course of her chemotherapy. She continues to play tennis. She also participated in the Susan Komen 5K Race for the Cure. Her only

---

other complaint at this time is decreased libido. She denies fever, chills, rash, shortness of breath, cough or chest pain. Her nausea is resolved at this time, although, again, she did have a difficult time with the last cycle of therapy. Her bowels are moving regularly. She is urinating without difficulty. She does report an increase in her level of fatigue with this last cycle of therapy; however, as noted above, she remains extremely active. Her appetite remains good.

The race is a highpoint in my cancer battle, a time when sheer force of will and determination let me triumph over my alien body. But it is one battle of many, and I am not the victor in most of the others. I feel awful, truly awful, every day. Everything that is bad intensifies. The jolts of pain increase in both frequency and intensity. The nausea feels like it is filling a cup that is about to overflow. The patch and the meds have put the cup in place, keeping it at bay or at low-grade, manageable levels, but now the cup is full and there is nothing more to be done. I feel the nausea lurking just below the surface when I first wake up, and it accompanies me throughout the day, with constant reminders that it is here, taunting me both physically and emotionally. I am terrified of returning to my early days of nausea hell and I worry that each low wave of it is signaling the tsunami to come.

I am told that each cycle is cumulative and that the fifth is the hardest one. I am not sure why that is. It stands to reason that if the cycles get progressively worse, the last one should be the hardest. But brought almost to my knees by the building pain, nausea and symphony of side effects, I am only too happy to consider it the peak, and hope that things ease up a bit with the final one. I try to take each hard day as a sign that the poisons are doing their thing. If I feel this shitty, I tell myself, think how the cancer – getting the full force of the fifth cycle's fury – feels.

But the mind games do not always work, and there are some tough days. I think my feelings can best be summarized thusly: I am sick of this shit.

I am sick of being sick.

221

CHAPTER TWENTY-FOUR

Noah comes home for an NCSSM Extended Weekend, his last before Thanksgiving Break. He gets in Thursday night, and I have planned a fun day for us on Friday, including lunch out and a matinee (which feels so decadent on a weekday). But I have been in bad shape and we end up spending almost the entire day in the infusion room. Noah works on his Harvard application in the chair next to me, keeping me company but averting his eyes or getting up to grab a snack or go to the bathroom whenever they do anything with my veins or needles. He is decidedly squeamish about all things medical and would no doubt rather not be with me in this room that is filled with everything he hates. But he offers to come and, selfishly, I want his company. I miss him dearly and this is supposed to be our special day together, so we're both trying to roll with the punches and simply change the venue.

On Saturday, he takes the SAT Subject Tests all day, and then goes out with some of his friends from East Mecklenburg High School on Saturday night. On Sunday, we do our traditional bagel run in the morning and then he plops down on the couch, with considerable prodding, to finish his college essays. He has written the main essay for the Common Application and is now working on his Harvard supplemental essay. This is our last weekend together before it is due (for early admission) and I know he will be crazy busy and distracted once he gets back to school, so I am riding him hard to write it now.

I am busy in the kitchen, making brownies and cookies for him to take back to his dorm, but I hear periodic whininess from the living room couch about how hard this is and how he doesn't want to do it. I finally lose it and tell him to suck it up. I know this is not how he wants to spend what remains of his Extended Weekend, but it has to be done and he needs to stop complaining.

"No Mom," Noah says, tears in his eyes. "That's not why it's hard." He pauses, lifting me up the computer so that I can come take a look at what he's written so far. "I'm writing about you and it's, well, it's really hard. I hate thinking about this stuff."

I feel about one inch tall. So much for my "suck it up" speech. I head in to the living room to give him a hug. I read the essay, which makes me cry as well.

David walks in, takes one look at us, and asks in bewilderment, "What is going on with you two?"

Here is Noah's essay that he submitted to Harvard:

I am a man of science. I believe in evolution, global warming, the big bang, and I trust in the opinion of scientists. I like the finality of data and the fact that it can be interpreted many ways, but never changes. Its constancy is comforting. This is why it is so hard for me to deal with my mom's cancer. While I have studied the science behind chemotherapy and know what's happening inside my mom's body as ovarian cancer cells multiply, spread and are hopefully killed and eradicated, I still feel anxious and vulnerable about what's happening. I've learned about the technicalities of cancer in biology, but still feel overwhelmed by the life-changing events that have rocked my family. It is hard to be a scientist when it is your mom facing this debilitating disease instead of a hypothetical person in a biology textbook.

I was ecstatic to get into the North Carolina School of Science and Math because I knew I'd be able to take the kind of high-level math and science classes that excite me. Not only were many of these classes not available at my former high school, but my excitement about them would have come at a huge social cost. I have stayed up late discussing super numbers, taken classes in graph theory, modern physics, and advanced topics in evolution, and I have loved every minute of it. But I was also somewhat reluctant to go to NCSSM because I was worried that I was going to get pigeonholed. Unlike some of my NCSSM peers, who are solely interested in math and science, I also love the humanities and I was unwilling to sacrifice them just to appease my inner mathematician and scientist. Sure, I love physics and get giddy over the concepts of topology, but if I can't act in a play, or get my hands on some Vonnegut, I don't feel fulfilled.

Fortunately, at NCSSM I get to do both. My humanities classes have been just as captivating as my math and science classes. In my American Studies class, I studied both the literature and

history of everything from Native American oral stories to the effects of beat poetry and rock and roll on 1950s suburbia. I wrote a paper about Americans' relationship with religion during Manifest Destiny and about the implications of Sinclair's The Jungle on American industry. I get to take theatre classes, act and direct in plays, and I participate in more sports at NCSSM than I ever did at home. All sides of me got to flourish.

But it is hard to reconcile both my sides – in this case, the scientist in me and the scared son – when dealing with my mom's cancer. If I only focused on the science of my mom's disease and the medicine behind her treatment, instead of confronting the emotions behind the incredibly strong and close relationship I have with her, a large part of me would be unexpressed. My mom is my greatest source of strength, and the reality that she could have been taken from me is just crippling. I am not sure how to cope with the fact that cancer – this fascinating scientific phenomenon I learned about in biology – could rob me of the one constant throughout my life. Seeing my mom, who is the toughest and most resilient person I know, brought to such lows is almost impossible to endure. And the fact that I have to do so from afar, that I am away at NCSSM while she is fighting this battle, makes it even harder. As a man of science, I know that each time the medicine (in her case, Cisplatin and Taxol) break her down, it is only so that the doctors can build her up. As a son who loves and admires his mom, I also know she can beat this. But at night, away from her and her comforting smile or hug, I am lost.

Moving forward, I want to continue to reconcile all of my different interests and sides. Harvard struck me as the ideal learning environment for someone like me who wants to pursue many different areas of study and who is excited about learning new things. I was particularly intrigued with Harvard's joint major program because I have always wanted to combine my love of political science and mathematics and to continue to explore the interconnection of physics and philosophy. And hopefully, by the time I am ready to enroll in college, I will no longer have to struggle with reconciling my roles as scared son and curious scientist. My mom's cancer will be a thing of the past and I can pursue this next chapter of my life without worrying that its bedrock is in any danger.

I bet Katya Lezin is really jealous...

Noah's Facebook post after getting a shot with Colin Firth (my chemo crush!) during a movie shoot at NCSSM.

Subject: Ovarian Odyssey
Date: October 16, 2011

Greetings from Lake George, NY, where I am treating myself to a Scrabble tournament getaway before starting my last cycle of chemo. That sounds so fabulous I think I'm going to have to repeat it ... my LAST cycle of chemo. I usually feel a mounting dread as my chemo days approach but this time I'm actually excited because I can't wait to knock them out and be done with chemo forever!

I had a rough go of it with Cycle 5 but this past week has been awesome. I have had lots of energy and feel as good as I can hope to feel in the midst of cancer and chemo, especially considering the fact that I'm nearing the end and it's all cumulative. I went in for a check up last week and my numbers all looked great so it's all systems go for this last round. I interviewed two fellow cancer patients recently for my column (I'll send a link to the column once it publishes) and they have both experienced delays in their treatment, so I feel very fortunate that mine stayed on schedule. I've had the October 24th end date in my head for so long that it would be truly demoralizing to have to extend my chemo into November.

A few new symptoms surfaced since I last wrote — my friend Lisa refers to them as the latest in my "parade of horribles" — but I'm happy to say they have not bothered me this week. The most distressing new chemo-related development was the sudden appearance of mouth sores (something I had dreaded more than anything else among the possible horrors I'd been warned about) but they have pretty much receded. I also noticed one day that my fingernails were horribly discolored — they'd turned a nasty shade of yellow — and my nurse told me they are also chemo casualties and that I shouldn't be surprised to lose them. Ah, the joys of filling your body with poison. But I just keep telling myself that this poison that's killing my mucous lining (how the mouth sores appear) and my fingernails and my hair follicles and umpteen other things is also killing my cancer, and that's the real poison. My medical team told me it is natural to start stressing about the cancer — whether we got it all, if it's going to come back — now that I'm nearing the end of my chemo. Ever since my diagnosis and the surgery and chemo that followed, I've been in fighter mode, and as horrible as the chemo has been, it! is at least something I am doing. The next phase, while I wait for my clean bill of health as I get periodically checked and scanned and examined — is much harder to bear because I'm essentially in wait and worry mode.

I must admit I've had several nightmares about the cancer reappearing and spots showing up on various tests, so getting the definitive "looks good" from my doctor will be a huge relief. He will take a look around when I have my surgery on December 15th and I will send an update about that once I enter the next phase of Katya, New and Improved. One of my infusion room buddies told me that she spends the week following her chemo in a fetal position, unable to move from her couch. Another friend, a fellow Scrabble player who is at this tournament, is in his second bout with lung cancer and his prognosis is not good. I feel so incredibly fortunate that my cancer was caught when it was and that I have essentially lived my life while fighting it. I have definitely had my share of aches and pains, but in the scope of how bad things could be — and are for so many people fighting cancer —

I have had it pretty good. Some people, when I share the

news or when they see my bald head, exclaim, "Oh, that's so unfair. Why you?" But really, why not me? And the fact that I am relatively young, healthy and fit — no doubt underlying the sense that it's unfair cancer picked me — is also why I have been able to fare as well as I have during treatment. I spent part of my lunch break yesterday walking around the gorgeous lake and feeling so thankful for everything and everyone who got me to this point. Cancer notwithstanding, I feel incredibly lucky.

Cycle 6 — my LAST one — here I come!

Love, Katya

At the Lake George Tournament with fellow Scrabblers. From left: Linda Oliva, Linda Wancel, Sue Gable and Cornelia Guest

That whole spiel the fine folks at the Blumenthal Cancer Center gave me about the fifth cycle being the hardest is pure and total bullshit. The sixth one is the worst, of course it is, it makes sense, and its only saving grace is the fact that it's the last one.

I tell David that I truly can't remember what it feels like to be free of pain and nausea. My new normal keeps changing, but its one consistency is that it is nothing like my old normal. I wake up and the feeling that I am on a wobbly boat is instantaneous. I try all day to steady the boat, and most days I succeed, but the water is never

228

totally still. I think my mind goes to a boat analogy because I get notoriously seasick. When we visited Venice during my childhood, I found the gondolas far more nauseating than enticing. When we visited my sister in California and Rusty, her husband who teaches sailing at UC Santa Cruz took us out on a 2-hour sail, it was about 2 hours too long for my liking. I love water, but I need to be *in* it. Being on top of it, especially in a vessel where you can feel the waves, is no fun at all. Comparing my chemo to a choppy boat ride is, in Katya speak, essentially saying that it sucks.

While the waters are very choppy, David and I attend a breast cancer reconstruction seminar at the Blumenthal Cancer Center. When we signed up for it earlier in the fall, I remember thinking that we could make a date night of it, line up rides home for the girls and go out to eat afterwards, just the two of us. Not quite. First off, I feel like shit. I would much rather be in bed right now, but these symposiums are only offered once each month and we need to get the information so that we can make an informed decision about the type of surgery I'm going to have. We also have to pick up Hannah *en route* from her cross- country practice, so she is with us. We set her up in the lobby, after she helps herself to the chips and soda they have available for attendees, and she settles in to do homework. We tell her we won't be long, thinking it can't possibly run more than an hour.

We are not even halfway through the program after an hour. Dr. Robinson begins by giving a brief overview of the history of breast re-construction, explaining that there have been many advances in recent years. The two options available to most women these days are to have silicone implants inserted or to create a new breast with fat from one's own body, usually from the stomach but butt and back fat can be used as well. I wonder if there is a boob bank somewhere, because I could surely donate enough for several women. My friends Cynthia and Alyssa, for example, both annoyingly thin, didn't have the option of having a DIEP (Deep Inferior Epigastric Perforator) procedure because they do not have enough body fat. No worries there.

As Dr. Robinson talks about the risk of infection with the sili- cone implants and the fact that the surgery is a multi-step process, with the breasts first inserted with fillers that expand the tissue for several months until the permanent implants can be safely inserted, I find myself leaning more and more towards the DIEP procedure. Yes, it is a longer and more involved surgery, but it is only one surgery. I like that, especially since my whole plan of meeting my insurance company's catastrophic cap before the end of the year would be for naught if a second surgery were required in the following year. I also like the idea of using my own body fat, not only because I have so much to give and having some of it surgically removed is a nice perk, but also because the breasts are more natural looking when made with fat versus silicone implants.

When he shows photos of women before and after their surgeries, David and I just look at each other. He silently takes my hand under the table. It is one thing to imagine the surgery and its aftermath on theoretical terms; it is quite another to be confronted with the stark photos of the women, their breasts a series of scars and discolored skin. It is jarring, but I feel so sick I can barely muster the energy to care or get upset.

I appear to be the only woman who is currently undergoing chemo in attendance and the only one whose husband came along. A woman who seems to be in her mid-sixties is introduced, and she proceeds to tell us her own cancer journey. She had the DIEP procedure, and I am eager to hear how she fared, how quickly she bounced back, if it was as brutal as everyone says it is. It takes her a long time to get to the actual surgery part of her story. There are pages and pages of notes that she reads aloud about her original diagnosis, her chemo, and how it impacted her.

She talks about how self-conscious she was when her hair first came back after her chemo regimen and, as is so often the case, it was nothing like it was before. Hers was half black and half white, which elicited a lot of comments and questions. "If there is one lesson I have learned from all of this," she says, "it is to be more charitable about people's appearances. Don't judge how someone looks because you don't know what they are going through."

After she is done talking, some representatives from the Pink House, a nonprofit dedicated to supporting women with breast cancer, get up to detail what services and products they can provide us. I feel weird sitting there, since I do not have breast cancer. The pink ribbon sisterhood does little for me. I am also fading fast. I just feel awful and I need to get to bed. I motion to David that it's time to go, especially since Hannah hasn't had dinner yet, Eliza has to be retrieved from Lorrina's house, and it is getting late.

We sneak out but right on our heels the previous speaker pops out, carrying a bag of stuff. She gives me a vest with strategically placed pockets to hold the pumps that will be a fixture for several days or weeks following the surgery. I can't quite get a handle on how that will work, how pumps will somehow emerge from my body, how I will have to squeeze them and drain them. It makes me even more nauseated to think about it, so I just thank her and hand it to David. She then gives me a hat, since I am the only woman who is bald in attendance, and tells me someone at her church knit it for her.

"I knew as soon as I saw you that it would fit you," she says proudly, "because you have such a big head."

Huh? A big head? Has everyone been lying to me when they tell me how nicely shaped my head is, how well I pull off the bald look? And what the hell happened to not passing judgment on people's appearance?

Subject: Ovarian Odyssey
Date: October 23, 2011

This past week has been emblematic of my overall cancer journey, in that! it was marked by some incredible highs and some terrible lows. I'll dispense with the lows first, since they are all attributable to feeling lousy. Let's just! say my last chemo did a! number on me and I had! the most pain I've felt !throughout the entire ordeal. Both the cumulative effect of it and the fact that my body appears to be in full revolt mode made this past week really miserable on a health front. I just never rebounded from last Monday's chemo or enjoyed the traditional respite from my aches and pains. I experienced cramps and the feeling that my stomach was being torn apart pretty much every waking moment, with the added bonus that this time the pain extended to my neck, back, hips and ankles. I interpreted it as my gut recruiting the rest of my body to ask, in no uncertain terms, "What the *&^(%$# are you doing to us?" I also had a harder time than usual with the nausea, and not being able to eat impacted my energy level. But knowing I was nearing the end certainly helped psychologically and each visit to the infusion room yielded examples of folks who had it worse than I do, if for no other reason than that they're at the beginning of their journeys and I, mercifully, am at the end.

*Okay, enough whining. Now for the highs! On our way in to the
Blumenthal Cancer Center for my last Day One chemo last Monday,
David told me to look up when we reached the busy intersection of
Queens and Providence near the hospital. There, holding balloons in
my honor, was the well-known Mr. McManaway statue, sporting one
of my customized cancer quotes t-shirts and adorned with a big sign
that read, "KATYA, LAST 1!" It instantly made me cry (agreed, no
small feat given that cheesy Commercials are equally effective at
bringing on the water works) because it so symbolized all of the
unbelievable support and love I have received throughout this
ordeal. Thank you, Lisa Z!*

*Another high was spending this past weekend in Asheville with
Hannah! and Eliza for the Asheville Scrabble Tournament. I almost
cancelled the trip, including twice when we were en route, because I
felt so lousy. But the girls had really been looking forward to our
time away together and I decided I could just take my aches and
pains on the road with me. On Saturday morning, I awoke exhausted
from yet another night of fitful sleep and frustrated that I was still
hurting. (Just as an aside, it is helpful to know that the chemo is
nearingthe end, but when you're in the thick of its side effects, that
holds little comfort. When you're hurting, the ordeal seems
interminable and even another day is one too many, so knowing that
pain stemmed from my nearing the finish line was of little comfort to
me.) I decided to go for a walk, hoping it would do me some good, so
I bundled up and headed outside. My friends JoAnn and Russ, with
whom we stayed, live deep in the woods, and it wasn't until I was
outside that I realized it was pitch black. There were no city lights,
no cars or really any other sign of civilization. I walked up the
mountain while the sun came up, and I'm here to tell you that's as
close to a spiritual experience as I'm going to have. It was just what
I needed to start the day with a new attitude and remind myself that I
am strong and can muster through the physical yukkiness (yes, that's
an official medical term).*

*It was also great getting to spend some quality time with the girls.
We devoted much of the journey home to discussing upcoming trips
and visits and events— all things we are looking forward to post-
cancer — and it was good for all three of us to know that the
proverbial corner is near. And the weekend was topped off by my
coming in third in my division at the tournament — no small feat
considering that chemo brain has me wondering what day of the
week it is and whether Colin Firth is accompanying me to the
hospital. I won $240, which is roughly .4% of a single chemo
treatment ... but I choose to look at is as part of the Italy fund.*

So I write to you on the eve of my very last chemo treatment with trepidation for the week ahead — I have no reason to doubt it will be just as brutal as this past week – but with overwhelming relief and gratitude that it marks the end. There are still parts of this journey that await me — the CAT scans and other diagnostic tests to ensure we got it all, the 14-hour surgery on December 15th — but this is the end of chemo. Yay! As my water bottle and brand new t-shirt (thank you, Marilyn!) say so succinctly, "Chemo sucks," and I am very glad to be done with it.

Love, Katya-

David takes me in for my last day of chemo. He says he doesn't care about the schedule, he'll be taking me in, thank you very much. My spirits are high but my body is not cooperating. I feel lousy, but I rebound when we get to the hospital. Friends are already there awaiting me and the excitement, the significance of this day, is palpable.

There is no attempt made to even try to abide by the visitor guidelines on my final day, and my room is a veritable party room. Lisa Miller confides that she will actually miss hanging out in my chemo room because we never do that otherwise. We meet for lunch or do things together, but just hanging out, talking for hours, that is something my chemo regimen provided us. We are forced to slow down, to just sit and be with each other, and I make a mental note to try not to forget the lesson that imparts.

Trish applauds my fortitude and the fact that I stayed on schedule. She tells me few people do so, that it is a really tough chemo regimen and most people have to take a break or stop altogether. I am just dumbfounded. "I never knew that was an option!" I say indignantly, and everyone laughs.

When we get home from the hospital, the house is filled with balloons and cards and gifts from a slew of people, all congratulating me on being done with chemo. I can't quite believe it. I want to celebrate and savor the moment but there is a chasm between the psychological and the physical, one I can't bridge. I'm so very happy to be done, I tell the girls that yes, I am relieved and excited and proud of myself, but what I don't tell them is that I have never felt

The sign that says it all. Whoohoo!

The statue dressed up for my final day of chemo.

Hanging out in my party private room with, counterclockwise from me, Iris, Lisa M., Marni and Gabi.

worse. I crawl into bed, most of the cards and gifts unopened downstairs.

It feels anticlimactic.

CHAPTER TWENTY-FIVE

On Friday, October 28th, I get up at 5:15 am to get Hannah moving. She has an alarm clock and is supposed to get herself up and ready each morning for her ridiculously early 5:50 am bus, but she has discovered the snooze button and often falls back asleep. David and I wait with her at the bus stop, as is our custom, and we then walk the dogs around the Grimmersborough loop. I come home and dutifully guzzle down my LaxaClear concoction before getting Eliza up and moving. It is my turn to drive for our carpool with Preston and Joel so I pick the boys up and we head in to school.

The whole morning, something feels different. I can't put my finger on it, but I can tell something is off, something is significant about this day. About mid-morning, it hits me. I am feeling no pain. I am still sluggish, bloated and bald, but *I don't feel sick*. No jolts of pain! No nausea!

I call David, so that he can proceed with the rest of his day without worrying. When he leaves for work each morning, I can see the concern in his eyes when he implores me to take it easy. When we talk during the day, as we inevitably do, I don't always share my lows with him, how lousy I am feeling, but he can hear it in my voice. Now he can hear the corner I've turned in my voice as well. He tells me I didn't need to tell him I am feeling better because he could tell as soon as I started talking. Lorrina says the same thing when I talk to her later in the day.

We head to Durham the next day to see Noah's play. It is my third visit to NCSSM this fall (the first two being a one-day Scrabble tournament in Durham and Family Day) but it is the first when I am not fighting nausea and assorted other aches and pains. I am so excited to be with Noah and really *be with* Noah, to enjoy a visit to his campus without the distraction of feeling lousy.

We host our annual dessert party, that this year serves as a celebration of the end of chemo, and over 100 people fill our house to toast my accomplishment... and to eat Oreo cheesecake and chocolate mousse. Several members of my medical team come to the party, as do some of my fellow infusion room patients. My friends, who have heard about these folks and read about them in my OO missives, treat them like minor celebrities. Madeline, the woman from the Congo whom I met on my first day of chemo and for whom I've often translated, comes with her entire family, all dressed in traditional garb with bright colorful abacosts and tall, magnificent head scarves, and holds court for hours in my living room.

I cater a lunch for all of the infusion room nurses and my medial team, bringing it as a small gesture of thanks for the excellent care I have received. I also bring Rodney, the front desk manager who is always dressed to the nines, even on dress-down Fridays, a t-shirt on which I've painted a tie that reads, on the back, *Rodney's Dress Down Shirt*. Rodney puts it on over his shirt and tie (his concession to Dress Down Fridays is that he does not wear his suit jacket) and we all have a good laugh. Bringing the food in, I feel triumphant and jubilant walking into the infusion room, knowing I am only there because I want to be, because I chose to come in, not because I have been summoned for treatment. A woman sitting forlornly in her chair, who is clearly at the beginning of her journey because she still has hair, gives me a sad, shy smile. I offer to fix her a plate of the food I have brought in and she shakes her head no, she has no appetite, but then changes her mind and asks for one of the rolls and some of the cookies. When I bring it over to her, I tell her it will get better. I tell her I was in her chair, quite literally, only a few short weeks ago. She looks incredulous.

I also host a party at my house for all of the women who rallied around me during my journey, who strengthened and supported me in every way imaginable, with gestures small and large. In a nod to Lisa M's comment about hanging out in my infusion room, I open up my house for the entire day, inviting everyone to come for as little or as long as they'd like. I put out breakfast fare in the morning and then set up a lunch spread and women trickle in and out all day. Many bring congratulatory gifts and the pile of Italy books – books about what to eat while in Italy, where to stay, Italian phrase books, Italian dictionaries – begin to pile up on my coffee table. I guess my mantra of "First chemo, then Italy" really resonated with people.

10/25/11 Hi Fabulous Female Friends!

I am so happy to be done with chemo and I would like to celebrate with my female friends and thank you for all you did -- big and small - to get me through the last five months of Taxol and Cisplatin hell.

One of few upsides to chemo was hanging out in in my chemo room with my friends. I love meeting folks for breakfast and lunch, but really, when do we take the time to just hang out? So what I'm offering you is an opportunity to do just that. I say this knowing you many of you do not have the flexibility with your jobs and lives to take me up on that, but come stop by for whatever works for you - stay the whole time, pop in and out, up to you. Just give me a sense of what your plans are so that I can have enough food ready.

So the deal is that I will have both breakfast yummies and a lunch spread available on TUESDAY, NOVEMBER 8th. Stop by any time from 9:30 am to 2 pm, or hang out the entire time. In anticipation of the inevitable query... no, there is nothing you can bring. This is my way of thanking you all for everything you have done for me and my family.

I hope you can make it. If you can't, I hope to see you at the dessert party on the 12th (hubbies included for that one) or at some

other point in the nice lull between the end of
chemo and my surgery on December 15th.

Cheers, Katya ------

11/10/11
Katya,
*Thank you for your hospitality today. You are blessed to have such
wonderful friends, I enjoyed meeting them. You certainly have a gift
for bringing people together, even in unfortunate circumstances...or
should I say in the happiness of conquering a major life obstacle.
The positive attitude you exude is remarkable and contagious.
If there is anything you need as you enter the next phase please let
me know,*
Michale(Michale Evans , a fellow East Meck HS parent) ------

Subject: Ovarian Odyssey
Date: November 9, 2011

*I am happy to report that, after months of neglect, my kitchen is
again a! hub of activity. Last Friday, I brought lunch in for the
nurses and staff at the Blumenthal Cancer Center. It was great to see
everyone again but it was equally great to visit the infusion center
without getting pricked and prodded. Yesterday, I hosted a Chemo
Conclusion Open House for all of the local folks who supported me
in so many ways over these past five months. I served both breakfast
and lunch and encouraged everyone to stay as long as they wanted
because one of the things my chemo buddies and I liked about my
chemo days was the fact that we all got to hang out together for
hours. I mention this because I think it is one of the lessons gleaned
from my cancer. Take the time to relax and hang out ... some of us
don't need help in this regard, so if you've already mastered the
slowing down/hanging out life lesson, good for you. And this
Saturday is our annual dessert party, so I'll be happily baking up a
storm and looking forward to celebrating the end of my chemo yet
again. .*

*I have cursed Cisplatin so many times during this journey that I
thought I owed it an apology, so here it is...in rhyme, no less! I am*

240

also attaching today's Charlotte Observer column about some of my fellow patients.

Love, Katya

ODE TO CISPLATIN

So often in life, time speeds by...
The kids grow a foot in the blink of an eye;
A trip or vacation that seems far away
Is suddenly over in less than a day.
But for me, back in June, it was hard to believe
That I'd ever make it to my chemo reprieve.
Five months lay interminably ahead
And seemed destined to be spent in bed.
.I stared at the calendar in dismay –
The end of October was light years away.
I knew I'd have to struggle through it,
But I truly wondered if I could do it.
The nausea and the surgical pain
Would it ever cease and wane?
I lost my hair and my energy,
And kissed goodbye to my vanity.
Eyebrows and eyelashes disappeared,
Leaving me looking decidedly weird.
A bloated stomach, baggy clothes...
I just kept adding to my list of woes.
Mouth sores, a stomach in knots,
And oh so many, many shots
Needles aplenty were my fate,
With veins that refused to cooperate.
A digestive system all out of whack,
Queasy Pops, my newfound snack.
The list is long... I could go on...
But no need, for these ills are gone!
Cisplatin and Taxol did their thing
And now their praises I do sing!
They filled me up and made me sick,
But, in the end, they did their trick.
My final CATscan came back clean!
No sign of cancer could be seen!
Those drugs I cursed and really hated,
Whose benefits seemed overrated,
Have now earned my highest praise
For no longer am I on borrowed days.

I'm good to go, back on track,
Confident my cancer won't come back.
So hooray for those drugs that did me in,
But ultimately helped me win.
The journey, while long, was a worthwhile one
And I'm oh so glad that it is done!

I receive a few rhymes in return, including this limerick from my parents' good friend, Elliott Morrison.

There was a young lady named Katya
The cancer god said "I gotya".
"Not yet you don't and I think you won't
so go back to your hole and rot ya

---

3 women fighting cancer just like me

My own journey in treatment has many companions

Katya Lezin

Both Lauri Himmelman, 55, and Sandra Hardy, 67, were initially told not to worry.

Himmelman, a landscaper who lives just outside Boone, had suffered from cramps for months and the feeling that she was "carrying a brick around" in her lower abdomen. Her physical revealed a mass, but it was thought to be a benign tumor.

242

"I was worried it was ovarian cancer," she said, "but that was ruled out because my C-125 levels (a blood test that is used

as an indicator of cancer) were normal."

Hardy, who was born and raised in Charlotte and lives in south Charlotte, found out she had suspicious cells in her lymph nodes when she went in for a routine mammogram. "They thought I had inflammatory breast cancer," Hardy said, but a biopsy revealed, to her relief, that she did not have breast cancer.

I have just completed my sixth and final cycle of chemo- therapy for my own (ovarian) cancer. I am happy to report that my post-chemo CAT scan showed no signs of cancer. I will write another column about the next part of my journey, a double mastectomy and reconstruction surgery scheduled for mid-December.

For Himmelman and Hardy, both fellow patients of mine at the Blumenthal Cancer Center, the diagnoses they ultimately received illustrate how difficult cancer can be to spot and identify.

Himmelman's hysterectomy, intended to simply remove what they thought was a benign tumor, was supposed to take two hours but ended up taking all day.

"I knew as soon as I woke up from surgery and saw the clock that I had cancer," she said. She was right.

Sandra Hardy appreciates the support of her family, including daughter Allison Neilsen, grandson Jack Neilsen and husband Jack Hardy.

She was diagnosed with a rare form of ovarian cancer, clear cell carcinoma, and was told it was already at Stage 3.
Hardy was diagnosed with peritoneal cancer (a cancer of the abdominal lining) that had spread up to the lymph nodes in her arm.

Both the location of the cancer cells and the fact that breast cancer cells and ovarian cancer cells are very similar made it difficult to initially diagnose.

Madeilene Mangabu, 55, has her daughter, Christine, to thank for catching her cancer. She came to visit Christine and her family from the Congo (formerly

Zaire), where Mangabu worked as a seamstress in Kinshasa. She had been suffering from headaches for quite a while so Christine insisted that her mother get a full checkup in the U.S.

The checkup led to a diagnosis of breast cancer, and Mangabu is thankful because she doubts "it would have been caught in the Congo."

Her initial plans to visit for a month have been indefinitely extended while she gets treated here, at the Blumenthal Cancer Center, because, as she said, "there is no comparison between the care I'm receiving here and what I would get in the Congo."

It has been a bumpy road for all three women. Himmelman has lost 20 pounds and has twice had her treatments delayed because she was too weak to stay on schedule. She has suffered mouth sores, an infection in her toe (due to her diminished white blood cell count) and spends the five days following each treatment curled in a fetal position.

Hardy has just completed her sixth and final cycle. Her type of cancer responds well to chemo, but it often recurs, so she will be checked frequently. She cites her bone pain as the worst part of her treatment.

Mangabu, who doesn't speak English, must rely on her daughter or a translator to be understood. "But everyone is so nice and patient," she said.

And all three women have rave reviews for the support they've received from friends and family.

Himmelman's sister encouraged her to view her chemo as an elixir, rather than poison, and made her a bracelet that reads, "Lauri's elixir." Hardy, who has been married for 46 years, says her husband, Jack, has been "the best care- giver."

And Mangabu, no doubt speaking for all three women, says the care she's received at the Blumenthal Cancer Center has made her treatment as bearable as possible.

Katya Lezin is a freelance writer for South Charlotte News. Have a story idea for Katya? Email her at bowserwoof@mindspring.com.

Reprinted with permission of South Charlotte News, a Charlotte Observer publication.

I feel my strength coming back, my energy builds with each day, and I try not to think about the surgery that looms large on the horizon. I try to just enjoy being done with chemo. Every once in a while, my mind goes there, to that dark *What if it comes back?* place. I honestly don't think I could do chemo again. My body might be able to hack it physically, but the emotional hurdle would be insurmountable. I get nauseated just thinking about it. So I don't. I banish those thoughts. Surely, this napalm attack killed everything off.

My friend Cynthia Frank sets up a lunch with a friend of hers, Shraddha Mehta, who has had the DIEP surgery with Dr. Robinson. We meet at Fran's Filling Station and I grill her about the surgery itself, the recovery, and how she is faring now, almost one year out. She offers to take me back to the bathroom and show me what her breasts look like now so off we go, two women in a stall, hoping no one comes in to find us saying things like "You can touch them if you'd like" (her) and "Wow, they're really firm" (me). That afternoon, I am driving Eliza to ballet while talking to David about my day. Eliza dashes out (we are always late to her class because of how late her school lets out) but she ends up coming right back to the van moments later to get the ballet shoes she forgot. She gives me an 11-year old WTF expression as she overhears me telling David, "She not only let me see her boobs, but she let me touch them as well!"

I am not just on the receiving end of such encounters. Friends also call or email me and ask me to serve as a resource for people they know going through chemo. "Every journey is different," I tell them, but I'm happy to offer encouragement and answer any questions I can. Both Amy Marx and Anne Sinsheimer, a Pilates instructor who has been giving me free private lessons as her get-well gesture, ask me to call a friend of theirs, Sue Coben, someone I have never met but whose name I have heard bandied about over the years. We play phone tag for a while and finally connect just before her first round of chemo. She is curious how incapacitated she'll feel and the worry and fear in her voice is palpable. Her chemo is relatively minor (as much as any chemo, a poisoning of the body, can be called minor) and is only scheduled to last a couple of hours at a time. I tell her the anticipation is worse than the actual process, and that I was pretty much able to live my life on a much more invasive chemo regimen. "You've got this," I tell her. I am just over a month past my last chemo session and it feels like a lifetime ago. I am no longer defined by my cancer. I tell Sue we will both go out and celebrate when she's done with hers.

My parents get to see for themselves that I am truly better, on the road to a full recovery, when they visit for Thanksgiving. In another nod to the perks of cancer, to one of the many silver linings that the disease brings with it, is the addition of my brother Ben, and his wife, Celine, to our Thanksgiving table. My brother has not visited us in Charlotte in the 12 years we've lived here and I have only met Celine once, when David and I were in Seattle for his work. Ben has been deeply moved by my cancer, sending me loving and encouraging emails, calling, and now agreeing to come spend Thanksgiving with us. I love getting to know Celine, who is lovely, and it is a fun, festive visit.

We have Thanksgiving at Iris and Dan's house, a yearly tradition that I thought we'd have to skip this year what with the addition of four extra people to our party, but Iris insists that there is room for everyone. Sitting at the table, pleasantly full on the smorgasbord of delicious fare (both Iris and Dan are excellent cooks), I look around at my family and friends and feel truly grateful. Thanksgiving is, after all, about giving thanks, and I am so thankful to have made it through, to have such phenomenal support, and to be here, enjoying this meal.

I am thankful for my kids, who are laughing and entertaining us with stories and songs, and who seem to have emerged from the cancer hell that defined our family life for the last six months relatively unscathed. I am thankful for my husband and for the opportunity this disease afforded us to confirm the strength of our love and our marriage. I am thankful for my parents, whom I love dearly, and the respite they will now get from the stress and worry of having a child facing a major illness across the country. I know it has been particularly hard on them and I am so glad to be able to send them back to Oregon with this behind me. I am thankful to have my brother and his wife at the table, and in our lives, and I am so thankful for my sister, not with us, who has been such a rock and who will be visiting us in December. I am thankful for my friends, like Iris, busy pouring wine and serving food and being a hostess extraordinaire, who was there for me on my darkest days. I imagine my other friends at their own Thanksgiving tables and I send out a heartfelt thanks for their companionship, their humor, their ability to laugh and cry with me and simply share the journey with me, making sure I never felt that it was mine alone.

And I am thankful for Dan's deep-fried turkey, especially the crispy pieces of skin, which I look forward to all year long.

Every cancer patient should be so lucky. With my chemo buddy coordinator Lisa Z. and my point person extraordinaire Lorrina.

With Lorrina and our mothers at a brunch I hosted over Thnaksgiving weekend.

CHAPTER TWENTY-SIX

Subject: Ovarian Odyssey
Date: December 1, 2011

Happy post-Thanksgiving to you all! We had a houseful for the week, with Noah home and visits from my parents and my brother, Ben, and his wife, Celine. It was great fun to have everyone here (I'm getting quite adept at playing the cancer card) and it was especially nice to feel good during the visit. My eyesight and hearing are both still reeling from the five months of chemo, but there do not seem to be any other lasting effects from my cancer ordeal. Physical effects, that is. The other long-lasting impact from my ovarian odyssey is actually a positive. I will never again feel sheepish or naïve about my belief that there is more good in the world than bad, or that random acts of kindness abound. I have five months' worth of proof that people are incredibly generous and loving and I have to say that the outpouring of love and friendship I continue to enjoy from folks of all ages and every walk of life, near and far, truly makes the journey — with all of its pain and angst and hair loss — almost worthwhile.

And speaking of hair loss, I am happy to report that I have definitive fuzz growing. I'm eager to see what it's going to look like when it finally comes in, and it seems right that it is growing in concurrent with my recovery. I look less and less like a cancer patient every day, which is exactly how I feel. In another month or so, I suspect I will look like I chose a really short hairdo on purpose (or had a hairdresser who had a vendetta against me) and the looks of pity and/or commiseration I get whenever my bald head and I are out and about will wane and then cease altogether. There will soon be no outward signs that I had cancer, which makes me realize that I probably encounter people every day who suffered a similar fate and have now moved on with their lives. And, of course, I think about those folks who were not as lucky as I have been and who are no longer here to tell their cancer stories. I am so very grateful that I get to be one of the ones who is on the other side of this.

I have enjoyed my respite from needles and hospital visits, but I am gearing up again for the next phase of my journey. Next week I have a slew of appointments to prepare me for my surgery on December 15th. It is a! 12-14 hour surgery because I am having the double mastectomy and reconstruction, using the fat from my stomach, done simultaneously. (Actually, concurrently is probably a more apt way of describing the surgery – simultaneously would not be very pretty!). It is a very involved and difficult surgery, but it has the advantage of being done in one day and – as I'm sure most women reading this have already figured out – I basically get a tummy tuck out of the deal. You have to find your silver linings where you can and that is definitely one of them, so I'm psyched I get some surgical assistance getting rid of my chemo gut! Recovery, I am told, is painful in that the reconstruction part of the surgery involves my being dissected from one hip to the other and a 4-inch swath of skin will be removed (in addition to my fat) so it will be difficult to straighten up at first as the remaining skin stretches and readjusts itself. I am hoping to stick to our holiday travel plans but I will just have to wait and see how I fare in the days following the surgery. I will be in the hospital for at least three days and I will try to send out an update as soon as I am able to do so.

I am attaching a photo of me and the girls in the JCC play we are in, A Year with Frog and Toad, which opens tonight. If you are local, come see us! If you're unable to see the show, know that yet another perk of cancer is that it provides a perfect bald head for mouse ears to sit atop!

Cheers, Katya

I visit with all of my doctors – I now have three overseeing my care (Dr. Naumann, my gynecological oncologist; Dr. Flippo, my breast oncologist; and Dr. Robinson, my plastic surgeon) and all three agree that I am able to handle the brutal surgery that is now just around the corner. I would not have scheduled it so soon after completing my chemo, since my poor body is still trying to rebound from all that trauma, but it will require no copay on my part if I squeeze it in to this calendar year since I have already met my catastrophic cap of $5000. (That was surprisingly and alarmingly easy to meet, since my copay for each day of chemo was over $1500.) Many people voice concern over the timing of my surgery, including my parents, who tell me I should remove the money from the equation when evaluating my options. I appreciate the sentiment, and the generosity behind it, but I can't do that. I decide to meet with all three doctors to ensure that I am not putting my health at risk. If there are any reasons to delay it, I will not proceed, even if it means having to shell out another $5000. I am relieved to get the blessing of all three.

And now that the surgery looms right around the corner, I am glad to be having it so soon. I want to enjoy the winter holidays with it behind me. I want to start the New Year afresh, with nothing but recovery and regaining my strength on the calendar. I am surprisingly okay with losing my breasts. They have always been a big part of my identity because they are large, which turns out to be both a positive (good cleavage, easy breastfeeding) and a negative (underwire bras; smushing them into sports bras) and I feel particularly indebted to them because they were the source of sustenance for all three of my babies. I have distinct memories of bonding with each child, in the dark of the night, listening to that rhythmic and endearing suckling. I take a bath and they float on the surface of the water and I wait for the tears to flow, but I am, instead, philosophical and dry-eyed. "You have served me well," I tell them, "but now it seems likely you will try to kill me, so buh-bye."

On the Saturday before my surgery, I meet Marni, Laura, Gabi, Lorrina, Iris, Amy, Lisa Z. and Lisa M. at Café Monte for brunch. We laugh about some of the funnier moments of my cancer journey and everyone compares notes and tells Katya chemo stories, most involving my Ativan-induced loopiness. Lisa Z. recounts how I was totally out of it, barely able to make it to the bathroom unassisted, the Benadryl kicking in and knocking me out. But when I am shuffling back to my room, I encounter Madeline Mangabou, and suddenly I'm speaking rapid and animated French. Lisa and my nurse just look at each other, in bewilderment, while I shuffle back to bed and promptly conk out. Lorrina shares how she finagled getting an Ativan shift, since she was usually the one bringing me in or bringing me home, because she wanted to see my legendary loopiness for herself, and how disappointed she was that for her I just snoozed. Until I woke up abruptly, looked at her with dead seriousness, and implored her not to drive to Kentucky by herself. "It's just too dangerous," I said, and Lorrina, who had no plans to drive to Kentucky, agreed. Iris tells everyone how I was the queen of the infusion room and knew everybody by name. "Man, they are going to miss having Katya coming in, that's for sure," Iris says. We laugh about the text mischief I enjoyed with Laura and Jen's pointed questions for my medical team and her exasperation with my boundary stretching. We reminisce about Gabi's picnic lunches and the day Marni handed me the plush robe and blanket they'd all bought me at the start of my journey and how very long ago that now seems.

Next on the agenda is a pedicure next door at a salon that can accommodate all of us, all in a row. First, however, I head to the bathroom. Washing my hands, I look in the mirror and notice with alarm that my face appears to be covered in something. I look closely, not sure if the mirror is playing tricks on me, but no, a feel of my face confirms it is true, I seem to somehow be covered in tiny little *hairs!* What the hell? From my ears, down my cheeks and across my chin, I am covered in a light layer of fuzz. It seems to have cropped up over- night or, more accurately, over the course of my brunch!

I head back to the table, thoroughly freaked out, and Iris explains that facial hair growth is a common menopausal side effect. The chemo that made me bald also kept my facial hair from growing, but now that I'm getting fuzz atop my head, it appears the coast is clear for hair growth everywhere. *Seriously?* Iris tries to find a bright side, telling me that I should be glad my hair appears to be blonde. She says it is much worse for dark-haired women because it is much more visible. I try to find comfort in the fact that, if I'm going to have a beard, at least mine is a blonde beard.

Marni and Gabi decide that the pedicure is not enough pamp- ering, so they arrange to meet me on Tuesday, the day before my surgery, for a massage. I have never had one and I tell the woman that I doubt I will need or be able to last for the full hour they have paid for because that is just too long for me to be still. Wrong. The only massaging I've ever had is when David treats me to some, but there's usually a payback involved. This is an entirely different experience and I am able to just totally relax and escape. For all of you out there struggling to find the perfect gift for a loved one facing surgery, let me assure you a massage fits the bill. I am as limber and relaxed as a woman facing a 14-hour surgery to lop off both of her breasts could possibly be.

CHAPTER TWENTY-SEVEN

My datebook's square for December 15th is chock-full of scribbles. There's Hannah's chamber choir winter concert, one she promises me would be much more to my liking than the fall one, with upbeat, holiday songs. Lorrina will be going in my stead, taking Eliza as well. It's also the day Noah finds out if he was accepted early to Harvard, his college of choice. I hate that I will be the last to know, because I will be unconscious when he gets the email. And it is the day I go under the knife.

I have to be at the hospital at 5:30 in the morning, even though there is minimal pre-op because I did that on a separate day. The early start time is because the surgery, really two separate surgeries done by two separate teams, will last the entire day. When we arrive, we check in and then I am whisked back to the holding cell (I know that's lawyer speak rather than doctor speak, but that's what it feels like to me) to await my docs. There will be three operating on me plus an anesthesiologist overseeing my sedation. I talk with him first, letting him know my nausea issues and what a hard time I had bouncing back from my hysterectomy. He decides to give me a prophylactic anti-nausea patch in addition to the meds that are already in the queue for my veins.

First up for the surgeons is Dr. Flippo, who will cut off both of my breasts. Her part of the surgery is slated to last several hours. She will then hand me off to Dr. Robinson and one of his partners, who will slice open my abdomen from hip to hip (it will literally look like I have been sliced in half) and remove the fat they will use to make my new breasts. About four inches of my stomach will be removed, including my belly button, and the remaining layer beneath my breasts will be stretched down and sewn to my abdomen. My belly button will then be added back to my new stomach. Four drains are inserted, one at each hip and one in each armpit, that will help drain my surgical sites of the fluids that accumulate after so much trauma to the body.

I will awaken in a special recovery room reserved for patients of this surgery because special nurses are needed to keep an eye on me and the room is kept at an unseasonably warm temperature to facilitate blood flow. The first 24 hours are critical. If the new breasts are going to fail, they will most likely do so overnight. I will then be moved to a regular room in the morning, where I will stay for at least three or four days before heading home.

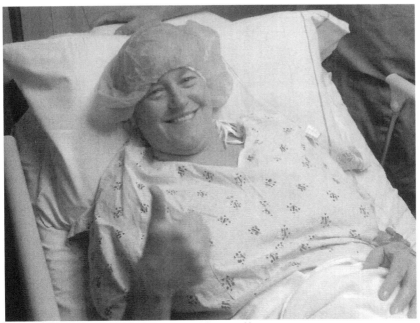

A groggy thumbs up before heading off to surgery.

When I groggily open my eyes, it is dark out. I have missed breakfast, lunch and dinner. Not that I have any kind of appetite at all, but it is a good marker of how much time has elapsed. There is no way, but for surgery, that I am missing three meals in a row! Dr. Robinson, his kind face grinning at me, disconnected from the rest of his body, just hanging in the air above my bed, smiling, tells me everything went well and that I'm doing great. I am in pain but it is not acute. Thank you, morphine. I am very out of it but I do manage to ask David one question that keeps nagging me as I drift in and out of consciousness.

"Did Noah get in to Harvard?" "No," David says, "he was deferred." "How's he doing?" I ask, worried that he'll be crestfallen.

"He's fine. He's taking it really well," David assures me.

And then I pass back out. The next day I am wheeled to my new room. I am now awake and alert enough to register the symphony of protests that my body is sounding. Every square inch of me seems to be demanding *What the hell happened here?*

I feel as if I have been brutally attacked by a bear, and I am sure I look the part as well. I am covered in angry, red scars and the black threads of my dissolving stitches stick out in unsightly zigzags all over. I look down at my breasts and am surprised to see them looking as large as before, since I had asked to have my new ones made significantly smaller. I later learn that they are disproportionately swollen and they will calm down once the trauma of the surgery wears off.

My stomach is the flattest I have ever seen it. Even more disconcerting is my missing appendix scar. The unsightly six-inch scar that has been a familiar feature on my abdomen ever since my 1977 emergency appendectomy in Islamabad, Pakistan is suddenly gone. It has been replaced with a scar that runs the entire width of my gut, just above my pelvis, and is straight across rather than diagonal. I look to see if my appendectomy scar is now adorning my left breast, as Dr. Robinson had warned me it might (because that is the patch of skin used to create the new breast) but I cannot see it. What I do see are the drains and they freak me out. It is one thing to be cut open and sewn back up again, but to have these tubes coming out of your body, to watch fluid from your own body accumulate in the plastic, balloon-like bubbles at the end of each tube, is quite another. They also hurt.

Every time I move or inadvertently stretch one too far or snag them on something, the stitches holding them in pull and tear. The nurses measure the liquid that is collected and mark it on a chart, then rinse the plastic balloons and replace them. David and I will have to do this on our own when we get home. In my present state, heavily sedated, in pain and pretty much unable to move, this seems like an impossible task.

David brings the kids in for a visit on Day Two, and I am happy to see them and know that we can now move forward as a family. I am chatting with them, discussing Hannah's concert, Noah's exams, Eliza's Chanukah and Christmas wish list, when I can feel the familiar wave of pain coming on. No problem. Without breaking stride in the conversation, I reach for my morphine pump, my savior from the pain that accompanies getting hundreds of stitches, both internal and external. My hand pats the sheet around me, in increasing desperation, as I search for the pump. I need the pump. Where is the pump?

"What do you need, hon?" David asks.

"I'm looking for the pump," I explain, imploring him to please help me find it.

David looks at me with pity. "Oh hon, you don't have it anymore. The nurse took it away this morning. Don't you remember her explaining that to you?"

No, I don't remember because I was on a morphine high at the time. No pump? I am in a small panic. How will I manage my pain? My "it's all good" façade crumbles and I tell David to take the kids home. I know I am quickly going to that place I don't want them to see.

Subject: Ovarian Odyssey
Date: December 20, 2011

I am happy to report that my new boobs and I are home from the hospital. The surgery was every bit as complex and brutal as was described to us, (with us being me and David, not me and my boobs) and we are glad to have it behind us.

Unfortunately, the recovery is equally brutal. I look like I was in! a battle with a big bear or Mack truck ... and that I lost the battle handily. A scar stretches from one hip to the other, my belly button is in a new place, and my significantly smaller breasts are covered in stitches and bruises. Adding to my post-surgery beauty are the four drains that hang from my breasts and abdomen that collect the liquid that now fills the new vacancies in my body. David and I are looking at the joint ritual of squeezing and emptying them as yet another opportunity for marital bonding. And I am still slowly emerging from 12 hours of sedation coupled with more drugs than should! ever be pumped into a body. When my vein again collapsed and a pool of morphine swelled in my wrist, making it seem like it was on fire, and the nurses commented, "That's just bizarre. We've never seen that before," I was so over it. My veins were speaking for the rest of my body parts, and the message was a loud and clear: "Leave us alone!" Enough poking and prodding for one year, thank you very much. Enough needles and catheters and pain pills and... well, you get the picture.

I will not lie. This is not easy. And there were times, lying there in my hospital bed, feeling immense pain every time I so much as shifted the pillow or moved my body, that I was consumed with frustration and sadness. It is hard to be so incapacitated at this time of year, when I want to be enjoying the fact that Noah is home and that my sister and brother-in-law are visiting. I relish all of the holiday activities that make this time of year so festive and it is really hard to sit on the sidelines. The six weeks of restricted strenuous activity will also be really challenging for me ... I will feel definite withdrawal from the pool and tennis courts and working up a good sweat on the elliptical machine. But I never want to hurt like this again, and I want all of this pain to have been worthwhile, so I will be a good patient and follow doctors' orders. Thank goodness Scrabble-playing is not prohibited! We meet with my doctors on the 21st for follow- up visits and, pending their approval, plan to head out shortly thereafter for family visits and Scrabble tournaments on the East Coast. Here's hoping the Scrabble Gods again recognize who is due for some blanks and bingos!

The kids seem quite relieved to have the surgery behind me! (Eliza actually offered me her lifesavings of $43.77 if I would cancel it) and we are all looking forward! to marching into 2012 healthy and cancer-free. It is often overwhelming to me to ponder how much! has happened in the past six months. It is not a journey I would choose to take, but given that I had no choice, I have to say it is one that was filled with more good than bad, more highpoints than low ones. The physical traumas and hardships were awful, but the emotional highs were magnificent, and I truly cherish them. Being treated to daily kindnesses from my warm, loving, supportive and funny family, friends and neighbors is what undoubtedly got me through the toughest times. I emerge from this whole experience feeling more grateful than unlucky, and more appreciative of all of the good things in my life that I can now continue to enjoy.

I wish you all the happiest of holidays and I sincerely thank you for everything you have done – big and small — to make this ovarian odyssey such a shared journey. We always felt we were doing this with the support and love of so many and all those calls, emails, cards, meals, gifts and caring words helped immensely. We knew we were not doing this alone.

Love, Katya
(aka, the woman whose 1977 Pakistani appendectomy scar now
adorns her left breast!)

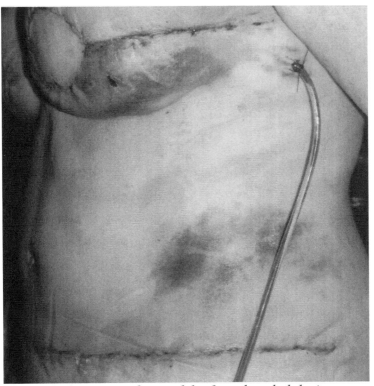

My scars, bruises and one of the four dreaded drains.

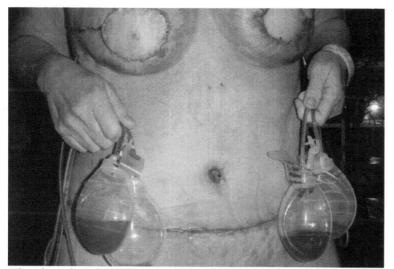

The dreaded drains, my constant companions.

Heading home after my double mastectomy.

Many of the folks on my Ovarian Odyssey distribution list also get our annual holiday letter, but there are some folks who will be hearing about my cancer for the first time. Our dog, Darcy, writes the letter, but I help him mull over the past year, and it feels good to reflect on things other than cancer, to have family highlights to share that are not dominated by diagnoses and disease. The holiday photo we include with each letter was taken at Thanksgiving, when I was still totally bald, so I'm sure it is a jarring shot for anyone who has not yet heard my news.

December 2011

Dear friends and family (furry and not),

The human members of the family have been a bit preoccupied lately so it once again falls to me to write our annual holiday letter. My first draft was short and sweet, reporting on the number of rawhides I have managed to stash under the couch this year and the fact that I have secured a permanent spot on the master bed each night, but the humans protested that you want to hear about them too. Sheesh. So here you go...

Katya and David celebrated their twentieth wedding anniversary in August and are looking forward to a trip to Italy this spring or summer. The trip will commemorate not only their wedded bliss (okay, bliss may be overstating it on some days, but they do seem to have a pretty good thing going) but also Katya's completion of chemotherapy and surgery. She was diagnosed with ovarian cancer last May and endured five months of intensive chemo plus two major surgeries. There were obvious downsides (the loss of her hair and assorted organs and body parts, thanks to a hysterectomy and double mastectomy) but there were many upsides as well, such as the phenomenal outpouring of love and support from friends and family, the all-purpose and ongoing "chemo brain" excuse, and the many perks that come with playing the cancer card. Nonetheless, both Katya and David are very happy to start the New Year with the Big C behind them.

Noah is finishing up his senior year at the North Carolina School of Science and Math, where he is taking courses for which the syllabi read like ancient Greek texts to his parents. He has continued to enjoy his extra-curricular pursuits as well, such as heading up the Young Democrats and the Space Settlement Club and acting in the school's theatrical productions – all things he duly noted on his college applications. He enjoyed his 1-95 college tour this summer and is now focused on finding scholarships for red-haired Scrabble players.

Speaking of redheads (pretty smooth transition for a dog, eh?), Hannah is as busy as ever. She continues to enjoy musical theatre and also sings in her school's chamber choir and the Teen Vocal

Ensemble at the Temple. She is still running cross-country and track and won her team's most improved runner award again this year, but could easily have walked away with the "biggest pre- and post-race whiner" award as well. David helps out with the team whenever he can, no doubt so that he can brag about the 5:32 mile he ran at the Emory Alumnae race last spring.

Eliza shares her sister's musical talents (having heard Katya singing in the shower, I can assure you none of her genes are at work) and sings in her school's choir and glee club. She has also taken up dance (ballet and modern) and is joining forces with Noah and Hannah again to compete on a 3-person Odyssey of the Mind team. She is also vying for top honors in the messy room department, but the competition is stiff, with Noah and Hannah equally deserving of a gold medal.

As I write this, the human members of the family are about to desert us (the canine members) for a trip up the East Coast, where four of them will be playing in Scrabble tournaments and one of them will be shaking his head and wondering how his wife managed to warp all three kids into becoming as obsessed as she is with that silly game. Molly and I will hold down the fort (translation: I will sit on the forbidden couch to my heart's delight while Molly will bark ferociously at every squirrel that dares cross our yard) and await their return in January.

We know Fuzzhead (our new nickname for Katya, formerly Baldy) and the rest of the crew join us in sending you best wishes for a wonderful holiday season and year.

Love, Darcy

Our holiday photo 2011 – touching my bald head for good luck!

CHAPTER TWENTY-EIGHT

I hate these fucking drains. They pull and pinch and are just gross. David and I get to experience yet another marital bonding opportunity with our new drain ritual. You have to start at the incision site, squeezing any bodily fluid and blood that has accumulated in the tubing, pushing it through until you reach the plastic balloon receptacle. You then squeeze the contents into a measuring cup, measure the amount, record it, dump it out, and start all over again a few hours later. I am reminded of the old Dunkin Donuts commercial, when the bleary- eyed doughnut baker wearily says, "Time to make the doughnuts" over and over again. I feel like those first few days at home are a constant refrain of David saying, "Time to do your drains."

Nicole and Rusty visit but I spend most of the time ensconced on the couch, waving as various family members come and go. When I walk, it is bent over because it feels as if I will break if I stand upright. I was warned about this phenomenon, the stretching of the skin that needs time to adjust and recalibrate. I knew it was coming, but the reality of it is something else entirely. It is hard to imagine ever being able to stand up straight.

On my second day home, I learn from David that Sue Coben, the woman with breast cancer whom I counseled prior to her first round of chemo, has died. *Wait, what?* She died two days after my surgery. Her chemo was on the Monday of that week, and it went well. On Friday, she went out for lunch with friends, then felt sick to her stomach. By the time she got to the hospital, the infection she had suddenly developed had gone septic. She died in the hospital, a few floors below where I was recuperating, on Saturday morning. *But I just talked to her,* I tell David. I am just devastated. Her kids, a son and two daughters, are roughly the same ages as mine. I can't imagine. And both David and I are so humbled by how lucky we are. My chemo was so much worse, both in its intensity and its duration, I have just emerged from a major surgery, my third in the past six months. And yet here I am and Sue is dead.

The following day we go in to the hospital for my post-op appointments and I am delighted to learn that three of my four drains can come out. There is still a significant amount of fluid in the fourth drain, the one on my right abdomen, to warrant leaving it in for a bit longer. But it is the boob drains that wreak havoc with any wardrobe choices I make, so I am stoked to get rid of them.

The nurse clips the stitches holding them in and then proceeds to pull them out. Whoa! I imagined that there were maybe a couple of inches of the tubing inside my body, but the length of the internal drains is astoundingly long. David and I both watch, mouths agape, as the never-ending tubes are pulled out, inch by inch, from my body. I am starring in my very own sci-fi movie, except the special effects don't only *look* real, they *are* real. Each drain is several feet long and I watch in bewilderment as it snakes its way through my body, something I can both see and feel. It is a totally bizarre experience and I once again announce that this would be totally fascinating if it were happening to someone other than me.

I get the thumbs up from both docs that I can leave for our holiday road trip, our annual Albany New Year's Scrabble pilgrimage that looked in serious danger of needing to be cancelled this year. We do make accommodations, however, and decide to only play in the Early Bird since the New Year's tournament would require the kids to miss two days of school. I am advised to stop frequently on the long car ride and get my blood circulating and to not overdo it (word has gotten around) but I am otherwise given permission to go. I will have to travel with my remaining drain, which is a colossal pain in the butt (or side, as the case may be), but no so much so that it justifies staying home. There are the usual post-surgery restrictions – no bathing, no lifting, no strenuous exercise – but I am told that all looks good and to enjoy my trip.

On Christmas Eve day, I am starting to move around a bit more and I decide that it is time to get back in the kitchen. I want to make Christmas Eve dinner. Everyone has been so kind but it is time for me to cook for my family. I plan the menu and David and I head out to get the groceries. It feels so cathartic to be doing this errand, to be out in the bright, chilly day and to be out and about in society. I am also enjoying the fact that public outings do not seem to require a bra. The swelling in my breasts has greatly subsided, but they are still solid and firm. They do not move. When I put shirts on, they stay put, like well behaved dogs that heel on command. I decide that this is a very nice perk, no pun intended, for all the hell I've been through.

I am very good about delegating the lifting of pots and

anything that might possibly violate my post-surgery restrictions.

The menu includes spaetzle, a Swiss dumpling-like side dish that is a family favorite. I make the dough and then knead it into a spaetlze grater (looks like a cheese grater, but with a container for the dough) over a pot of boiling water. When I am done, I feel sore and I worry that I have overdone it. I use that as my excuse not to do the dishes, and instead go lie on the couch while the rest of my family puts the kitchen back in order.

On Christmas Day, we head over to our friends Mara and Tony's house for a brunch. While there, I show Marc Lewin my red and swollen boobs. He says the kneading probably irritated them but that he does not see a need to call it in unless it gets worse. I have no problem lifting my shirt for him, or for anyone else who wants to see Dr. Robinson's creations. I view it as akin to lifting a shirtsleeve to show off an impressive scar on one's forearm. I do not feel any sense of sexuality or privacy about my new breasts. They are, after all, more stomach than breasts. I am in awe of what the doctors were able to do, how they represent the latest developments in medical science, and I'm also just blown away by the stitches and scars, the way a 3rd grader would want to show off a really impressive skinned knee.

When we get home, I go rest while David tries to get the house in order before we leave on our trip. He opens up the kitchen drawer that is stocked with sharp knives and Cuisinart blades and slices open his finger. Marc Lewin does his second Christmas Day consult for the Lezin Lieberman family and tells David stiches are in order and he should head to the ER. We have plans to go out for the traditional Jewish Christmas Day feast of Chinese food with Lorrina and her family, so I call and propose the new plan. David and I drop Eliza off to her, we will then head to the ER at CMC-Pineville with Noah and Hannah and we will all meet at the restaurant as planned.

Of course that's not how it goes down. David spends over 5 hours in the ER, and when he is finally seen, too much time has elapsed to close the wound with stitches and surgical glue is used instead. Something Marc could have done earlier in the day. Arghhh. David insists that we still salvage our dinner without him, so Lorrina picks us up at the hospital and we go out to eat and then head home, where David returns close to 11 pm. While I am waiting for David back at the house, I start thinking that I should have hung out in the

ER with him and had someone check out my breasts. They are now twice as big as they were before, which is concerning because the swelling is supposed to be going down, not up. They also really hurt.

I call the service for Dr. Robinson's group and I'm told that Dr. Fisher, who is on call, will call me first thing in the morning to arrange my coming in to see him. We both get up at 5:00 am, both of us unable to sleep, and walk the dogs. At around 8:00 am, we head up- town, thinking we'll at least be closer to the hospital when we get the call. We wait until 10:00 am. The call never comes. I call the service back and am told very snippily that the doctor will call me and that I should be patient. I explain that I was told he'd call first thing in the morning and that 10:00 am is not first thing by anyone's standards. I finally get through to a supervisor who pages the doctor and off I go to the emergency room, where he meets me.

Dr. Fisher confirms that my breasts are swollen and angry, a surefire sign of overdoing it. He queries me about what I've done and when I explain how good I was about following every prohibition on the *Do not* list, he tells me that it was surely the kneading, the repetitive back and forth motion, that caused the flare up.

"But nowhere on there does it say *no kneading,*" I say in my defense.

"That's not exactly something we feel a need to point out to our patients," he says, no doubt glad I'm not *his* patient. "We don't have a lot of folks emerging from this kind of major surgery wanting to knead something,"

He tells me the swelling should go down and still gives us a green light to go on our trip, but says that under no circumstances am I to lift anything or do anything at all strenuous. I promise to be good. David pipes up, "Really good, Katya. Not *Katya* good."

Dr. Fisher does notice that there is a spot on my right breast scar that appears to be agitated. He orders a sulfa cream for it and says that the emergency room nurse, who is very nice and supplies us with all sorts of bandages and surgical tape, will explain how to apply it. The nurse goes so far as to put the first dose on for me, slathering it liberally across the scars on my entire right breast, not just the small, agitated area. He then does so on the left breast too, saying it will help those scars heal faster as well. He tells us to apply a new layer of cream several times each day.

We head off and I dutifully apply the cream. We stop at Juli and Willy's house in Virginia Beach for the night, and Willy makes me the ribs and crab leg dinner I have missed so much since they moved away and that he promised me as a prize for getting through chemo. I apply the cream and the bandages. No discernible improvement, but these things take time. We stop at Norman and Susanne's house in Maryland. I show Susanne my breasts and I notice that they are somewhat blotchy. We arrive in Albany and I continue to apply the sulfa, but it is stinging now and I have developed small blisters across and under my breasts. I continue applying the cream but it is increasingly painful to do so and the blisters have now turned into what appears to be hives.

"This," I think, and David concurs, "is not right."

I call my docs back in Charlotte and Sandra, Dr. Robinson's nurse, tells me to stop using the cream immediately.

When we stop back in Maryland on our way home, Norman and Susanne (retired doctor and former nurse, respectively) look at my breasts and say I am having an acute allergic reaction to the sulfa cream. They give me Benadryl. I feel as miserable as I look.

"Why didn't you stop using the cream right away?" Susanne asks. "It's clear you were having an allergic reaction."

David and I just sigh. Nothing is clear. My entire body is a freak show. The swelling, the blisters, the scars – they change every day and nothing ever looks right. I am really frustrated because my emergency room visit actually made things much worse, not better.

David and I go out for New Year's Eve dinner, just the two of us, a night I had imbued with all sorts of significance. This would be our opportunity to toast the New Year, a clean start, all medical woes well behind us. Instead, I struggle to sit upright and keep my eyes open, the Benadryl doing its thing. I am sore, tired and woozy. I ask David to take me home.

Happy New Year.

Our Maryland visit ends on a high note with an open house Susanne hosts so that we can visit with as many people as possible in the short time we are there. It is yet another reminder of how lucky we are to be surrounded by so much love and support. I spend the afternoon on the couch, regaling folks with some of the lighter moments of my cancer journey, and I am, in turn, congratulated for getting through it all. My friends Cathy Bledsoe and Jean Sedlacko from law school sit with David's high school buddies Mike Carlson and Blake Fetrow and Norman and Susanne's Havarah (a Jewish friends club) and other long- time neighbors and friends and everyone toasts my recovery.

Happy New Year, it is.

CHAPTER TWENTY-NINE

Wednesday, Jan. 11, 2012

My doctor is a leader fighting ovarian cancer
Katya Lezin

He battles on despite drug shortages, not enough research funding.

COURTESY OF R. WENDELL NAUMANN

Dr. R. Wendell Naumann is excited about the many advances that have been made in the field of gynecological oncology.

For information about the Gynecologic Oncology Group or o learn how best to advocate for drug reform, visit www.gog.org.

Editor's note: This is another installment in Correspondent Katya Lezin's "Cancer journey," in which she chronicles her battle with ovarian cancer.

When I first met Dr. R. Wendell Naumann, 49, the gynecological oncologist to whom I was referred once I was diagnosed with ovarian cancer, he explained to me that he would be the doctor seeing me through my entire cancer ordeal.

He would perform the surgery - in my case, a laparoscopic hysterectomy - and oversee the chemotherapy and treatment that followed. It turns out that patient-centric approach is unique to gynecological oncology and is one of the things that drew Naumann to the field.

"Rather than handing the patient from doctor to doctor, the physicians center themselves around the patient and the care the patient receives is much less fragmented," Naumann said.

Naumann touts this centralized approach with leading to many of the advances that recently have been made with ovarian cancer.

The improvements in chemotherapy, especially the development of IP (intraperitoneal) chemo, in which a port is inserted in the abdomen so that the chemo drugs can be concentrated where the cancer is located, and the ability to do laparoscopic surgery have led to advances in both the length of time before the cancer comes back and the overall survival rate for ovarian cancer.

"People think of oncology as a depressing field," Naumann said. "But the vast majority of my patients do well and I cure them."

Naumann initially went to medical school, at the University of Alabama Birmingham, with hopes of becoming a cardiothoracic surgeon, but he switched to gynecological oncology because "the divorce rate in the surgery department was over 100 percent."

He met his wife, Jan Naumann, an OBGYN in Charlotte, while both were residents and they married in 1991. Naumann switched to oncology at an exciting time in the field, when both the medical profession and the country had declared war on cancer, leading to both increased funding and the discovery of new chemotherapy drugs. The advances in his field have been exhilarating both medically and personally.

"The side effects from the chemo drugs we used to administer were so horrific that patients couldn't finish the chemo regimen," Naumann said.

Great strides have been made in minimizing the side effects and finding more palatable drugs that are equally effective in killing the cancer cells, both of which I can personally vouch. I was able to pretty much live my life while undergoing the five months of chemo that my treatment entailed.

But Naumann, who says "it is very rewarding to see patients do well," notes that the survival rate for ovarian cancer is still significantly lower than other cancers because it is often detected late.

"By the time symptoms appear, it is often Stage 3 or 4." This low survival rate means that the numbers of survivors – who can advocate for more research and attention - are politically small in number.

Naumann finds the short shrift ovarian cancer receives - both in research dollars and in political clout - extremely frustrating.

"Research cures cancer," Naumann said. "Clinical trials are needed to develop new drugs, but the funding of ovarian cancer is significantly less than that of other cancers."

Another frustration of Naumann's, and one he hopes people will educate themselves about and advocate for legislative intervention, is the recent shortage of drugs used to combat the recurrence of ovarian cancer.

"There are drugs that significantly change the cure rate for cancer, "and our system does not ensure that there is an effective supply of them," Naumann said.

Naumann recently explained how dire the drug shortage situation is on CNN's "Sanjay Gupta MD."

Naumann does not blame the drug companies, for whom the profit margin on producing some of these drugs is extremely small, but he believes there should be a legislative requirement that "these drugs be stockpiled and that the companies who make them guarantee a supply of them."

In addition to deriving tremendous satisfaction from seeing his patients do well, Naumann also enjoys teaching and conducting research as part of the Gynecologic Oncology Group, a cooperative group of gynecological oncologists.

He is always engaged in research and has become an expert in his field.

"I'm the person they call when they don't know what to do," Naumann said. "And that challenges me to be my best."

Katya Lezin is a freelance writer for South Charlotte News. Do you have a story idea for Katya? Email her at bowserwoof@mindspring.com.

Reprinted with permission of South Charlotte News, a Charlotte Observer publication.

I have so much time on my hands, I don't know what to do with myself. Gone is the time suck of daily trips across town to the Blumenthal Cancer Center. My post-op appointments, both for my surgeries and for my cancer, are sporadic. Weeks can go by without my needing to set foot in a medical office of any kind. I am a free woman.

At a birthday party for our friend (who also happens to be our pediatrician) Matt Samarel, I am seated next to Phil Solomon, my friend and OB/GYN who is the one who found my cancer. He tells me again what a hard call that was for him to make. We are talking about how fortuitous it was that I went to see him. I tell him that I'm going to be much better about going in to see him regularly from now on.

"Umm," Phil says, smiling at me sheepishly. "You're not really my patient anymore. "

I look at him quizzically. "You've got nothing for me," he says. His comment comes on the heels of an email Iris sends me about my facial hair, which she ends by reassuring me that I'm still very much a woman. It is one of those reassurances that is meant well, but ends up being more disconcerting that reassuring because I did not think my femininity was in question until she felt a need to reassure me on that front.

"Great," I say to David. "I'm bald, I have no breasts, I'm growing a beard, Iris feels a need to tell me I'm still a woman, and I no longer have an OB/GYN because I have no female parts left. "

"At least your hair's starting to grow back," David says.

Sometimes David does *not* know the right thing to say. I can feel my body bouncing back (except for my boobs, which do no bouncing of any kind. Still no bra necessary – whoohoo!) and my scars are healing nicely. There is one stubborn scab on my left breast that is slow to heal, but I am sure it is simply a question of time. The fuzz on my head is like a buzz cut, only the hair is unbelievably soft, like a baby's. I know I have reached a milestone when there is enough to warrant shampoo, and David has hinted that a brush might be in order as well.

Hannah's spring concert is scheduled for the end of February, and she has been practicing for hours each day. There is complicated choreography to accompany the singing and she shows me little snippets at the bus stop each morning.

I volunteer to staff the ticket table for the Thursday night performance and I buy tickets for us to see the Friday night performance. Ivy Zerkle expresses interest in seeing the show as well, so I arrange to bring her with us on Friday night, February 24th.

When I am selling tickets, I am tempted to peek in. The bright costumes, the audience applause and the short bursts of singing I hear when the auditorium doors open momentarily to let in a latecomer have me excited to see the show. Ms. Heinen, the choral director, comes out to tell me and the other volunteer that we can come in and see the show for free when we are done selling tickets. I demur, choosing instead to get work done while waiting for it to be over so that I can give Hannah a ride home. I'd rather see the show the whole way through, sitting properly in my paid seat.

On Friday, I feel sluggish. I walk the dogs around the Grimmersborough loop and I am out of breath going up the hill. *Man, I am out of shape* I think to myself, frustrated that I am once again presented with evidence of the new normal I have to accept post-cancer. When Eliza comes home from school, she is full of plans for celebrating her birthday on Sunday. We will be having a bunch of girls over to bake and hang out.

When I am changing clothes, Eliza notices that there is a new and decidedly pink spot on my left breast.

"Does it hurt?" she asks. Nope. Not a bit. But I don't feel great.

Eliza and I pick up Ivy and we meet David at a sandwich shop near Hannah's school to scarf down a quick dinner before the concert. I don't have much appetite and I tell David that I don't feel good. He feels my forehead and tells me I don't have a temperature. We get to the concert early, as instructed by Hannah to get good seats, and I am finding the hard, wooden auditorium chairs really uncomfortable. I really just need to lay my head down. I tell David that I am going to go lie in the van until the concert starts. He looks surprised.

"You really feel that bad?" he asks.

I do.

When I get to the van, I check on the pink spot. It is larger and looks like it is turning from pink to red. I call David, hoping to catch him before he turns his cell phone off, and I tell him that I will not be going to the concert. I'm going to drive myself home and go to bed.

David knows how much I've been looking forward to this concert, especially since I missed the last one. He also knows I am usually someone who plows through, who thinks the headache will go away, the pain will subside.

"You really feel that bad?" he asks again.

I do.

We agree that I should first call the doctor on call, just in case the spot on my breast is anything to worry about. Sue Coben's rapid decline is fresh in our minds.

When I reach Dr. Getz, he tells me he is going to call in an antibiotic for me. He asks me for the number for the pharmacy. I don't have it and ask him if he wants me to put him on speaker while I look it up on my iPhone. No, he says, I'll call you back in a few minutes.

I wait. I wait some more. Ten minutes go by. Fifteen. I am annoyed, because he could have looked up the number just as easily. I call the Harris Teeter pharmacy at the Arboretum Shopping Center near our house to see if maybe he called it in without calling me back, but they have not heard from him. They confirm that they will be open until 9 pm, so I decide to start driving over there so that I'll be closer to home when he calls, and I can just pop in, pick up my pills, pop them, and go to bed.

I get to the Arboretum and I wait in the parking lot for Dr. Getz to call. I am going downhill fast. When he finally calls, he asks me how I'm doing and I say I feel awful, worse than when we first spoke. (A *full half hour ago!* I want to yell.)

He asks me to look at my breast and tell him if it looks the same. Oh my God. It is much worse. In the time it took for me to drive across town, the pink spot has turned red and is now covering my entire breast. I tell Dr. Getz and he changes his mind about the antibiotics.

"You know what?" he says. "We're just going to have you head straight to the emergency room."

I agree that's the most prudent course. I am annoyed, though, because I was much closer to the hospital when I called the first time, from the East Meck High School parking lot. Now I am almost home, clear across town. I call David, but my call goes straight to his voicemail because he has turned off his phone for the concert. I leave him a message telling him that I am driving myself in to the emergency room.

I feel decidedly shitty. Every red light seems interminable. I grip the steering wheel and put every ounce of energy I can summon into driving and getting myself there. I consider calling a friend but by the time I reach someone by phone and she then reaches me by car, more time would elapse. So I somehow get myself there and I know this is the right call because I am going downhill fast.

When I get to the hospital, I park in the closest lot I can find to the emergency room. David has always dropped me off right at the entrance in the past, so parking and walking there seems like a huge ordeal. This is another sign that I am very ill. The distance is not that far, yet I have to lay my head on the steering wheel and steel myself for it. I walk by the emergency room waiting area on my way in to the hospital and I can see that it is totally packed. Shit.

A quick scan reveals very few veritable emergencies. This is what is wrong with our health care system. I check in and I am told that it will be at least a 3-hour wait. *This is what is wrong with our health care system!*

I honestly don't think I'm going to make it. I know I am feverish because I am both freezing and burning, my discomfort rocking back and forth between the two extremes. I send a text to friends who live relatively nearby, on the off chance they are home on a Friday night, asking for a blanket and some water, but the text can't go out because there is no cell phone coverage in this part of the hospital.

I am asked to step behind the registration desk to get my vitals taken. The room is so crowded that the traditional chair opposite the desk is taken, so I make my way around it to where the admitting clerk usually sits. I read a notice to all emergency room personnel directing them to no longer refer to triage patients as such but instead call them trigger patients.

I wonder why that is and my lawyer's mind ponders what lawsuit they're trying to avoid. A nurse's aide takes my temperature. 102.7. David didn't even think I felt warm when he felt my forehead at dinner, less than two hours earlier. The aide then takes my blood pressure and pulse. I see in his face that it is not good. Not good at all.

"We've got a triage here," he says loudly, almost yelling.

He summons over the nurse who has come in to bring back the next few patients. She walks over and he shows her the numbers he has written down. Her eyebrows arch and she looks at me, then redoes the tests herself. They apparently yield the same results because she says. "You're coming with me right now." She turns to the aide and tells him to alert the nurses that she's bringing back a triage patient.

Nobody is obeying the new trigger versus triage directive I think to myself, and then I realize I can't be that ill if I am focusing on things like that.

When I am back in the emergency room, I lie down on a gurney and change into a hospital gown. I look at my breast and I gasp. The infection, and it is now clear that's what is ailing me, has spread across both breasts, up to my neck, and down to my pelvis. My breasts are swollen and blistered. *What the hell?* The emergency room doctor who is quickly summoned takes a sharpie and draws an outline around the infection. It is an oblong circle that outlines my entire torso.

Dr. Getz arrives and tells me what I now know. I am fighting a very serious infection. He will put me on several IV antibiotics. I already know I'll be spending the night, but I ask him how quickly I'll bounce back once he gives me the antibiotics. I'm wondering if I'll be able to leave in the morning.

He just looks at me. His look says, very plainly, I don't think you get it.

"You will be here the entire weekend. Probably longer. You are very, very sick."

Eliza's birthday is Sunday. *Crap.*

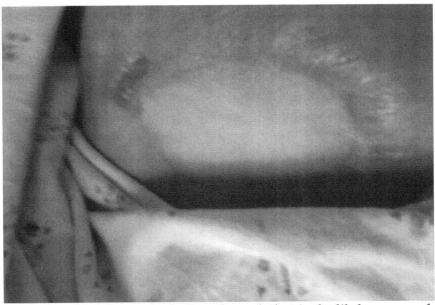

My infected left breast, including the scab that is the likely source of the infection.

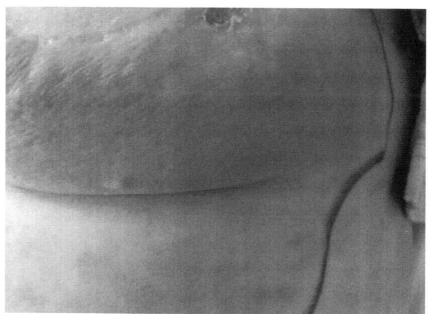

The blue Sharpie line delineating the path of the infection.

Subject: Ovarian Odyssey
Date: February 26, 2012

I figured it was time to send out another Ovarian Odyssey update because I have received quite a few "How are you doing?" emails lately. I was planning to wait until Wednesday, when the last of my cancer journey columns (this one profiling the surgeon responsible for my reconstruction surgery) will be published in the Charlotte Observer, and I was going to assure you all that I was doing great and basically had nothing to report. Obviously, that was going to make for too boring an update, so I had to add another hospital visit to the mix to spice things up.

That's right, I'm writing this from the hospital, where I've been ensconced since Friday night. I really had been doing great, and I even felt fine on Friday. I walked the dogs and felt somewhat sluggish, but I chalked that up to a heavy workout with weights (newly reintroduced to my workouts) the day before. Back at the house, I noticed that I was feeling pain under my left breast and that I was slightly swollen and red. I made a mental note to keep an eye on the redness, because I knew a woman who died tragically and unexpectedly from a chemo-related infection the week of my surgery and it served as a warning to take any signs of infection seriously.

By the time I got to Hannah's choir concert, I was quite ill. I had missed her last two concerts due to chemo and surgery so I was excited to finally get to see her perform, but it was not to be. I felt awful, and when I described my symptoms to the doctor on call (the swelling and redness had spread and I felt feverish), I was told to head in to the emergency room. I reluctantly left David and the girls at the concert and headed to the hospital. By the time I got there, I was dismayed to see a roomful of people and I was told the wait would be at least 3 hours. There was no room to sit down and I was shivering and miserable. But fear not... the silver lining to how quickly my symptoms (a rash and swelling that now extended over both my breasts and across my stomach; a 102.7 fever and uncontrollable shaking) spiraled downwards... no waiting for me! I was immediately triaged and given a room and medical care.
So I am now hooked up to my old friend, Mr. IV, getting a cocktail of antibiotics that is working wonders. I am doing infinitely better and hope to get out of here within the next few days. I hated missing Eliza's birthday today but, on the bright side, I get to watch the Oscars uninterrupted tonight. And, as always, in a perverse way, being sick is a reminder of how lucky I am. I have once again received great care, including from Angelo, a nurse's assistant, who works 16-hour shifts taking blood pressures and temperatures and filling ice buckets with a smile on his face and a genuine enjoyment of his job. I again feel humbled to be here (not necessarily here in the hospital, but here in general) and to have made it through another bump in the road that could have been so much worse.

I thank you all for your good wishes and concern. I'll be back in touch on Weds. to send along my latest column. And thanks to all of you who have encouraged me to put my cancer musings into a book – I am working on doing just that. I recently spoke about my journey at the hospital's breast cancer reconstruction symposium and I have been asked to be on an advisory council at the hospital, so none of this has been in vain.

Love, Katya

Subject: Ovarian Odyssey
Date: February 28, 2012

*I am happy to report that I am home from the hospital and right back
in the swing of things. I have a few minor vestiges of my infection
and hospital stay (including the Sharpie boundary they used to
delineate the spread of the infection, which is impossible to wash off
and will no doubt garner many a stare when I change in the locker
room) but, for the most part, I'm good to go.*

*They are still not sure what caused the infection, but the general
consensus is that I got to the hospital in the nick of time. Once again,
within the realm of cancer, I am extremely lucky. Among the many
nicknames I've had throughout this journey, such as Baldy and
Fuzzhead, I think perhaps the most apt is Weebles, because the
mantra that kept running through my head during this last health
scare was, "Weebles wobble but they don't fall down." As far as
commercial references go, it sure beats, "I've fallen and I can't get
up."*
*Anyway, here, as promised, is today's Charlotte Observer column
about my final surgery.*

Love, Katya

Wednesday, Feb. 29, 2012

Major surgery marks the end of personal battle

And I start 2012 afresh with great hope for the future

Katya Lezin

One of the many surreal moments during my cancer
journey was when my husband and I attended the

287

breast cancer reconstruction symposium at Charlotte Medical Center.

Sitting in the audience of women, some of whom had already had mastectomies, others who were, like me, still under-going chemotherapy and looking ahead to the next surgery, I stared at slides of patients with no breasts and myriad examples of reconstructed breasts.

I also examined silicone implants and listened as Dr. John Michael Robinson explained all of the options available. "Some date night," I whispered to my husband.

Even though I did not have breast cancer, the genetic mutation that was detected at the time of my ovarian cancer diagnosis made my odds of getting breast cancer intolerably high. I opted for a prophylactic double mastectomy so that I could reduce my risk to practically nil.

After attending the symposium and consulting with Dr. Robinson, I decided to have perforator flap breast reconstruction, a surgery that was not available in Charlotte until Dr. Robinson, 43, joined the CMC's Carolinas Cosmetic and Plastic Surgery practice in 2009.

Most people are familiar with implants, the silicone inserts that replace the breast tissue that is removed following a mastectomy

Unbeknownst to me prior to the symposium, another option is to replace the fatty tissue with one's own fat... something, I might add, I had no problem supplying.

The old TRAM (transverse rectus abdominal muscle) flap procedure involved taking the abdominal muscle along with the skin and fat to recreate the missing breast. My surgery, a DIEP flap, is a more advanced procedure that leaves the muscle intact, but instead takes blood vessels that perforate through the muscle and keep the skin and fat alive for reconstruction.

It is not, as one can imagine, a simple surgery.

Dr. Robinson, who received his medical degree at Philadelphia's Jefferson Medical College and worked alongside his father, also a plastic surgeon, at the University of South Carolina's Plastic Surgery Program, enjoys being able to give his patients a choice.

He is one of approximately 300 surgeons in the country doing perforator flap reconstruction surgery and he is "doing more and more each year." He finds what he does extremely rewarding, whether it's inserts or a perforator flap surgery, because, as he puts it, "I get to give my patients something back that was taken from them."

For me, the surgery marked the end of a long journey, but also marks the beginning of a new chapter in my life. It was scheduled to fall within the calendar year for financial reasons (because I had

already met my medical insurance's catastrophic cap for the year) but the timing was also good in that it marked the end of the year.

I was able to start 2012 afresh, all cancer, chemo, and surgeries behind me. I am so grateful to have emerged from all of this relatively unscathed and I am humbled to know others are not as lucky.

I am in awe of what my body was able to endure and what my medical team was able to do to it.

And thanks to Dr. Robinson and my new flat tummy, I just may have to invest in a this summer.

Katya Lezin and Dr. John Michael Robinson

If you are interested in attending one of the monthly breast cancer reconstruction symposiums hosted by Carolinas Cosmetic and Plastic Surgery at CMC, call 704-446-6810.

Katya Lezin is a freelance writer for South Charlotte News. Have a story idea for Katya? Email her at bowserwoof@mindspring.com.

Reprinted with permission of South Charlotte News, a Charlotte Observer publication.

CHAPTER THIRTY

I am sitting in the big private room at George's Brasserie, one of my favorite Charlotte restaurants. On the table in front of me are a big plate of mussels in white wine sauce, frites, and an arugula salad with pears and hazelnuts. Seated around the table are many of my dearest Charlotte friends: Lorrina, Jen, three Lisas (Zerkle, Miller and Ruben- son), Alyssa, Marni, Gabi, Margie Pokorney (one of Eliza's teachers), Bridgette and Katie Fine. We are celebrating my birthday, and I feel so fortunate to be surrounded by such wonderful women, both tonight and in my life. I owe them a lot, these women who helped me through the hardest year of my life.

Amidst the laughter and joking (we comment that it's a good thing we have a private room), I propose a toast to my fabulous friends. I want to formally acknowledge the role they played in my recovery.

"Do you guys remember, early on in this whole journey, when my neighbor ran up to me while I was walking around the neighborhood after my surgery to tell me that he was lifting me up every day?"

Nods from everyone who has heard the story.
"I was puzzled at first. I took him literally. Then I realized he meant it spiritually. He was lifting me up with his *prayer*. But you all," I say, looking around at my dear friends, who have sat with me during chemo and with David during my surgeries, brought me meals and goodies galore, taken care of my kids in ways big and small, and sent me constant reminders that they were thinking of me and made sure I never felt that I was fighting this battle alone, "you have truly lifted me up. Your friendship and support made this so much more bearable."

I am particularly emotional about this birthday, my 47th, because it truly feels like the demarcation between the old, sick me and the new, healthy me. David's birthday is the day before mine and we go out to eat together and toast the year and years ahead.

"Just think," I say to David, "last year when we celebrated our birthdays, we had no idea this was looming on the horizon."

"You were probably already sick," David surmises.
"We just didn't know it yet."

We are both very glad that I had the prophylactic double mastectomy. It is so much more gratifying to toast the end of the year behind us without having any lingering fears about a cancer lurking in my breasts. I know I would worry every day about that and I am so glad I removed that concern, that gnawing fear, from

One of my many birthday celebrations with, from left, Iris, Betsy Rosen, Tiz Benson and Rabbi Judy Schindler. In the background is one of two cakes Tiz brought from her scrumptious bakery Tizzerts.

the equation. I have already had my first post-chemo blood test to measure my CA-125 level. My concern about the recurrence of my ovarian cancer simmers on low on the back burner, but on the day of my blood test, it boils over on the front burner. I am extremely relieved when my numbers come back low. My CA-125 is 14. When I had cancer, it was 1315. My new baseline is now 14. I am cancer-free.... and worry-free, until the next blood test three months from now.

In April, I head back in for more surgery. Unlike the last time I went under the knife, this one will be an outpatient procedure. We will show up first thing in the morning and we will go home before dinnertime. The primary objective is to remove the scar tissue that has built up in both breasts. The one in my left breast is the size of a fist and is starting to impede my arm's mobility. Dr. Robinson also plans to fix what he calls the "tags" (the slight lifting of the skin and scar tissue) on the ends of my abdominal scar. And, best of all, he will liposuction fat from my hips to help lift and contour my breasts.

Carolinas Medical Center

Office /Clinic Visit Notes

GENITOURINARY: Normal external genitalia, vagina, urethra, and urethral meatus. Cervix and uterus surgically absent. Anus and rectum are unremarkable.

IMPRESSION; 1. .Ovarian carcinoma. She is now without disease. Her CA-125 was initially elevated at 1315. It rapidly returned to normal at today's value was 14.3 after she had her catheter removed. She is otherwise doing well and regaining her energy and has had minimal side effects from her chemotherapy. 2. .BRCA positivity, status post prophylactic mastectomy, as noted above. 3. Estrogen deprivation. She is currently asymptomatic.

PLAN: We will continue to watch her closely and plan on seeing her back in 3 months for continued surveillance.

Electronically Signed By: NAUMANN, ROBERT W MD 03/06/2012 10:18 am

---

When we meet with Dr. Robinson while I am being prepped for surgery, he tells me the scar tissue in my breasts is more pervasive than he had realized when he saw me for my pre-op appointment the week before. He tells me he will remove it today and also take care of the skin tags on my hips but he will not be contouring the breasts (so no liposuction) because it won't work if he does it all in one fell swoop. The scar tissue he removes will leave a big void that needs time to heal before he fills it with new fat. He will take care of that in a second surgery sometime in the summer.

I am crestfallen. *Another* surgery? This isn't it?

I have to recalibrate, adjust my expectations. I had it in my head that I was all done. It takes some effort, more than I can handle, lying there in my hospital gown, facing imminent surgery. Surgery I thought was the very last one.

Dr. Robinson assures me that this surgery is nothing

compared to my initial surgery in December. I will be a little sore, but nothing like what I experienced in December. "You can probably hit the tennis courts in the next day or two," he tells me.

This time, it is Dr. Robinson who needs to manage his expectations. *Tennis? Are you kidding me?* I spend the next week in acute pain. It feels worse to me than the first surgery, and I realize it is because I am not in the hospital on a morphine drip. I am back home, but I was still sliced open and my body was still traumatized. I am given painkillers but I don't take them. It's not that I'm some kind of stoic martyr. I hurt. I complain bitterly that I hurt. I'm not hiding that fact or going for some kind of courage award. But I would rather deal with the pain than risk the nausea that painkillers seem sure to engender. Pain is physical. With nausea, it gets emotional. I can't go there.

Subject: Ovarian Odyssey
Date: April 18, 2012

I'm writing to let you all know that I went in for a tune up today and I am now back home, thanks to the wonders of modern medicine and the cost-cutting wizardry of insurance coverage. In at 6:30 this morning, lots of pre- op pokes and prods, a 2 hour surgery, a couple hours of post-op recovery, and then back in my own bed with Nurses Molly and Darcy on duty by mid-afternoon. I can't say I feel great at the moment but, compared to what I've been through, this isn't too bad. The main issue is, yet again, one of managing my expectations. I had it in my head that this would be a simple surgery with minimal recovery time, due to my own bounce right back attitude, but also due to Dr. Robinson's assurances that I could schedule a tennis match for the next day. Unfortunately, the surgery ended up being longer and more complex than anticipated because, as we've firmly established by now, I tend to go for the outer edges of the bell curve. I had quite a bit of scar tissue built up around both my breasts, especially the left one, and they were no longer symmetrical (both in size and location) after fighting off the infection that had me hospitalized in February. Dr. Robinson's plan had been to go in via my old incision sites, remove the scar tissue, and then contour each breast with fat from my hips (my favorite part of the plan since I am able to apply that fat in spades). The scar tissue was far worse than expected so he could only take care of that part of the plan for today. Insert big, audible sigh here.

That means I am not done with surgery and will have to again get cut open in about 3 months. Cue sigh number two. The lifting and cutting he did today has left me in a considerable amount of pain, but I am confident it will be short-lived. And my trusty drains are back – yay. (Instructions for that last sentiment are to add a heavy dose of sarcasm.) I have to keep the drains in until next Tuesday – ugh! – so David and I are again bonding over this uniquely personal marital task.

On the positive side, my hair is coming back in with a style all its own. It looks like I stuck my finger in an electrical socket that, I am told, is a look some women pay top dollar to achieve. I've also been plowing ahead with my book on this whole cancer ride of mine, which is why I know my current surgical woes are no big deal, because I've been reliving my early days (via notes and saved emails) when my gripes were far greater. I also know a few people who are struggling right now with their own cancer diagnoses and I am once again so grateful to be at the end of my journey, albeit an end that is a little more prolonged than I had hoped.

Happy Spring to you all!

Love, Katya

I remind myself that this pain and these scars are worth it because, even at its worst, it still beats cancer. I have to laugh when, on the heels of my second surgery on my reconstructed breasts, I receive an email that jumps to the top of this journey's *Really?!?* moments.

April 20, 2012
Dear Ms. Lezin

It is time for your screening mammogram. You are due for your next appointment on or after 5/11/2012. If you have recently returned for this examination, please disregard this reminder.
Please schedule your appointment using the link below
Thank you for choosing Charlotte Radiology Breast Center. Please visit www.beatcancerCR.com to find out how you can spread the word about the importance of breast health and annual mammography.

Thank You, Charlotte Radiology Breast Center

A few days after the surgery, I notice David staring at me intently as I am getting dressed. It's not the way a husband who hasn't had any in a while might stare at his naked wife. I know it's not because he's hot for me since my new, red scars (my old ones, reopened) and bruised and battered body are not likely to elicit any *hubba, hubba* comments these days. I might as well have a big, neon sign above me that flashes the warning DON'T EVEN THINK ABOUT TOUCHING ME. I am that sore. Tennis? Not even close.

"Hon," David says, walking up to me for a closer look. "Your breasts look red. Redder than they were yesterday."

I look in the mirror. He's right.

"I want you to go in there. Today. Call them first thing in the morning," David says, in his *this is not negotiable* voice. The doctors told him my February infection was the closest call I've had during this entire journey. There will be no wait and see. We get how serious these infections can be, how quickly they can turn on you. I promise him I will call.

Sandra, Dr. Robinson's nurse, tells me to come in. Dr. Robinson takes a look and says it does look like the beginnings of an infection. He prescribes an antibiotic and tells me to keep an eye on it. I am to report back if anything changes.

I go back the next day and the next. On the third day, an additional antibiotic is prescribed. I spend more time driving back and forth to the hospital, in the waiting room, at appointments, and back and forth to the pharmacy, than I do on anything else. I think to myself that it would be logistically easier if I just stayed at the hospital, since I've been there every day of the week. I jinx myself. On Friday, one of Dr. Robinson's partners sees me (because Dr. Robinson is in surgery) and decides to admit me. It's time to give me more powerful antibiotics intravenously.

Here we go again.

David meets me at the hospital and we wait forever for a room to be assigned to me because the hospital is chock full. Finally, a room becomes available on the 4th floor. I've never been to that floor, and David and I comment on how sad it is that I actually have a repertoire of hospital floors, a firsthand knowledge of how the hospital works and what the different towers and wings are like. Iris, who has come to find us after David texted her, is surprised at my room assignment. She informs us that the 4th floor is a transitional floor, intended for patients who have just had surgery or who are waiting to be transferred else- where.

I am trying to be a trooper about having to be admitted and spending yet another weekend holed up inside the hospital, but my *let's make the best out of it* attitude crumbles when we get to my room. It is decidedly smaller and more bare bones than any other room I've seen (and I'm developing quite an impressive basis of comparison) but the clincher is the toilet. Instead of having a bathroom with a door, this charming room comes equipped with a pull out toilet. I kid you not! The maximum security prisoners I taught in Virginia had it better than this! To make matters worse, the toilet is right by the door, with only a flimsy curtain to draw around it separating you from anyone walking in.

I really have to pee so Iris suggests I just use the bathroom down the hall, seeing as it actually has a door. As I'm heading down there, a nurse stops me.

"Are you a patient?" she asks.

"Yes, I have just been admitted. I'm in that room right there." I tell her, as I turn to keep walking down the hallway. My need to pee is now dire.

"Just where do you think you're going?" she asks me, gruffly. She is the first hospital personnel in all of my visits to address me with anything other than kindness and sympathy.

"To the bathroom." I'm about to explain how the one in my room is totally unacceptable when she interrupts me.

"You need to use the toilet in your room" She turns me around as she continues, her no-nonsense voice and attitude making it clear she means business. "The hall bathroom is not for patients." I return to my room, tears from this latest frustration welling up in my eyes. Iris is having none of it. She goes out in the hallway, her badge identifying her as a doctor prominently displayed, and comes back a few minutes later to tell me it's fine for me to use the bathroom down the hall. It turns out that patients skirt the no smoking policy by using the hallway bathrooms so their usage is strictly monitored. Iris assures the nurse that I am not a smoking risk.

Fortunately, I am only in the room intended for unconscious patients for a couple of hours before a new room is located on the 6th floor. Hallelujah. I send David home to deal with the girls and tell him I can certainly handle getting settled in my new room by myself. Unlike February, when my infection was accompanied by a fever and overall malaise that had me feeling horrible, I feel perfectly fine. There is a horrible rash on my breasts, but I am otherwise unaffected. It feels weird to be in a hospital, ready to spend the night, when I am otherwise symptom-free.

I try to walk upstairs by myself but they insist on wheeling me up in a wheelchair. I am deposited in my new room and the volunteer who brings me up wishes me well and leaves. I wait. I wait some more. Surely a nurse will be in to welcome me and get my IV line started. Surely a nurse's aid will be in to get my vitals. Nothing. I wait a full half hour before ringing my call button. My nurse seems surprised to hear from me. "We didn't even know you were here, " she says. Good thing I called.

She struggles to find a line on me and I tell her that my veins are notoriously difficult. She says she's not even going to mess around with them and instead calls the hospital's IV therapy team. The *what,* I ask. She explains that the hospital has nurses on call around-the-clock whose sole job is to start IV lines in patients whose veins are problematic. *Really?* I can't believe this is the first I'm hearing of this. Sure enough, the IV therapy nurse comes in and starts a line no problem.

"Good to know for the next time," I tell David when he visits later that night.

David looks at me wearily. "How about not having a next time," he says.

Good point.

My rash does not respond to the antibiotic so I am put on a new one, Vancomycin. David has brought the girls in for a visit and we have just started chatting when the Vancomycin is administered. I am in the middle of telling the girls about my toilet woes from the day before when I suddenly feel as if my hair has caught on fire. My scalp has a horrific burning sensation and I am in agony.
David and the girls look at me in horror as I scream and start pulling at my hair.

The nurse immediately stops the Vancomycin. There are now hives popping up on my collarbone and neck.

"You are having an acute allergic reaction," she explains, the stress in her voice evident as she asks me how I feel, if I can breathe okay. I can, now that I am no longer on fire. She tells me an allergic reaction to Vancomycin is so common that it has its own name, Red Man's Syndrome

She administers Benadryl through my IV to offset the allergic reaction, which always knocks me out and makes me instantly woozy.

"Mommy's okay, girls," I tell Hannah and Eliza, who are looking at me with big eyes. "I'm just a little sleepy," I say, slurring my words. "But I'm just fine. Just sleepy. Very, very sleepy."

David ushers them out of the room while I nod off.

Never a dull moment.

Subject: Ovarian Odyssey
Date: April 28, 2012

The best way to summarize the week I've had is to share with you that my medical team officially dubbed me a "problem child." I saw them every day last week, and my pharmacist almost as frequently, and the week also included a hospital stay and several doctors scratching their heads. As I've said so often during this journey, this would be fascinating if it weren't happening to me!

On Monday, I went in to get my drains removed. I was in considerable pain and discomfort and I'd hoped that saying goodbye to the drains would improve things dramatically. It did not. On Tuesday, when I saw Dr. Robinson for my post-op visit, he said that

I looked somewhat pink and enlarged so he put me on an antibiotic and an ibuprofen to get the swelling down. On Wednesday, when there was no improvement, he added a second antibiotic. On Thursday, all four surgical sites (my breasts and both hips) were bright red and swollen.

There was much debate among Dr. Robinson and his partners as to what was causing my redness and swelling. It looked like an allergic reaction because it was limited to my four surgical sites, rather than spreading all over my torso the way it did when I was hospitalized in February. On the other hand, my skin was thick and filled with fluid, arguing in favor of an infection.
They decided to admit me and give me another antibiotic intravenously to try to get ahead of whatever was attacking my body. In the "never take the easy road" approach I've apparently decided to take lately, I developed an allergic reaction to the antibiotic. I started pulling at my hair because it felt like my scalp was on fire and my neck and torso broke out in red splotches and hives. My nurse immediately stopped my antibiotic and I was given Benadryl intravenously, my old chemo friend that knocks me out almost immediately. A few hours later, while my nurse was checking on me, I broke out in another reaction, so the doctor on call ordered a steroid for me and then I was put on yet another antibiotic.

The next morning I felt and looked much better, so Dr. Robinson agreed to spring me. I was given one more dose of the antibiotic intravenously and then given yet another one to take orally. So here's hoping antibiotic number five is the winner. I will see Dr. Robinson again on Tuesday, when I will hopefully get the green light to travel to Boston on Weds. for the IECA (Independent Educational Consultants Association) conference. I suspect it will be a cathartic trip because I was at this conference last year when I received the Big C call. What a ride it has been, and one I had hoped would be over by now (the illness part of it, that is!). I am still red and swollen and my body is clearly still fighting something, but I am happy to be home. The girls and I went to the farmer's market this morning and I was so glad to be out with them rather than confined to a hospital room, which is where I thought I'd be spending the weekend. So here's to modern medicine, which doesn't always have the answers but can still get us back on our feet and back to our lives.

Love,
Katya

CHAPTER THIRTY-ONE

I am so frustrated about my weight. Whatever poundage I lost lopping off my boobs has magically glommed on to other parts of my body. I love my tight, flat stomach, something I haven't had since elementary school, but pretty much every other part of my body is much bigger than it was pre-cancer. I couldn't lift weights for so long that my strong, muscular arms and back are now just large, fatty and unsightly. My butt and thighs seem to have inherited all the fat that can no longer fill my stomach. I can't get most of my pants past my upper thighs. It is hugely discouraging because I work out like a banchee, but it seems to be having no effect. Could I eat better? Sure. My daily coffee is more a vehicle for half and half than it is a caffeine fix and I have not purged my diet of bread and sweets. But my new nonexistent metabolism (thank you, instant menopause) and my shifting of body weight and fat has conspired to make me the heaviest I have ever been in my life. It is bizarre because I don't look it. I actually prefer my figure to the one that was reflected in the pre-cancer mirror, but the scale says otherwise. This, I am ashamed to admit because of the vanity and shallowness it reflects, has me saying *That's not fair!* far more than I ever have about the injustice of my cancer diagnosis and the treatment that followed.

I had so hoped to show off a new, svelte figure when I see my folks and my sister in Colorado for our annual Mother's Day weekend. I have not seen my parents since Thanksgiving and my sister shortly thereafter, when she visited right after my December surgery, so it has been a while. I have a new crop of curly hair for them to admire and my scars have healed nicely. But my figure? Not so much.

The girls and I missed last year's Mother's Day race, something we did for the first time back in 2006 and every year since as a way to have a girls-only weekend together, because I was in Philadelphia for the IECA conference. That was also the year I got the call about my cancer. So this year, sitting between Hannah and Eliza on the Delta flight that my sister has finagled for us with her free miles, I am so thankful to be making the trip, to have this time with my girls, and to be able to get in a bonus visit with my parents and my sister.

Title IX, a women's athletic clothing line that sponsors the annual race, a 9.9 K around the Boulder Reservoir, asked for participants

Check out my curls!

to tell their stories. In the week leading up to the race, I struggled mightily with insomnia and the inevitable digestion issues that seem to follow any surgery I endure. I take a break from playing online Scrabble at 2 am, during one of my many wakeful nights when I am physically exhausted but sleep eludes me, to send in my submission for what the race means to me:

May 2, 2012

My Title 9 Race Story

I could play on the number 9 and tell you the many multiples of that number that factor into my race participation. How 3 generations of women (my mom, my sister and my two daughters and I) picked this race as our Mother's Day tradition, something we have done together for 6 years. Or how we come from 3 different states -- Oregon, California and North Carolina - to enjoy the weekend together because we don't get to see each other nearly enough. In fact, I wrote something along those lines two years ago, the last time I ran the race, and won a prize in that year's story competition.

The reason I didn't run the race last year -- the first one I missed in five years -- is because it coincided with a conference I had to attend. My mom and my sister participated without me while I was across the country in Philadelphia, which is where I was when I got the dreaded call from my OB/GYN telling me I had ovarian cancer. This year, the race will mark exactly one year from the time of my diagnosis. A year filled with four surgeries (because I also learned I have a genetic mutation that significantly increased my odds of getting breast cancer), five months of chemotherapy, and many unwelcome changes to my body and my life.

But my story is not a sad one, because I am back this year -- albeit without any of my female parts! - to run this race that celebrates women and the bonds that women share. Running the race in the Boulder sun with my daughters and my mom and my sister all there to enjoy the day with me will be that much more poignant because I feel so fortunate to still be here. The race is a good excuse to get together and it will be the first time my parents (we convinced my dad to come along too this year) and my sister have seen me post-mastectomy, with my new crop of hair and my new breasts. It will be a great way to show them and my daughters, who have seen their mom hit some pretty low points, that I am strong and healthy and happy. I doubt my time will be anything to brag about, but I also doubt there will be anyone prouder or happier crossing the finish line.

Katya Lezin Charlotte, NC Age 47

Running with daughters Hannah Lieberman (15) and Eliza Lieberman (12), sister Nicole Lezin (49) and mom Alice Lezin (75). Dad Art Lezin (83) will be cheering us all on.

I am right that my time is nothing to brag about. Eliza and I do a combination of walking and running to cross the finish line, and Hannah (who is the first family member by far to finish, thanks to her cross- country and track training) and Nicole and my mom have all beat us across the finish line. I am not exactly out of shape – I still exercise a lot and can hold my own on the tennis court – but I am not in the shape I was pre-cancer. I have to accept that, this new normal, but it isn't always easy.

Subject: Ovarian Odyssey
Date: May 15, 2012

Well, I just passed the one year anniversary of getting the Big C call... and what a year it has been.

The girls and I marked the occasion by flying out to Colorado, where we joined my parents and my sister for our annual Mother's Day race in Boulder (We spend the entire weekend dreading the race that brought us out there!). We had a wonderful time and some of us (not Yours Truly) also turned in some impressive times in the race -- my mom, for example, came in 2nd in her age division. (And in typical Mom fashion, she is wishing she could have a do-over so she could make up the one minute that separated her and the first place winner, a sprightly 70-year old.)

My parents had not seen me since Thanksgiving...for those keeping count, that's two surgeries, two infections, and four hospitalizations ago. They were happy to see my full head of hair and pronounced me "surprisingly healthy."

My scars are all starting to heal and I am looking forward to a run of good health before my next surgery in mid-July. I have gone through a lot but my body has borne it all astonishingly well, and I am grateful to it for seeing me through all this with only the occasional protest. I wish that one of my many side effects could have included inexplicable weight loss rather than the post-menopausal gain I am now enjoying (and by enjoy, I mean just the opposite) but I am choosing to interpret it all as symbols of strength and health. And it sure beats the alternative... I am happy to be here, to be enjoying the spring, to be looking forward to the summer and all of the fun things that we have planned, and to know that none of our plans have to be scheduled around chemo. Every once in a while a smell or taste will take me back to my chemo regimen and I am just so grateful to be done with that. So let's hear it for a chemo-free summer!

Happy belated Mother's Day to all of you moms out there and happy May 15th to the rest of you. Here I am with Eliza and Hannah and Mom and Nicole... and yes, I am now the shortest member of the family!

Love, Katya

3 generations enjoying the post-race euphoria. We did it!

     We come back from Colorado to the jam-packed end of the school year calendar that was so daunting last year, when I was still reeling from my cancer diagnosis. I again coordinate the Randolph Middle School Scrabble tournament, where each student is paired with a parent or teacher. I lay a bunch of games, t-shirts and Scrabble paraphernalia on the prize table, and the student coming in first gets first dibs, the second goes next, and so on.

     As I start the prize ceremony, Andy Zerkle (who paired with his son Eli, placing first) presents me with a card signed by all of the kids and a generous gift card from everyone. I get choked up as I accept this lovely gesture, reminiscing aloud about the state I was in at last year's tournament. I tell the collected parents and teachers that these kids have seen me through a lot – several surgeries and hospitalizations, and days I dragged myself in for club even though I looked and felt like hell. It feels so cathartic to end the year on such a happier note.

Eli, as the first place student finisher, then proceeds to pick the iTunes gift card as his prize. Eliza, who paired with Mr. Oreskovic, an 8th grade social studies teacher, and came in second, gets to come up next to pick a prize. She makes it clear that Eli has already picked the prize she wants, while simultaneously mocking my tearful thank you comments.

"Now *I'm* going to cry," Eliza announces to much laughter.

So much for my little girl being traumatized by my Ovarian Odyssey.

CHAPTER THIRTY-TWO

I am such a well-known sap that I am sure I would have cried at Noah's high school graduation even if I hadn't faced my own mortality in the year preceding it, but sitting in the Durham sunshine, looking at Noah so tall and handsome in his cap and gown, I am overcome with emotion. I just feel so grateful to be here, to be able to enjoy this day and this milestone, and to know that Noah will be heading off to college without my illness hanging over his head.

Noah's graduation from NCSSM.

With each day that passes and each new hair follicle that grows, I feel further and further removed from my cancer. I can feel us all rebounding, getting back into the groove of what our life was like before the cancer grenade blew everything up. But as my 3-month check up and blood test draws near, I can feel the anxiety mounting. Most of the time, I tend to ignore or quell the fear of recurrence, the knowledge that my IIB classification was on the cusp of being classified as advanced, and that the recurrence rate for advanced ovarian cancer is what makes it so insidious. But in the days preceding my blood test, the discouraging statistics float to the surface of my subconscious and take up residence in my daily thoughts. The blood test forces me to think about something I'd rather not.

My first post-chemo CA-125 reading was in March. It was 14. This, I was told, is my baseline. It might go up or down a few points, but as long as I remain cancer-free, my CA-125 should hover right around 14. I go back for my second reading in early June. Trish also decides to check my thyroid since I complain bitterly at our appointment about my weight. She calls me the next day.

"Well," she says, "your thyroid is fine." I can feel the big "but" hanging in the air.

"Your CA-125, though, is up," Trish tells me.

My heart sinks. I think of the cancer growing and festering within me. I feel sick to my stomach.

"It's a 27," Trish tells me, sensing my immediate panic. "That's not terribly alarming, but it's an upward trend we don't like. It has almost doubled, and I think I'd feel better getting a scan to just make sure there's nothing going on."

Me too.

A CT scan is scheduled for the next day. I drink the cups of nastiness I'd hoped to never imbibe again, I get a line started in the veins I'd hoped would have a nice, long vacation from being pricked, and I lie back on the gurney while the contrast die makes me flush, burns my throat, heats my body from head to toes, and leaves me with the sensation that I have peed in my pants even though I haven't. It is an extremely bizarre experience, and one I didn't feel a need to repeat. "Please, please, please," I plead to no one in particular, "let this find nothing."

Trish calls me the next day. "Good news!" she says, wasting no time in calming my nerves.

Hannah is home because she is done with her final exams, so I listen and offer innocuous responses like "that's great" and "got it" to what Trish tells me. I fire off an email to the few family and friends who knew about my elevated count and were worrying right along with me.

June 5, 2012

Hi all. Hannah is home so I'm sending out this email rather than calling. My scan came back totally clean. It shows a lot of trauma (scarring and inflammation) from all of my surgeries, which is what is probably to blame for my elevated CA-125 count. My docs have scheduled another blood test for the morning of my next surgery on July 11th to get another baseline, but hopefully it will either plateau or go back down. The only reason we'd be concerned is if it spiked again. For now, no reason to worry and I am good to go. I plan on sleeping well tonight!

Love, Katya

I am beyond relieved. We have a fantastic summer ahead of us and I am so glad it will not be marred by a return of the cancer and all that entails. Noah will be interning for the Democratic National Convention, a plum position that is perfectly in line with his passion for politics and takes full advantage of the fortuitous location of this year's DNC in Charlotte. He received permission up front for two trips we will be making in the summer, both for two weeks, and will take the bus uptown to the DNC Headquarters on all other days. He will be attending the Honors College at UNC-Chapel Hill in the fall (Harvard did not have the good sense to admit him and the other schools that wanted him – Emory and Georgetown – were on crack as far as what they thought we could pay). In the *everything happens for a reason* department, he learns on the first day of his internship that he will be expected to come back and work the entire week of the convention in September, after school has started. This exciting development would be much more logistically challenging if he were attending any other school. He is all smiles, looking forward to a fun summer and a promising future.

Eliza will attend her first sleepover camp, a choral camp for which her RMS choir teacher not only recommended her but is also footing half the bill. I was reluctant to give my permission at first because Eliza has struggled with sleepovers and being away from us in the past, a problem that was exacerbated during my year of cancer, but she assures me she will be just fine. I tell her she has to be since the camp is at East Carolina University, a 5-hour drive from Charlotte, and Noah and I will be dropping her off there on our way up the East Coast for two Scrabble tournaments (the first of Noah's two pre-approved trips), the Albany 4th of July tournament and the MidSummer Madness in Delaware. Eliza also gets to go to a tournament in Knoxville, Tennessee with me at the start of the summer, a trip I am combining with looking at schools for my Perfect Fit College business.

Hannah is not part of any of these plans because she is heading off to France for the entire summer to be an *au pair* for Celine's sister. When the opportunity first presented itself to us, I raised all sorts of red flags to Hannah. She doesn't speak a word of French. Taking care of three kids (ages 2, 5 and 7) all day, every day, is a far cry from the occasional babysitting job. And the entire summer, June 11th to August 18th, is a *really* long time to be away. Hannah insists she can do it, that it is an amazing opportunity (we need only pay for her airfare) and that she will be fine. I was an *au pair* in France at exactly her age and I do think travel and experiencing other countries and cultures is life-transforming, so we agree to let her go.

Within days of arriving in France, Hannah totally falls apart. She is miserably homesick, which I at first attribute to the jet lag and the language barrier, but it soon becomes clear that it is not temporary or surmountable. She emails around the clock begging us to let her come home. We finally reach a compromise, working with her patient and understanding French host family, which has her staying for a month and then returning home prematurely in July.

Hannah's homesickness can be attributed to several factors, but the most salient one is that the solitude and separation has her finally confronting my cancer for the first time. Her resilience, both commend- able and at times insulting in that she seemed impervious to what was happening to me and to our family, now comes crashing down. She sends me email after email expressing a fear that I'm going to die, irrationally asking me to promise to live forever, and vowing to never leave my side again

When Eliza and I go to Tennessee, she sees how Hannah's breakdown impacts me. I tell her she cannot get homesick like this when she goes to camp, that if she's having second thoughts, I'd rather know now than take her there and have her fall apart. She promises me she's got this. When Noah and I drop her off, I give her a big hug and I try to hide my trepidation. She calls two days later, and I fear the worst.

"Mom, I don't want to upset you," she begins, and I think, *here we go...*

"But I don't miss you *at all,*" she concludes.

Music to my ears. Noah and I have a great road trip together and we devote many of the hours of our long car rides together processing everything that has happened over the last year. He tells me it was hard to be away from home while I was sick, but I assure him that I felt his support and love from afar. I am so glad to have this time with him before he leaves for college.

We visit Carl and Beth and Grandpa Joe on our way to Albany and Beth tells me not to have this next surgery. She sees it as taking an unnecessary risk, especially given my infections, and it does give me pause. I have always scoffed at cosmetic surgery, and now I am some- one who has her very own plastic surgeon. I agree that the third —and I hope final—breast reconstruction is not a necessity, but I don't see it as purely aesthetic or frivolous either. One of my breasts is concave, making it look ridiculous under shirts. And my breasts are uneven, although my friends tell me that is something that afflicts many women and is not just a surgical mishap. I also have to admit that the prospect of lipo- suctioning some of the fat from my hips to contour the breasts is mightily appealing. I am not above using surgical assistance to get my post-cancer body back in pre-cancer shape.

Hannah's flight home is scheduled for July 11th, a date her host family picked as the most convenient for them, which happens to coincide with my surgery. David and I head in to the hospital in the morning to get my blood drawn, and we then kill some time walking along the Greenway while we await my 11 am check-in time. We have spent many hours over the course of my appoint-ments, hospitalizations and doctors' visits walking along this Greenway, and we talk about how glad we are that it was built. The

---

315

only down side is having to walk through a cloud of smoke as we near the hospital.

"Good to see the hospital employees enjoying the Greenway," I say to David sarcastically.

I have not been allowed to eat since the night before and I am cranky hungry at this point. My nurses (one is being trained so I have two at a time) are a lot of fun. They tell me they love Dr. Robinson and that he is one of the nicest doctors around. I agree. They admire his handiwork and I tell them the best part is that I never have to wear a bra. We laugh about that being a real *perk* of the surgery. They both have large breasts and they are quite envious.

"Even running, playing tennis," I tell them. "No bra."

"No way!" they say in unison.

They go over my medical history, my meds, my allergies, and they ask me if I have any complaints.

"Yes," I say emphatically, "I'm *hungry.*"

Dr. Robinson shows up and tells us his morning surgery has become more complicated and time-consuming. He's going to have to push back my surgery for a couple of hours. Major bummer, mainly because that's more time my stomach will be grumbling.

My nurses sheepishly tell me they are heading off to lunch but they'll be back to prep me for the surgery. When they return, I tease them.

"Are you *licking your lips?*" I ask in mock indignation. "Yes, it was so tasty," they tease me right back. "Well," I say, "tomorrow *I'll* be able to eat, but *you'll* still be wearing bras."

Game, set, match.

While we are waiting for Dr. Robinson to return, I ask the nurses to see if my blood work has been uploaded on my digital medical records. They look and report that my CA-125 is 28. David and I are relieved, and we assume that means it essentially plateaued, but we hope Trish or Dr. Naumann will call and confirm that it is good news. We never hear from them.

When I awaken after the surgery, I am incredibly sore. There was minimal slicing this time, mercifully, but I feel as if I've been hit by a Mack truck. Liposuction is a pretty brutal assault on the body, if you think about it, and I already have some impressive bruising to prove it. My breasts are sore and swollen but only the right one, which was lifted up to match the left, was cut open. I am again given prescriptions for painkillers I have no plans to fill, because I'll take this pain, even if it intensifies, over nausea any day. Besides, I am buoyed by the knowledge that this is my last surgery. As I recuperate at home, David and Noah head out late at night to retrieve Hannah, who missed her connecting flight at JFK, from the airport. We are all under one roof, in varying stages of exhaustion.

On the day after my surgery, I venture out to get bagels with David. I continue to be sore and stiff, but it is manageable. The next day, I feel fine but David thinks my breast looks pink and more swollen. I promise to call Dr. Robinson as soon as the office opens at 9:00. I drop Hannah off at a babysitting job, Eliza off at her aerial dancing day camp in NoDa and Noah off at his internship uptown. With all three kids where they need to be for the day, I head to Terrace Café, where I am meeting Lorrina and Jen to celebrate Lisa Miller's birthday. I get as far as ordering coffee before I get the return call from Sandra, Dr.Robin- son's nurse. I describe what I see and feel and she doesn't hesitate. We have been down this road before.

"Come on in," she tells me. I take my coffee to go.

Dr. Robinson is in surgery so Dr. Lefaivre sees me. He gives me the choice of being admitted for IV antibiotics or going home and trying them orally first. It is a Friday. I have gone the route of trying to get medical attention on a weekend. I have also seen how quickly infec- tions can spiral out of control, and, on top of that, I have firsthand knowledge of how impervious to antibiotics my own infections seem to be. I opt for being admitted.

The hospital is again totally full so this time a room is found for me on the 11th floor.

"Oh, I've never been to that floor," I say, and everyone laughs. I am getting to be quite the connoisseur of what Carolinas Medical Center has to offer. The 11th floor is the orthopedic floor.

Walking in on my own two feet, I pass by rooms with patients who look longingly at my mobility. They are hooked up to scary-looking pulleys and contraptions, their limbs in casts and slings. Once I am hooked up to my IV pole, getting the inevitable antibiotics that seem to follow any surgery for me, I take it along with me for laps of my floor. The nurses have assorted nicknames for me *Speedy, Marathoner, Energizer Bunny* and they call out to me as I pass their stations. I see that almost every door but my own has a gold star.

317

"Why don't I get a gold star?" I ask my nurse. I mean, I'm friendly and obliging. Surely, I deserve a gold star too.

"That designates a patient who isn't mobile," she explains. "That's definitely *not* you."

That night, Dr. Robinson comes to visit me after his surgery. He looks exhausted.

"Hello, problem child," he says, by way of greeting.

I smile sheepishly.

"Trust me," I tell him, "I'm not trying to make this a habit."

He is perplexed. He tells me they used a different type of suture, a different type of soap, and different gloves. He can't imagine what it is that is causing these reactions. He sinks down on the couch in my spacious room. He is despondent because the DIEP he just performed did not take. It happens infrequently, but when it does, it slays him. He tells me that the unlucky woman did not have proper blood flow in her breasts. He thinks they are unsalvageable. I can't imagine waking up from that long, dreaded surgery to discover that it was all in vain, that it will have to be done again.

The next morning, Dr. Robinson visits me again on his rounds. He is ebullient because they were able to save his patient's breasts. I tell him she may very well not even know what a close call it was. I remember how groggy I was just after the surgery. She may not even realize things weren't looking good there for a while.

"Oh no, she knows," he tells me, grinning.

"Why? How can you be sure?" I ask.

He pauses for dramatic effect.

"Because her breasts are covered in leeches."

"In *what?*"

It turns out, despite all the medical advances and modern technology available today, there are a few old world cures that just can't be beat. When you need to get rid of extra blood that has accumulated in the body, nothing seems to beat a bunch of leeches! I shudder to think of that poor woman, waking up to find *that* all over her new rack.

As is often the case, any pity party I might have entertained for myself is cut short by this hands-down winner of the I've-got-it-worse game.

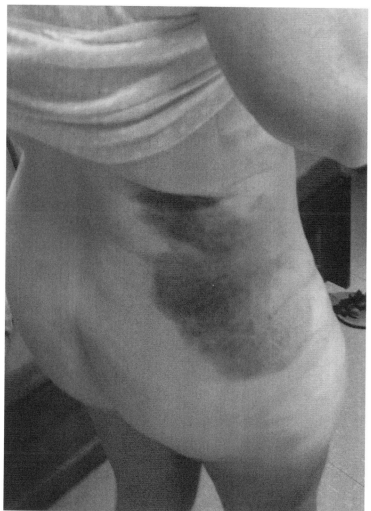

My impressive bruising after my July liposuction surgery.

Subject: Ovarian Odyssey
Date: July 13, 2012

Well, here we go again. As many of you know, I had my fifth and (hopefully) final surgery this past Wednesday. It went well and I was back home the same day, following doctor's orders to indulge in laziness and pampering. (I am getting quite adept at lounging around.) I was a bit sore and stiff but otherwise fine and David and I were both thinking we had finally cleared a hurdle without any complications or setbacks. Wrong.

I woke up this morning to a very red, swollen and – I am convinced – pissed off breast. I drove Hannah (who just arrived home from France) to a babysitting job, dropped Noah off uptown for his DNC internship, and brought Eliza to her dance camp. It was as if the infection were waiting for me to fulfill my morning carpool duties. As soon as I'd dropped Eliza off, the infection kicked it up a notch. I came in to my doctor's office and they decided to admit me. The infection, once again of unknown origin, has spread quickly. It has moved over to my second breast and is straining the stitches of my incisions. I am receiving intravenous antibiotics and the hope is that I will get out of here on Sunday or Monday once the infection calms down.

So that's the bad news. Obviously, I'd rather not be spending yet another weekend in the hospital. But I have lovely nurses, a big, spacious room, and lots of visitors. And other than the infection, I feel pretty good. I'm on the orthopedic floor, because there was no room else- where in the hospital, so my room comes equipped with all sorts of chains and levers, all of which make me feel grateful that they are not needed in my case. It's a physical reminder that it could always be worse.

More good news – my CA-125 count has stabilized. My last count was worrisome and we were looking to this one to confirm that the cancer has not returned. I have yet to discuss it with my doctors, but it only went up a fraction and I'm choosing to interpret that as a positive. Phew! Again, it's all relative. A few days fighting an infection in the hospital sure beats having to undergo chemo again. I've got this.

So there you have it. I truly hope this is the last missive I will send out from the hospital! But if I had to schedule a hospital visit, I couldn't have timed this one better. I just got back from a Scrabble road trip with Noah and we are all heading out to the West Coast on the 23rd, so another silver lining is that the infection did not interfere with any of my travel plans.

Here's hoping you are all enjoying a fun, relaxing and infection-free summer.

Fondly, Katya

I leave several messages for Dr. Naumann and Trish asking them to please interpret my latest blood test for me. I want to confirm that the slight rise, from 27 to 28, is statistically a plateau, and that the undercurrent of concern that has been buzzing within me ever since I got the news, unofficially, can be turned off. Finally, on my third day in the hospital, I get a call from Trish. She has been away and didn't get any of my messages. Yes, the blood test is fine. Then, the next day, Keisha, Dr. Naumann's nurse, unaware that Trish has called me in response to my messages, calls to tell me the same thing, almost a week after I had the blood test done. I do not think they comprehend what it is like to wait on the results and a medical analysis of what they mean. It is extremely trying and worrisome, oh medical team, and it only takes a couple of minutes to call and put me out of my misery. I am told that my next appointment and blood work will be in late September.

Being in the hospital provides yet another opportunity to see how kind people are. My close friends and family have already firmly established that they are going to make sure I feel as comfortable and supported as possible while going through this ovarian odyssey, but I am also continuously touched by the kindnesses of people I know less well. Neighbors and acquaintances I rarely see in my day-to-day life come by to visit, bearing gifts and giving up valuable weekend time to trek out to the hospital to see me. It also makes for some amusing overlapping of visitors, when the room holds people who have never met and probably never would have but for my hospitalization.

I also continue to get bombarded (in a good way) with cyber messages of support. Each time I send out an Ovarian Odyssey email, I get a steady stream of responses within minutes of hitting the send button. Some people respond every single time, some only once or twice throughout my journey, but all leave me feeling validated (variations of "that really sucks"), empowered (you're so strong and brave) and, most of all, loved (we are here for you, we're thinking of you). Again, never hesitate to let someone know you're thinking of her. I just cannot imagine a scenario when that isn't a good idea, a welcome sentiment.

Heather Steffy, a Scrabble friend of mine, sends me a mnemonic she thinks is particularly apt. I rarely study Scrabble words and am woefully inept at anagramming and memorizing word lists, but this one I think might hold some extra sway in my stubbornly resistant brain. The mnemonic, a way of memorizing all of the letters that can be added to a stem word to form a bingo (a word using all 7 tiles on your rack, meriting an extra 50 points) is LESION + TUMOR? PAGE SKILLFUL DOCTOR. (For example, lesion plus P forms the word epsilon, lesion plus A forms the word anisole and so on.)

It is also an apt mnemonic to send to me because a skillful doc is summoned in my case as well. Dr. Robinson is mystified as to why my body keeps attacking his handiwork. In addition to my post-surgical infections, I seem hypersensitive to antibiotics and meds. While I am in the hospital, a nurse puts some hydrocortisone cream on my scar and rash to help it heal and ease my discomfort, and I break out in hives. I am having some kind of reaction, an immediate and definitive rejection, to a cream I have used many times in the past. It is as if my body has been rewired and is now on high alert to combat anything that is done to it. It has lost its ability to discern what is helpful intervention and what should be fought off.

Even if my layperson take on all this were accurate, it does not explain why or how we should combat this new enemy status, so Dr. Robinson has an infectious disease specialist come and see me while I am still in the hospital. Dr. Lovell examines me, utters many "hmmms" and "I sees" and ends up prescribing a different antibiotic for me. I am released with a prescription for the pill form of the antibiotic and instructions to see him in his office in a few days.

When I meet with Dr. Lovell again one week later, he says that he thinks my last two rashes have been allergic reactions rather than infections. Neither was accompanied by a fever, unlike the February infection that almost killed me. He thinks perhaps I am allergic to the sutures, since that appears to be the physical source of my rashes and reactions. It is possible the problem arises from something my body generates or does when the internal sutures begin to dissolve, which explains the delay of a day or two in the reaction.

He takes me off the antibiotics and wishes me a good trip to Oregon, where I am headed in two days with the rest of the family for our big West Coast trip. I leave with strict instructions to call him if I notice any swelling, redness or any other signs that my breasts are angry (my words, not his). I am so relieved to be heading off on this trip with no medications to take, no medical procedures to incorporate into my vacation. I am taking Diamox, a pill to help offset the effects of high altitude (having once succumbed to high altitude sickness in Colorado, I now take it prophylactically whenever I head to potential trouble spots), but that's it. No other meds. It is the first time in ages that I am free of any prescriptions, there are no surgeries or procedures looming in my future, and I can now totally focus on being well and cancer-free. What a great way to start a vacation.

CHAPTER THIRTY-THREE

On the night before we leave for Oregon, we have Noah's DNC boss and fellow interns, along with Dan Murrey (the chair of the DNC Host Committee) and his wife Katie Oates and their kids, over for dinner. My feet hurt, but I attribute it to being on them all day. When I'm cooking a big meal, I rarely get a chance to sit down, so I figure my feet are simply protesting the extra work shift they were given.

The next day, I hit the gym before our afternoon flight and there is no denying that there is something wrong with my feet. They tingle and almost buzz with annoyance. It is not a painful sensation, but it is extremely annoying and uncomfortable, as if they are either on the verge of falling asleep or are coming out of being asleep. But while that sensation only lasts a few minutes, this goes on, intermittently, all day.

When we land in Chicago, waiting for our final flight to Portland, I decide to call Maggie Hield, who has taken over as Dr. Naumann's chemo coordinator (Nichole Filyaw has decided to stay home with her baby). I remember hearing about this very symptom as a possible side effect from chemo, but surely this can't be that. I finished chemo on October 24th, more than nine months ago. Surely this couldn't be Cisplatin rearing its ugly head again.

Wrong. That unnervingly powerful drug's long and insidious tentacles can still lash out and zap me, literally unnerving me.

"It's called neuropathy," Maggie explains to me. "The Cisplatin killed your nerve endings."

I am just incredulous that I could still be feeling the effects of chemo nine months later. That a new symptom could crop up *now*, just when I thought I was finally free and clear of all things cancer-related.

Maggie asks if I have any tingling sensation in my hands. No, thank goodness, I don't. *Yet.* I don't even let my mind go there. The feet are bad enough.

There is nothing much to be done, although assorted vitamins and supplements can sometimes diminish the tingling. I shelve that information for future use. For now, I am tired of popping pills. I am sick of putting anything not manufactured *by* my body – even a vitamin or supplement – *into* my body.

I was really good about ignoring the Internet when I was fighting my cancer, learning early on that it was far more alarming than informative. But I do a quick cyber search of neuropathy, hoping I'll find patient accounts that say the first few days after it first manifests itself are the worst; that the discomfort is totally manageable and becomes barely noticeable. That is not what I find. Shit. The amounts of Cisplatin I was given make it a certainty my neuropathy will be severe. Maggie actually told me my medical team had been surprised I'd emerged from chemo without any neuropathy because I was given Cisplatin in such high doses that it was extremely surprising I was able to duck this common side effect. The web warns that it is even worse when it gets in your hands. It can make it hard to do things like buttons and one's handwriting suffers. Shit, shit, shit. The tingling is now constant. At best, it is an annoyance, a falling asleep sensation. At worst, it feels like walking on crumbled glass.

But it is hard to be in a funk when surrounded by such magnificent landscape. My parents' house in Bend, Oregon is carved onto a mountainside, with a clear, breathtaking view of snow-capped mountains, the very mountains I skied on as a child and that lured my parents back here for their retirement. One day, we drive out to Elk Lake, one of the many that surround my parents' house, and enjoy a day of swimming and relaxing in yet another pristine spot. Hannah and I decide to swim across the lake (something my parents later chastise me for and outright forbid me from doing again) and we enjoy some quality time together as we make our way across the water. When we are in the middle of the lake, we lie on our backs and admire the eerie quiet that comes from having no one else within sight. All around us are tall, majestic trees and snow-capped mountains. Above us is a clear, beautiful blue sky with clouds that seem to be painted on it to complete the picture-perfect view. I feel strong and resilient and so happy to be in this spot, at this moment. Our next stop is Santa Cruz, California, a day's drive away, where Nicole and Rusty live. We will visit with them and David's sister, Carolyn, and her family, who are driving up from their home in San Diego to spend a few days with us. On the long car ride, one I cherish because I think it may be one of our last as a family, with Noah heading off to college and the family dynamic changing forever, I feel a bizarre tingling in my hands. I don't get it at first. I think maybe the car's vibration is getting to me. I wonder if I am dehydrated. And then it hits me. *Shit.*

Subject: Ovarian Odyssey
Date: July 31, 2012

I am happy to report that I am healing well and my breasts and the rest of my body have called a truce and seem to be getting along. That's the good news. The bad news is that, in what can only be seen as more of that good ol' cancer irony, I had about a day of enjoying my newfound good health before a new, pesky symptom showed up. Yet another "REALLY?!??!" moment in the long litany of this-would-be-fascinating-if-it-weren't- happening-to-me medical curiosities that have defined both my body and my life lately. Just before leaving for the West Coast, where we are enjoying a fabulous family vacation, I started feeling an annoying and persistent tingling in my feet. I remembered that sensory neuropathy is a common symptom of Cisplatin, especially in the doses I received, but I thought I'd somehow managed to escape it. My last dose of chemotherapy was nine months ago. I thought I was in the clear. This couldn't possibly be Cisplatin rearing its ugly head. Wrong. I called my docs and found out that's exactly what this is. Sigh. At best, it's a low-grade discomfort, akin to the feeling you have when your feet are either just falling asleep or just coming out of that state. At worst, it feels as if you are walking on crumbled glass or have little sharp stones under your skin. And the really discouraging part is that it can be long-lasting or – gasp! – permanent. Right now I'm trying to console myself with the fact that it's not in my hands, which is apparently even more debilitating. My docs are putting me on Vitamin B in the hope it will help relieve it somewhat and I will remind myself that it could be worse.

My heart goes out to some of my friends who are not faring as well and it gives me perspective. I am reminded, again, how lucky I am that we caught my cancer early and that, even considering some of my hiccups, I have had a relatively easy go of it.

On a much more positive note, I am attaching my latest column about my cancer journey. The reception to the column – and the chemo buddy program I initiated - has been extremely touching and gratifying. The hospital received over 25 volunteer applications the day my column ran, and the calls keep coming in. I also just got word that I'm going to be interviewed on the local news, which will no doubt help bring in even more volunteers. Cancer stinks, but it makes it so much more bearable to know that good things have come of my own battle with it. Here's the link for the article and I'm attaching a photo of all of us enjoying Elk Lake near my parents' home in Bend, Oregon.

Fondly, Katya

Wanted: Volunteers to be chemo buddies

Levine Cancer Institute starts program to aid cancer patients

Learn more: For information or to sign up for a Chemo Buddy training session, contact Malinda Bivens, 704-355-2105.

Editor's note: This column is part of a series about Katya Lezin's ovarian cancer diagnosis and treatment.

One of the many lessons stemming from my cancer journey is that I am not alone.

Each time I headed into the Blumenthal Cancer Center (now the Levine Cancer Institute) for treatment, a chemotherapy regimen that left me bald, drained and nauseous, I had to fight the urge to engage in a pity party about my misfortune

But a look around me at my fellow patients confirmed that, as is true with most things in life, it is all relative.

There were plenty of people who had it so much worse than I did, either because their cancer was more advanced, their treatment more brutal, or they did not have the support system I did to help make their visits to the infusion room as palatable as possible.

Several of Katya Lezin's friends took her out for a pedicure before her last surgery, from left, Jen Davis-Martin, Lisa Zerkle, Amy Marx, Lisa Miller, Iris Cheng, Marni Eisner, Lezin and Lorrina Eastman

I was lucky.

There was not much I could do about the medical issues that plagued my cancer peers, but the disparities in our support systems did seem like something I could tackle.

I wanted to offset the embarrassment of riches that was my circle of friends and family and find some way of leveling the playing field, so that those patients who appeared to have no one at their side could also benefit from the companionship and support that was a key factor in my recovery.

When my chemo concluded in late October, I approached my care team at Levine Cancer Institute with my idea of a chemo buddy system.

I proposed lining up volunteers who would be available to serve as a companion to any cancer patients who self- identified as wanting a chemo buddy.

I explained that I was in no way disparaging the infusion room nurses, who do an amazing job meeting each patient's needs, but their focus is and should be on the patient's medical needs.

Those patients wanting companionship could now opt to be assigned a chemo buddy.

The Levine Cancer Institute program development team conducted a survey, gauging patient interest in a chemo buddy program.

The response was a resounding yes.

Several meetings ensued to iron out the logistics, such as the training for each volunteer and the necessity of assigning a volunteer to a particular day and time rather than to a specific patient so that patients don't get on one chemo buddy who may not be available each time they come in for treatment.

I am happy to report that the program is ready to launch.

It has been gratifying to learn there is minimal red tape when everyone agrees an initiative is worth pursuing.

The chemo buddy program will be available to patients in the new Levine Cancer Institute building when it opens on the Carolinas Medical Center campus in October.

Anyone interested in volunteering a minimum of one day per month to provide one-on-one companionship and caring to patients undergoing chemotherapy must undergo one of several chemo buddy training sessions that are being offered by Malinda Bivens, the Levine Cancer Institute's Volunteer Coordinator.

Issues such as confidentiality standards and how to be an empathetic listener will be discussed, but the main criteria for a chemo buddy is simply the willingness to be there for someone in whatever way he or she needs.

Cancer is hard enough. No one should have to face it alone.

Katya Lezin is a freelance writer. Do you have a story idea for Katya? Email her at bowserwoof@mindspring.com.

Reprinted with permission of South Charlotte News, a Charlotte Observer publication.

CHAPTER THIRTY-FOUR

There have been many full-circle moments throughout my journey, times when I reflect on all I have been through or significant dates or occasions that are imbued with extra significance because of what preceded them. Walking through the aquarium at Sea World, looking up at the sharks swimming directly over my head in the glass- encased walkway, staring right back and the myriad fish of every shape, size and color that seem to lock eyes with me on every turn, is one of those moments.

I had decided to forego the Scrabble Nationals this year, seeing as Noah couldn't take any more time off from his DNC internship, Hannah would be in France (even though it turns out she was home by then) and it would be a cost we didn't need to incur, with college tuition *and* medical bills unwelcome additions to our budget. But when David asked me, during one of my many unexpected hospitalizations in the spring, "Would it help you to look forward to Nationals?" I nodded yes (I'm no fool) and promptly found a great deal that bundled the airfare and hotel together. (I should have told him it would *really* help me to have a new Prius parked in the driveway when I got home.)

Eliza has been a reluctant Scrabble competitor. She likes it well enough and has a good eye for the board, but she refuses to study at all and has only recently started enjoying tournaments enough to have them trump whatever else she might have planned for that weekend. But she seemed excited about the prospect of going to Nationals, especially since it would be just the two of us. And her excitement grew exponentially when I realized, in that kind of epiphany that deserves the proverbial light bulb over my head, that *Sea World* is in Orlando!

"Eliza," I tell her one day when we are out waking the dogs, "remember how you thought I was telling you we were going to Sea World when I sat you down to have the cancer talk?"

"Yup," she smiles sheepishly. "I really thought that was your big announcement."

"Well, you know how we're going to Nationals in Orlando," I say.

She's looking at me expectantly. She's starting to sense where this is going.

"Well, guess what else is in Orlando?" I ask. Her eyes get big.

"SEA WORLD!" she squeals.

It feels cathartic to be here with her, to watch the shows with the seals and the whales and get splashed by the walrus and walk hand in hand in the Florida sunshine and reflect on how lucky we are to have made her Sea World wish, so endearingly off-base initially, a reality.

Eliza and I at Sea World.

Another full circle and cathartic experience is seeing the chemo buddies program I initiated come to life. I meet at the hospital with the administrators who are in charge of implementing it and we hash out some of the logistics and parameters. We establish some ground rules – each volunteer will be assigned to a day and time slot rather than a patient, there will be a chemo buddy training as well as a hospital orientation, and, my addition, there will be no proselytizing. Melinda Bivens, the hospital's volunteer coordinator, discloses that my column and then the Channel 36 story about the chemo buddy program have yielded many, many inquiry calls and requests for applications. She is inundated but says it is a nice problem to have. It is clear we have not only tapped into a need at the hospital (over 75 infusion patients surveyed indicated they would be interested in having a chemo buddy assigned to them) but also in the community, with a few callers redirected to other programs and social services since they appear to still be grieving the death of a loved one.

We establish a start date for the program – after the Blumenthal Cancer Center becomes the Levine Cancer Institute and the infusion room moves into its new digs across the street – and we set up the first training. The first date proposed doesn't work for me because, I tell the committee with minimal attempt to hide my excitement, I will be in Europe. So we set up the training for the day after I get back from my trip. Everyone wishes me bon voyage. Seeing it there, in big, bold letters in my datebook on September 27, KATYA AND DAVID LEAVE FOR EUROPE, is such a thrill. The trip that is finally, magically happening, represents perhaps the most full circle, cathartic experience of all.

I can still recall the agony of chemo, the bitter, metallic taste in my mouth, the sluggish, uncharacteristic fatigue that I seemed to don like a heavy coat every time I left my bed, the underlying nausea that was always pestering me, like an annoying little child, threatening to throw a full-blown tantrum at a moment's notice, the bloating, the baldness, the needles... I can bring it all back at a moment's notice. Each time I step into the hospital and smell that distinct hospital odor, a combination of disinfectant and sickness, or when I find a book or sweater or anything else that I associate with chemo, it all comes back. And I remember how whenever things got really bad, I would get through it by repeating the mantra David proposed, "First chemo, then Italy. First chemo, then Italy."
Back then, I couldn't imagine how I was going to get through six cycles of chemo, 12 long days of injections and drugs and feeling at war with my own body. The five months stretched ahead of me in an inter- minable series of pages in my datebook. Our Italy trip, while enticing and encouraging, seemed equally far off and unattainable. Even when I finished chemo, and the pile of Italy travel books took over our entire coffee table, the logistical hurdles to planning our trip seemed daunting.

I know David needs this trip as much as I do. I realize there will never be an ideal time to get away, to ditch our lives and obligations, not to mention the girls, and just go, so we pick a time in the fall and book the tickets. The anticipation of the trip is euphoric enough. I fill David in on the plans I make, describing the train ride we'll take from Milan to Lake Como or the hotel I've booked in Rome, and it becomes a favorite topic of conversation for us on our morning walk. Susanne, my mother- in-law, agrees to come watch the girls for us and we are good to go.

We decide to add France to our itinerary and we throw in a short visit to both Paris and Rome because David has never been to either city. We plan a trip that includes visits with friends as well as lots of time alone, planned excursions along with lots of unscheduled time to do with what we like. It feels like such an incredible indulgence – 12 days for just the two of us. I joke with the girls that their parents may no longer be married by the time we come back because we have never spent that much time together. Here's hoping we really do like each other, I say. Eliza tells me that's not funny. My parents were due to get back from their own European adventure the day before our departure, but their trip is cancelled when my dad suffers a massive heart attack just days before they are supposed to go. I know one has nothing to do with the other and I am so thankful and relieved to still have my dad alive and with us, but I can't help feeling a twinge of guilt that we are heading off on a trip they can no longer take. I know my mom counts on these trips of theirs to see her family, all of whom have remained in Switzerland, and that not going is a bitter pill to swallow.

Shortly before we leave, I go to the bank to take some money out of savings to take with us on the trip. When I see what is in our account, I gasp. Someone has stolen from us! The account is about $8000 short! I am ready to sound the alarm when it hits me, *I* took that money out! *I* pilfered thousands and thousands of dollars from our savings. I think the whole cancer ordeal was so surreal that I just didn't process or consciously account for the thousands and thousands of dollars I spent to pay the medical bills that came in a steady stream and, in fact, *continue* to pour in.

Most are in the several hundred dollar range, with some in the thousands. All are a pittance of what I would have to pay without insurance, but they nonetheless require funds that I do not have in our regular checking account. The one that makes me utter expletives immediately upon opening it is for $91,748.99 and covers the dates 12/15/11 to 12/18/11. The explanation of the coding for this charge, why I am responsible for it rather than my insurance company even though they pre-approved the surgery, is that my double mastectomy has been deemed cosmetic surgery.

When I call BlueCross/Blue Shield to ask how this could possibly be, since the hospital couldn't even schedule the surgery without first getting approval from my insurance company that it is covered in my plan, the female agent explains to me that this was optional, cosmetic surgery that is not authorized under my plan. I try to stay calm.

"So you're telling me that I *chose* to have both my breasts lopped off, that this was my cosmetic goal?" I ask.

"Ma'am," she says, her voice monotone, "it is coded as cosmetic surgery."

"But you *pre-approved* it," I stammer, beside myself. "You approved the payment for the genetic test that showed me to have an 85% chance of getting breast cancer, and you then approved my having the double mastectomy."

"Ma'am," she says again, her tone infuriating me. "Your uterine cancer did not cause your breast cancer."

Oh my God, *seriously?*

"First of all, I didn't have *uterine* cancer, I had ovarian cancer. They're not all interchangeable. Second of all, " I pause, wondering why I am arguing with this idiot. "You know what, I'd like to speak with a supervisor."

When I do, we figure out that the surgery was coded wrong. An error on the hospital's part. I am assured it will get resolved.

I continue to get the bills for this whopping amount, so astronomically beyond anything I can pay that it worries me much less than the bills that continue to trickle in for hundreds of dollars that I can, and do, pay. Finally, in September, I get a bill from the hospital for this same time frame, but indicating that I owe $6,500. *Your insurance company has already paid. You are responsible for the remaining balance in full.*

I'm confused. And a little panicked. This surgery was in December, back when I'd met my catastrophic cap. I should not be responsible for any amount, let alone thousands of dollars. I call the insurance company. They explain that the hospital forgot to charge for some equipment so they did so when they resubmitted the bill, with the proper coding, and it is that section of the bill that is under review. But why, I ask, did the hospital send me a bill indicating that I owe the balance?

A conference call ensues, and Blue Cross asks the hospital billing representative the same question. She tells me not to worry about it, that it is, in fact, under review with my insurance company. And my insurance company assures me that it will not be on me, regardless, since I have already met my catastrophic cap for that time period.

"Then why," I ask, my mounting frustration over this entire process culminating in this one bill, this one moment that is so emblematic of the confusing, aggravating and, I have come to believe, some- times deceitful rigamorale that is our health care system, "am I receiving a bill that tells me in no uncertain terms that I am to pay it?"

The hospital rep hems and haws, but really what she should say, if she were to respond with full disclosure and honesty, is "that's how we do it." We throw a bunch of papers out there and hope a few stick. We hope there will be enough saps out there who just pay these threatening and utterly deceitful bills. I ignored one, for a mere $25, because it looked duplicative (for the same day and service) of one I had already paid. The next time I saw that bill, it came from a collection agency, along with a threatening letter. Did I mention that the amount in question was $25?

And this, mind you, is with *good* health insurance. This is with intelligent people with multiple graduate degrees who can read, write and advocate for ourselves. This is with steady income and no major disruption to our livelihoods as a result of my illness. I can only imagine how this must go down when even just one of those factors is not present, as is true for so many Americans.

But I digress! Let's go back to the plane that is about to take off for Paris, the first stop on Katya and David's excellent European adventure. David and I clink glasses and kiss, we feel like giddy teenagers who have just escaped a boring school dance and the watchful eyes of the chaperones. We are FREE! We have nearly two weeks of fabulous food, sightseeing, and relaxation ahead of us. And David is hoping we will take full advantage of our hotel rooms. He is not disappointed.

While we stroll the streets of Paris or enjoy a leisurely dinner down a quaint back alley in Gravedona, we talk about the year behind us. We are hoping this trip serves as the final exclamation point on a journey that brought us to our knees, but also brought us closer together. I ask David when he was most worried and he confides that the February infection was the most trying time for him, rendered all the more difficult because it came out of nowhere. I tell him my darkest days were just after the hysterectomy, when I truly didn't think I could do it.

But I *did* do it. And we celebrate that fact for twelve glorious days.

Subject: Ovarian Odyssey
Date: October 4, 2012

Buonjiorno! I am happy to report that David and I have made it to Italy, where we are celebrating both our marriage (this is our belated 20th anniversary trip) and the conclusion of chemo, surgery, hospitalizations and all things cancer.

We started our European adventure by flying to Paris, where we dined with la famille Caubel, my adopted French family from the time I was an exchange student in Valenciennes 30 years ago! They met David for the first time and he concluded that it was easy to see why we are so fond of each other.

After a day touring Paris, including a romantic boat ride down the Seine, we took the train to Valence, in the South of France, and spent a few days with our French friends Catherine, Bernard and their daughter, Nina (whom we met by chance in San Francisco six years ago and they then visited us last summer in Charlotte). They took us to villages, castles and sights that were delightfully off the beaten path, but the highlight (at least for three kids awaiting gifts at home) was a visit to a world-renowned chocolate shop and factory near their lovely home.

We then flew from Lyon to Milan and enjoyed a quick visit to that beautiful city before traveling by train to Como. We are right on the lake, in a lovely town called Gravedona, and our days are pretty much spent eating and then hiking, walking and running in an attempt to stay just slightly ahead of our caloric consumption. Highlights so far include pumpkin gnocchi, tiramisu gelato and an octopus salad that might just be the best thing I have ever eaten. We head to Rome tomorrow, where we will spend a few days being tourists before flying home on the 8th. Anyone who gets to spend quality time together as we have, in the most beautiful of surroundings, indulging in unbelievable cuisine and sightseeing, is already incredibly lucky. But rest assured we feel especially fortunate to be able to enjoy this trip, given the year that preceded it.

Ciao!
Katya

On the streets in Bellagio on Lake Como.

On a romantic boat ride down the Seine in Paris.

CHAPTER THIRTY-FIVE

The day after we get back from Italy, I go in for my 3-month checkup and blood work. The appointment was originally scheduled for just before my departure, but that ended up being the move-in day to the new building (from the Blumenthal Cancer Center to the Levine Cancer Institute) so we rescheduled for after the trip. I tell David the timing is intentional. I am convinced all is well, but on the off chance the appointment and blood test yield worrisome results, I do not want that hanging over our heads during our trip. Nothing would kill the romance faster than the fear that my cancer has recurred.

Dr. Naumann, whom I have not seen in a long time, greets me like an old friend. He tells me he got more comments from the column I wrote about him than he did about his CNN appearance. He tells me to relax while he sticks his hand in places it shouldn't go and tells me I'm doing great. I have my blood drawn after my appointment and Dr. Naumann tells me he's looking for the number to stabilize or go down. If there's any trend upward, no matter how small, he'll want to do a CT scan to see what is going on. I instinctively gag at the thought of the scan, both for the physical ordeal of the scan itself and the emotional ordeal for what it signifies, and I hope it will not come to that. He tells me I'll get the results in the next day or two.

That night, Hannah and Eliza come in to my room together. They ask about the blood test and I tell them I don't have the results yet. They look at each other and nod. They have something they'd like to discuss with me.

"We understand why you lied the first time," Hannah says.

"But we want you to promise to tell us the truth this time," Eliza say.

"No matter what," Hannah says. "Even if it's not good." She pauses. "Even though we know it's going to be okay."

I have made my mom a similar promise. Whenever she asks me how I am, and I tell her I'm doing great, she wants to know if I'm telling her everything.

I get it. They were blindsided last time and were left playing catch up. I vow to tell them what I know, when I know it.

The next morning, I am sitting in the JCC parking lot with Eliza, waiting for her school bus to Randolph. My phone rings and I see it is Dr. Naumann's office. I know this can't be good. They have never been good about calling with good news. I know it is bad. I also know Eliza is sitting right next to me. I promised to tell her everything, but I'm certainly not going to send her off to school for the day reeling from bad news I haven't even had a chance to process myself. I turn my body as inconspicuously as possible and answer the call.

"Hi, this is Keisha, Dr. Naumann's nurse," the cheery voice informs me in a Southern drawl. "Your CA-125 came back and it has gone up, just a teeny bit, to 30. Dr. Naumann would like to do a CT scan, just as a precaution. They'll be calling you to set that up."

"Okay," I say. There's not much else I can say, or ask, with Eliza sitting right there.

I send David an email.

Sent: Wednesday, October 10, 2012 8:21 AM To: Lieberman, David C. Subject: Fuck
Dr. just called. It's up. I have to get a CT scan. I'll call you when I'm not with Eliza.

He shoots a response right back.

I don't know what to say other than I love you and we'll get through this.

That same day, I head over to the Levine Cancer Institute for the first chemo buddy training. I walk into a room filled with seventeen women and the nurse who will be overseeing the program. We start off by going around in a circle and introducing ourselves and explaining why we are here. My spirits, so low from the call earlier in the morning, my thoughts so distracted with the fear that I might be sick again, are given the best possible remedy as woman after woman says how excited she is to participate, how my column touched her and made her want to volunteer.

That sentiment is echoed in this email I received after the column describing the chemo buddy program ran in *The Charlotte Observer.*

Dear Katya,

I've been following your columns and pray you continue to be given everyone and everything good and great as your awesome journey unfolds. The chemo buddy program you're creating in tandem w/ the Levine Cancer institute is such a beautiful, loving concept. My only sister, age 59, lived in St. Petersburg, FL, and passed away two months ago from primary peritoneal carcinoma (PPC) which also is categorized as ovarian cancer for treatment purposes. Of course, I deeply miss her. She spoke so lovingly of her chemo nurse, Christina, though I often wished there had been a program for her to have a buddy alongside when she underwent her chemo treatments which sometimes lasted 3-4 hours as Christina, understandably, was spread very thin clinically attending all patients simultaneously. While my sister was very blessed w/ a devoted husband and local friends, they, too, were required to juggle busy lives and not always could be present w/ her during chemo. Upon reading your article, I felt such a calling. It touched my heart so much that your journey would be used to help others at such a critical juncture in life. Thank you so much for being so kind and loving to look way beyond yourself to help serve others who need this support. Please know I have called Malinda Bivens for the purpose of becoming a chemo buddy. You are an inspiration and blessing to our community. Thank you so much.

Sincerely, Renee Tomberlin

Meg Turner, the social worker for Levine Cancer Institute, stops by to share how much she values what we will be doing and how important it is. She tells the story of a woman who was just in her office, in tears, telling her that the only way she can steel herself for chemo each time is to wrap herself in the curtains of an adjoining room and sob. "I'm the only person who doesn't have anyone with me," the woman says. I tell this group of volunteers that no one should have to feel that way, to face that hardship on top of all of the others. We all feel motivated and moved.

We are taken on a tour of the new infusion room and I am blown away by the contrast to the old room across the street. It is enormous, with separate bays, each boasting its own kitchen, and an art room and music room, as well as an enormous waiting room. Several nurses give me quizzical looks until they recognize me, under my curls, and run up to hug me and congratulate me on how well I look.

It is so gratifying to see the chemo buddy program take flight and to know that some good came of my cancer journey. I feel touched that so many in the community have responded to my call for action and that so many patients will be helped. I am totally impressed with the new infusion center and I know that anyone receiving care there will be as comfortable as possible. But what I'm thinking most of all as I tour the facility and conduct the training is that I hope like hell I don't have to experience the infusion room and the chemo buddy program as a patient.

I share the news with the girls and my folks. I regret the promise I have made to them because they are all worried, and it is a worry that may be for naught. I could have spared them this stress; there will be time enough to worry once it is confirmed. I feel hypochondriacal about little aches and pains I feel that are no doubt just a function of my age, but in the context of the CA-125 and my looming scan, I fear they are signs that my body is again fighting cancer.

I receive a lovely email from a woman who attended the Chemo Buddy training, and it does a lot to snap me out of my pity party. I forward it to David and friends and family in the know, assuring them I am feeling better.

Note to self: when you have a shitty day, schedule a chemo buddy training where everyone will tell you how much they loved your article and are full of enthusiasm for your idea. :)

Begin forwarded message:
October 11, 2012
Hi Katya, You did an awesome job yesterday! There is no doubt I was exactly where I needed to be and look forward to being the best chemo buddy I can. You are a great speaker and I left the orientation ready to start!

346

If there is anything else I can do to help facilitate the implementation of this program, don't hesitate to contact me. You are in my thoughts.
Audrey Ashkin

The CT scan is scheduled for Friday at 11:30. I have to show up several hours ahead of time to drink the contrast solution. It is as nasty as ever, but I gulp it down because I want to get this over with. The nurse takes me back and asks me which arm is better for starting a line. I tell her it doesn't matter, they're both equally bad, but I can barely get the words out. The needle, the hospital setting, it's all coming back, and I am sitting there thinking, *I can't do this again. Please don't make me have to do this all over again.*

I lie on my back, hold my breath when the machine tells me to do so, feel the familiar sensation of heat permeate my body, and then I'm done. My fate lies in that image. I tell the technicians to sprinkle lots of mojo on it as they handle it. They wish me luck and assure me it will reach my doctor within a few hours. "You will definitely have the results today," they promise me.

I meet Jen and Lisa Z. for lunch. I go home and lie down, because I am still battling the cold the woman who was indiscriminately hacking on the plane gave me. At 4 pm, when I have heard nothing, I call and leave a message for Dr. Naumann or his nurse to please call me with the results. Nothing. I call again at 4:30. I leave another message. At 4:55 pm, I am seething. They're probably gone for the day, and I'm going to have to stew over this all weekend. My family will endure a weekend full of worry as well. It is unconscionable.

I call and ask to speak with the triage nurse. I explain the situation and she tells me that Dr. Naumann will be calling me. I tell her, as calmly as I can, that I know my results are up, that she can easily find them on the computer, and that I will not spend the entire weekend not knowing. In this case, I tell her, ignorance is definitely *not* bliss. She agrees to look it up.

"There is no sign of a recurrence of cancer," she reads aloud.

I thank her profusely and then waste no time in spreading the word to the few close friends and relatives who were worrying along with me.

Subject: CLEAN CT SCAN!!
Date: Fri, 12 Oct 2012 17:05:54 -0400

It was looking like I was going to have to worry about this all weekend because no one called from my doctor's office. I finally reached one of the triage nurses and implored her to look up my results, telling her it was unconscionable to make me wait through the weekend. She agreed and some very tense moments ensued while she brought the report up on the screen.

Great news. No evidence of cancer. Hallelujah.

I suspect I'll have an expedited (in 4-6 weeks, rather than 12) blood test to see if the CA-125 keeps trending up, but for now I'm going to just focus on the relief of knowing the scan found nothing.

Thanks for all the crossed fingers and good thoughts. PHEW!

Love, Katya

I will have to go through this emotional upheaval again a few months from now, and every three months for the first two years following my chemo. I will not be able to pronounce myself cured until five years out. But that's what the doctors say. For me, this clean CT scan marks the end. It is the demarcation of sick Katya and healthy Katya, the line dividing a year that was totally consumed by my cancer and all the years that will follow it, cancer-free.

I won't say it's the end of my cancer journey because I have come to realize that once you embark on this journey, you remain on it. My world will forever be colored by my cancer experience. I have faced my own mortality, I have felt betrayed by my own body and then felt swells of gratitude to that very same body for enduring so much and, in the end, saving me. I have had my world rocked but I have also seen the foundations of my world – my family, my friends, my own sense of self – stand strong and steady through all of the rocking. I have been tested and I will forever be changed by how I responded to that test, and how everyone around me did as well.

It is not something I would ever wish to happen, and I am not glad that it did. The low points were low indeed. But I wish I could have known, back when I took the *You have cancer* call, that there would be so much good coming out of the bad. That my naïve belief that everyone means well is, in fact, grounded in reality and borne out by how folks far and wide responded to every turn of my journey. I think of how it brought me closer to people around me, adding a depth and significance to my friendships and relationships that only this kind of shared experience could add. And how it introduced me to a whole new slice of life and characters, such as the pharmacists at the Harris Teeter at the Arboretum (who always inquired how the patch or a new medicine worked out for me and seemed to genuinely care about how I was feeling), the folks at Poppy's Bagels and Mezzanotte, both frequent stops on my way to and from chemo, and the readers of my columns chronicling my cancer journey, who sent me notes of appreciation and encouragement.

Most of all, I wish I could have known, back when I thought my life was over, that it would, in a bizarre but undeniable way, be enhanced and rendered fuller. That cancer would convert an already happy and appreciative optimist into someone who is even more aware of all that is good in her life and values it that much more, and that my love for my husband and my kids and my siblings and parents and dear friends would be strengthened, not threatened, by this disease.

And I would never have guessed that my sense of humor would not only remain intact, but would be fueled by so many unexpected moments of levity. Who knew cancer could be so damn funny? I chuckle aloud at totally inopportune moments (sitting in Temple for Yom Kippur, for instance) recalling some of the funniest episodes, laugh-out-loud moments rendered all the funnier because of the backdrop of cancer. I recall the looks of consternation and disdain when, sitting buck naked in the hot tub at the JCC, I try to rub my abdominal scar to help the scarring go down and then realize what that looks like under the bubbles! I remember inadvertently trying to take the elderly gentleman plugged in next to me in the infusion room to the bathroom with me and Hannah telling the hotel clerk, when asked to describe me after misplacing our room key, that I have shoulder-length hair and then changing her mind and saying no, never mind, I'm bald. And the moment I return to most often is David telling me he can't find my asshole. That low point epitomizes the bonding opportunities that an illness, with all of its moments of degradation and humiliation, can engender. David and I still use *I can't find it* as our code for anything that is so bad it's funny.

When I serve as the speaker at the hospital's monthly Breast Cancer Reconstruction Symposium, I usually have everyone in stitches. You wouldn't think talking about my double mastectomy and the cancer necessitating it would lend itself to the Katya Comedy Hour, but it does. My overarching message is that the anticipation of this major surgery that awaits them is so much worse than the reality of it, and I illustrate that by highlighting some of the funny experiences along the way. I haven't yet lifted my shirt to show off Dr. Robinson's handiwork, but I have certainly been tempted to do so. I want to show them my scars, my breasts that look nothing like they did before, my new short, curly hair, my abdominal scar that makes it seem as if I've been cut in half, and say, yes, almost everything about me changed, parts were taken out, new parts added, and all sorts of stuff was ingested, injected and zapped into me. But guess what? I'm still here. And I'm still me.

And I don't have to wear a bra anymore. Ever.

At our annual dessert party, happy that our most pressing problem is who gets the last slice of Oreo cheesecake.

I did it!